# Windows® XP
## in an instant

## Visual

*From*
### maranGraphics®

&

## Hungry Minds™

Best-Selling Books • Digital Downloads • e-books • Answer Networks •
e-Newsletters • Branded Web Sites • e-learning

New York, NY ♦ Cleveland, OH ♦ Indianapolis, IN

## Windows® XP In an Instant

Published by
**Hungry Minds, Inc.**
909 Third Avenue
New York, NY 10022
www.hungryminds.com

Copyright© 2001 by maranGraphics Inc.
    5755 Coopers Avenue
    Mississauga, Ontario, Canada
    L4Z 1R9

Library of Congress Control Number: 2001093183

ISBN: 0-7645-3625-7

Printed in the United States of America

10 9 8 7 6 5 4 3 2

1B/QR/QZ/QR/MG

Distributed in the United States by Hungry Minds, Inc.
Distributed by CDG Books Canada Inc. for Canada; by Transworld Publishers Limited in the United Kingdom; by IDG Norge Books for Norway; by IDG Sweden Books for Sweden; by IDG Books Australia Publishing Corporation Pty. Ltd. for Australia and New Zealand; by TransQuest Publishers Pte Ltd. for Singapore, Malaysia, Thailand, Indonesia, and Hong Kong; by Gotop Information Inc. for Taiwan; by ICG Muse, Inc. for Japan; by Intersoft for South Africa; by Eyrolles for France; by International Thomson Publishing for Germany, Austria and Switzerland; by Distribuidora Cuspide for Argentina; by LR International for Brazil; by Galileo Libros for Chile; by Ediciones ZETA S.C.R. Ltda. for Peru; by WS Computer Publishing Corporation, Inc. for the Philippines; by Contemporanea de Ediciones for Venezuela; by Express Computer Distributors for the Caribbean and West Indies; by Micronesia Media Distributor, Inc. for Micronesia; by Chips Computadoras S.A. de C.V. for Mexico; by Editorial Norma de Panama S.A. for Panama; by American Bookshops for Finland. For corporate orders, please call maranGraphics at 800-469-6616 or fax 905-890-9434.
For general information on Hungry Minds' products and services, please contact our Customer Care Department within the U.S. at 800-762-2974, outside the U.S. at 317-572-3993 or fax 317-572-4002.
For sales inquiries and reseller information, including discounts, premium and bulk quantity sales, and foreign-language translations, please contact our Customer Care Department at 800-434-3422, fax 317-572-4002, or write to Hungry Minds, Inc., Attn: Customer Care Department, 10475 Crosspoint Boulevard, Indianapolis, IN 46256.
For information on licensing foreign or domestic rights, please contact our Sub-Rights Customer Care Department at 212-844-5000.
For information on using Hungry Minds' products and services in the classroom or for ordering examination copies, please contact our Educational Sales Department at 800-434-2086 or fax 317-572-4005.
For press review copies, author interviews, or other publicity information, please contact our Public Relations department at 317-572-3168 or fax 317-572-4168.
For authorization to photocopy items for corporate, personal, or educational use, please contact Copyright Clearance Center, 222 Rosewood Drive, Danvers, MA 01923, or fax 978-750-4470.

## Trademark Acknowledgments

## Permissions

 is a trademark of Hungry Minds, Inc.

| U.S. Corporate Sales | U.S. Trade Sales |
| --- | --- |
| Contact maranGraphics at (800) 469-6616 or fax (905) 890-9434. | Contact Hungry Minds at (800) 434-3422 or fax (317) 572-4002. |

# Some comments from our readers...

"I have to praise you and your company on the fine products you turn out. I have twelve of the *Teach Yourself VISUALLY* and *Simplified* books in my house. They were instrumental in helping me pass a difficult computer course. Thank you for creating books that are easy to follow."

–*Gordon Justin (Brielle, NJ)*

"I commend your efforts and your success. I teach in an outreach program for the Dr. Eugene Clark Library in Lockhart, TX. Your *Teach Yourself VISUALLY* books are incredible and I use them in my computer classes. All my students love them!"

–*Michele Schalin (Lockhart, TX)*

"Thank you so much for helping people like me learn about computers. The Maran family is just what the doctor ordered. Thank you, thank you, thank you."

–*Carol Moten (New Kensington, PA)*

"I would like to take this time to compliment maranGraphics on creating such great books. Thank you for making it clear. Keep up the good work."

–*Kirk Santoro (Burbank, CA)*

"I write to extend my thanks and appreciation for your books. They are clear, easy to follow, and straight to the point. Keep up the good work!"

–*Seward Kollie (Dakar, Senegal)*

"What fantastic teaching books you have produced! Congratulations to you and your staff. You deserve the Nobel prize in Education in the Software category. Thanks for helping me to understand computers."

–*Bruno Tonon (Melbourne, Australia)*

"Over time, I have bought a number of your 'Read Less, Learn More' books. For me, they are THE way to learn anything easily."

–*José A. Mazón (Cuba, NY)*

"I was introduced to maranGraphics about four years ago and YOU ARE THE GREATEST THING THAT EVER HAPPENED TO INTRODUCTORY COMPUTER BOOKS!"

–*Glenn Nettleton (Huntsville, AL)*

"Compliments To The Chef!! Your books are extraordinary! Or, simply put, Extra-Ordinary, meaning way above the rest! THANK YOU THANK YOU THANK YOU! for creating these."

–*Christine J. Manfrin (Castle Rock, CO)*

"I'm a grandma who was pushed by an 11-year-old grandson to join the computer age. I found myself hopelessly confused and frustrated until I discovered the Visual series. I'm no expert by any means now, but I'm a lot further along than I would have been otherwise. Thank you!"

–*Carol Louthain (Logansport, IN)*

"Thank you, thank you, thank you...for making it so easy for me to break into this high-tech world. I now own four of your books. I recommend them to anyone who is a beginner like myself. Now... if you could just do one for programming VCRs, it would make my day!"

–*Gay O'Donnell (Calgary, Alberta, Canada)*

"You're marvelous! I am greatly in your debt."

–*Patrick Baird (Lacey, WA)*

**maranGraphics is a family-run business
located near Toronto, Canada.**

**At *maranGraphics*,** we believe in producing great computer books–one book at a time.

Each maranGraphics book uses the award-winning communication process that we have been developing over the last 25 years. Using this process, we organize screen shots and text in a way that makes it easy for you to learn new concepts and tasks.

We spend hours deciding the best way to perform each task, so you don't have to!

Our clear, easy-to-follow screen shots and instructions walk you through each task from beginning to end.

We want to thank you for purchasing what we feel are the best computer books money can buy. We hope you enjoy using this book as much as we enjoyed creating it!

Sincerely,

*The Maran Family*

Please visit us on the Web at:
# www.maran.com

## CREDITS

**Author:**
Ruth Maran

**Copy Development Director:**
Kelleigh Johnson

**Copy Editor:**
Raquel Scott

**Technical Consultant:**
Paul Whitehead

**Project Manager:**
Judy Maran

**Editors:**
Teri Lynn Pinsent
Norm Schumacher
Cathy Lo
Stacey Morrison
Roxanne Van Damme
Roderick Anatalio
Megan Kirby

**Screen Captures:**
Jill Maran

**Layout Artists:**
Hee-Jin Park
Paul Baker
Treena Lees

**Screen Artist:**
Darryl Grossi

**Indexer:**
Kelleigh Johnson

**Permissions Coordinator:**
Jennifer Amaral

**Senior Vice President and
Publisher, Hungry Minds
Technology Publishing Group:**
Richard Swadley

**Publishing Director,
Hungry Minds Technology
Publishing Group:**
Barry Pruett

**Editorial Support,
Hungry Minds Technology
Publishing Group:**
Jennifer Dorsey
Sandy Rodrigues
Lindsay Sandman

**Post Production:**
Robert Maran

## ACKNOWLEDGMENTS

Thanks to the dedicated staff of maranGraphics, including
Jennifer Amaral, Roderick Anatalio, Paul Baker,
Darryl Grossi, Kelleigh Johnson, Megan Kirby, Wanda Lawrie,
Treena Lees, Cathy Lo, Jill Maran, Judy Maran, Robert Maran,
Ruth Maran, Russ Marini, Suzana G. Miokovic, Stacey Morrison,
Hee-Jin Park, Teri Lynn Pinsent, Steven Schaerer, Norm Schumacher,
Raquel Scott, Roxanne Van Damme and Paul Whitehead.

Finally, to Richard Maran who originated the easy-to-use
graphic format of this guide. Thank you for your
inspiration and guidance.

# TABLE OF CONTENTS

# TABLE OF CONTENTS

# INTRODUCTION TO WINDOWS

Microsoft® Windows® XP is a program that controls the overall activity of your computer. Microsoft Windows XP ensures that all parts of your computer work together smoothly and efficiently. **XP** stands for experience.

## INTRODUCTION TO WINDOWS

## WORK WITH FILES

When you create and save a document, Windows stores the document as a file. You can sort, open, rename, print, delete, move, copy and search for files. If you accidentally delete a file, you can usually restore the file from the Recycle Bin. You can create folders to organize your files and place shortcuts on your desktop to help you easily access your favorite files and folders. You can also e-mail a file, publish a file to the Web and copy files to a floppy disk or recordable CD.

## WORK WITH PICTURES

Windows XP includes many features that allow you to work with pictures. Pictures you create can be inserted into other programs or displayed as wallpaper on your desktop. Windows provides the My Pictures folder, which is a convenient place to store and view pictures. The My Pictures folder provides a thumbnail view of pictures so you can preview the pictures in the folder without opening them.

Windows also allows you to easily manage pictures you create using devices such as scanners, digital cameras and image manipulation software.

## CUSTOMIZE WINDOWS

You can customize Windows to suit your preferences. You can display a picture on your desktop or change the colors used to display screen elements. You can also have a screen saver appear when you are not using your computer. You can also have programs start automatically each time you start Windows, have sound effects play when certain events occur on your computer and change the way your mouse works.

## WORK WITH MUSIC AND VIDEOS

Windows includes the Windows Media Player program, which allows you to play music CDs and listen to radio station broadcasts over the Internet on your computer. You can use the Media Guide feature to access the latest music and movies on the Internet. You can also copy songs from a music CD to your computer or copy songs from your computer to a CD or other portable device.

# in an instant

### CREATE MOVIES

Windows includes the Windows Movie Maker program, which allows you to transfer your home movies to your computer. You can then organize and edit the movies on your computer before sharing them with friends and family.

### SHARE YOUR COMPUTER

If you share your computer with other people, you can create user accounts to keep the personal files and settings for each person separate. You can assign a password to each user account and easily share files with other users. You can also make your personal folders private so that other users cannot view the contents of the personal folders.

### OPTIMIZE COMPUTER PERFORMANCE

Windows provides tools to help you optimize your computer's performance. You can update Windows, install and remove programs and schedule computer maintenance tasks to run at specific times. Windows makes it easy to remove unnecessary files to free up disk space on your computer and allows you to restore your computer to an earlier time if you experience problems. You can also allow a friend or colleague at another computer to view your computer screen and take control of your computer to help you solve a computer problem.

### WORK ON A NETWORK

Windows allows you to share information and equipment with other people on a network. You can share folders stored on your computer as well as a printer that is directly connected to your computer. Windows also provides a wizard to help you set up a home network.

### ACCESS THE WORLD WIDE WEB

Windows XP includes Internet Explorer, which allows you to browse through the information on the World Wide Web. You can search for and display Web pages of interest, change the Web page that appears each time you start Internet Explorer and create a list of your favorite Web pages.

### EXCHANGE E-MAIL AND INSTANT MESSAGES

Outlook Express allows you to exchange e-mail messages with people around the world. You can read, send, reply to, forward, print and delete e-mail messages. You can also use the address book to store the e-mail addresses of people you frequently send messages to.

The Windows Messenger program included with Windows allows you to see when contacts are online and exchange instant messages and files with other people over the Internet.

# USING THE START MENU

You can use the Start menu to access programs, files, computer settings and help information. You can access the Start menu while you are in any program. This is useful if you want to quickly start a new program without having to close or minimize the current program. The programs available on the Start menu depend on the software installed on your computer.

## USING THE START MENU

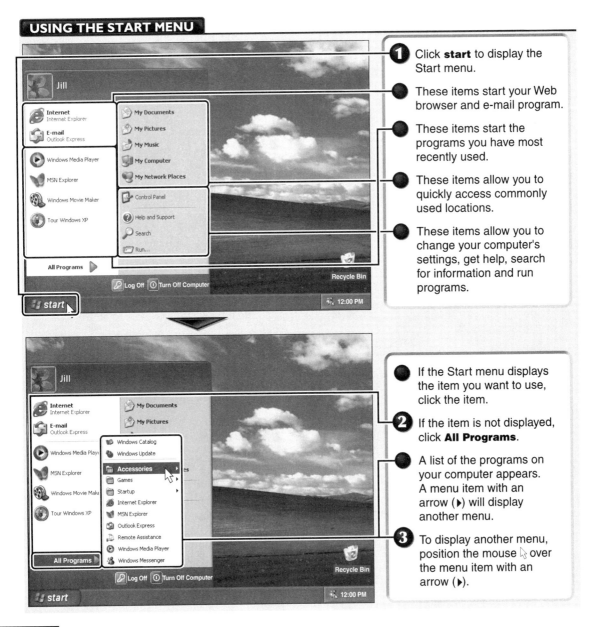

**1** Click **start** to display the Start menu.

● These items start your Web browser and e-mail program.

● These items start the programs you have most recently used.

● These items allow you to quickly access commonly used locations.

● These items allow you to change your computer's settings, get help, search for information and run programs.

● If the Start menu displays the item you want to use, click the item.

**2** If the item is not displayed, click **All Programs**.

● A list of the programs on your computer appears. A menu item with an arrow (▶) will display another menu.

**3** To display another menu, position the mouse ▷ over the menu item with an arrow (▶).

4

# in an instant

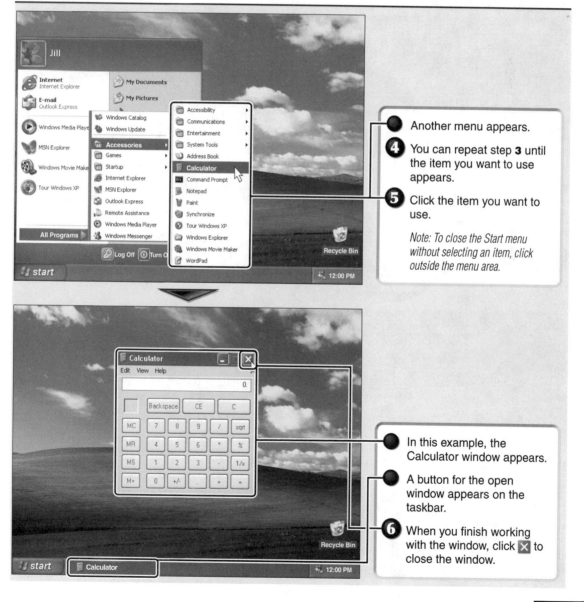

Another menu appears.

4 You can repeat step **3** until the item you want to use appears.

5 Click the item you want to use.

*Note: To close the Start menu without selecting an item, click outside the menu area.*

In this example, the Calculator window appears.

A button for the open window appears on the taskbar.

6 When you finish working with the window, click ✖ to close the window.

# MOVE A WINDOW

If a window covers items on your screen, you can move the window to a different location. If you have more than one window open, you can adjust the position of the windows to ensure that you can view the contents of each window.

MOVE A WINDOW

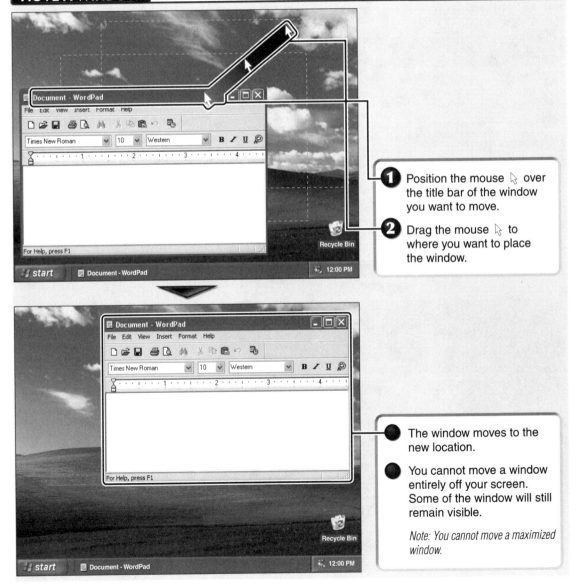

1 Position the mouse ⌖ over the title bar of the window you want to move.

2 Drag the mouse ⌖ to where you want to place the window.

● The window moves to the new location.

● You cannot move a window entirely off your screen. Some of the window will still remain visible.

*Note: You cannot move a maximized window.*

# RESIZE A WINDOW

You can easily change the size of a window displayed on your screen. Enlarging the size of a window allows you to view more information in the window, while reducing the size of a window allows you to view items covered by the window. You should keep in mind that some programs have windows that cannot be resized.

## RESIZE A WINDOW

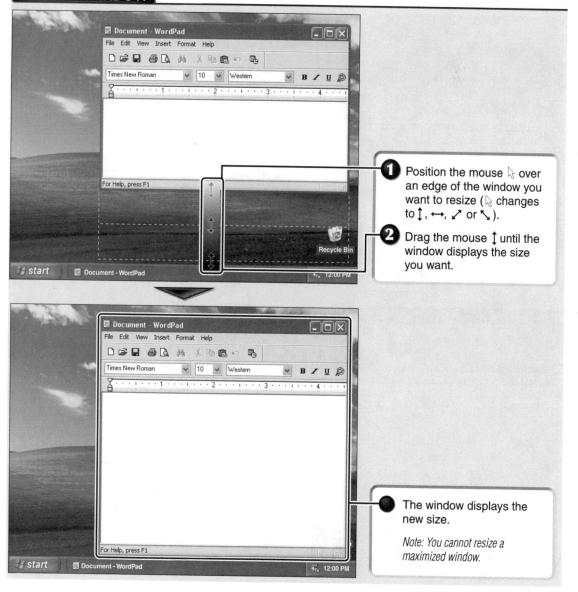

**1** Position the mouse ⌖ over an edge of the window you want to resize (⌖ changes to ↕, ↔, ⤢ or ⤡).

**2** Drag the mouse ↕ until the window displays the size you want.

● The window displays the new size.

*Note: You cannot resize a maximized window.*

# MAXIMIZE A WINDOW

You can maximize a window to fill your entire screen. Maximizing a window allows you to view more of the information in the window. For example, you may want to maximize a WordPad window to allow you to see more of a document you are reviewing.

## MAXIMIZE A WINDOW

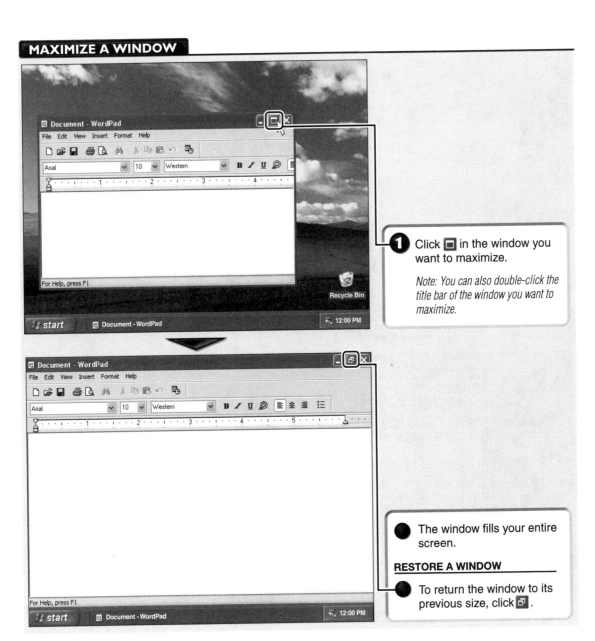

**1** Click ☐ in the window you want to maximize.

*Note: You can also double-click the title bar of the window you want to maximize.*

● The window fills your entire screen.

**RESTORE A WINDOW**

● To return the window to its previous size, click ☐.

# MINIMIZE A WINDOW

If you are not using a window, you can minimize the
window to temporarily remove it from your screen
so you can work on other tasks. Minimizing a window
reduces the window to a button on the taskbar. You
can redisplay a minimized window at any time.

## MINIMIZE A WINDOW

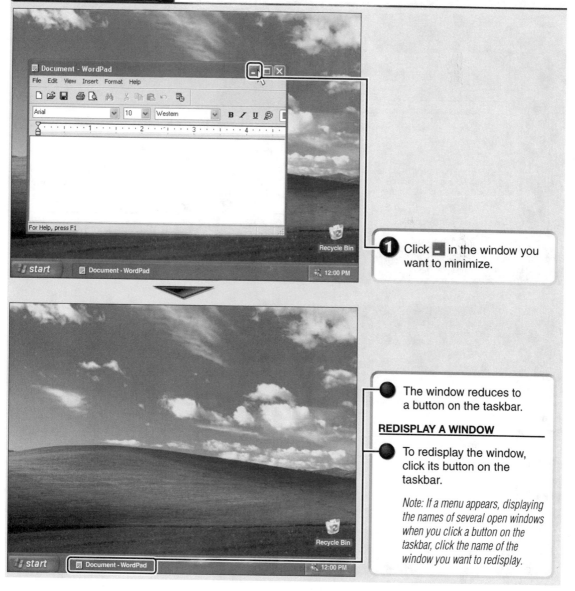

**1** Click ▬ in the window you
want to minimize.

■ The window reduces to
a button on the taskbar.

### REDISPLAY A WINDOW

To redisplay the window,
click its button on the
taskbar.

*Note: If a menu appears, displaying
the names of several open windows
when you click a button on the
taskbar, click the name of the
window you want to redisplay.*

**9**

# SCROLL THROUGH A WINDOW

You can use a scroll bar to browse through the information in a window. Scrolling is useful when a window is not large enough to display all the information it contains. You can also purchase a mouse that has a wheel between the left and right mouse buttons. This wheel allows you to scroll through information in a window.

## SCROLL THROUGH A WINDOW

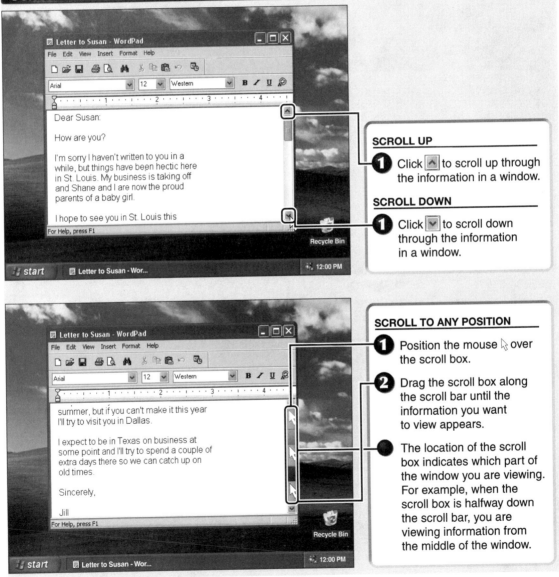

**SCROLL UP**

1 Click ▲ to scroll up through the information in a window.

**SCROLL DOWN**

1 Click ▼ to scroll down through the information in a window.

**SCROLL TO ANY POSITION**

1 Position the mouse ▷ over the scroll box.

2 Drag the scroll box along the scroll bar until the information you want to view appears.

● The location of the scroll box indicates which part of the window you are viewing. For example, when the scroll box is halfway down the scroll bar, you are viewing information from the middle of the window.

# SWITCH BETWEEN WINDOWS

If you have more than one window open on your screen, you can easily switch between the windows. Each window is like a separate piece of paper. Switching between windows is like placing a different piece of paper at the top of the pile. You can only work in the active window, which appears in front of all other windows and displays a dark title bar.

## SWITCH BETWEEN WINDOWS

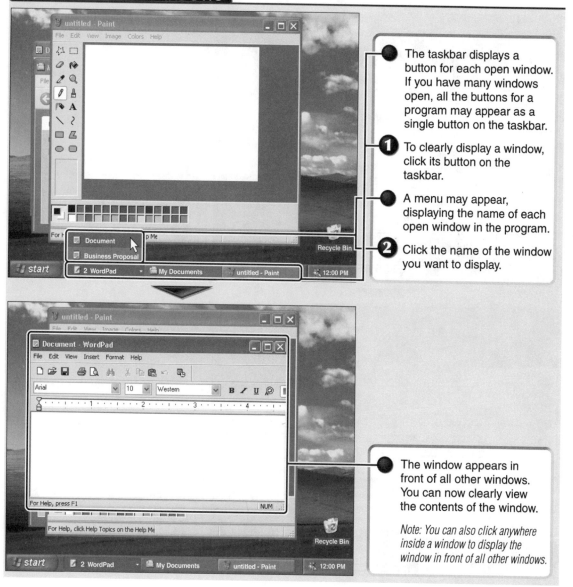

The taskbar displays a button for each open window. If you have many windows open, all the buttons for a program may appear as a single button on the taskbar.

**1** To clearly display a window, click its button on the taskbar.

A menu may appear, displaying the name of each open window in the program.

**2** Click the name of the window you want to display.

The window appears in front of all other windows. You can now clearly view the contents of the window.

*Note: You can also click anywhere inside a window to display the window in front of all other windows.*

# PLAY GAMES

Windows includes several games that you can play on your computer. Games are a fun way to improve your mouse skills and hand-eye coordination. If you are connected to the Internet, you can play some games, such as Checkers, with other people over the Internet. Windows will match you with other players from around the world.

## PLAY GAMES

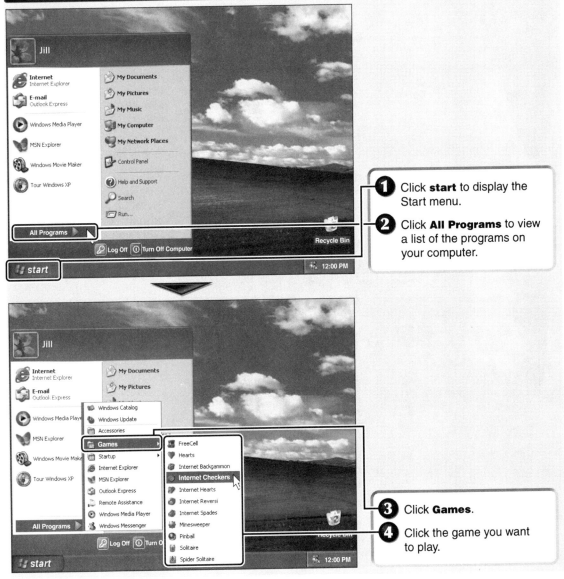

**1** Click **start** to display the Start menu.

**2** Click **All Programs** to view a list of the programs on your computer.

**3** Click **Games**.

**4** Click the game you want to play.

# in an instant

● If you selected an Internet game, a dialog box appears that displays information about playing games on the Internet.

*Note: If you selected a non-Internet game, skip to step 6.*

**5** Click **Play** to continue.

*Note: If you are not currently connected to the Internet, a dialog box will appear that allows you to connect.*

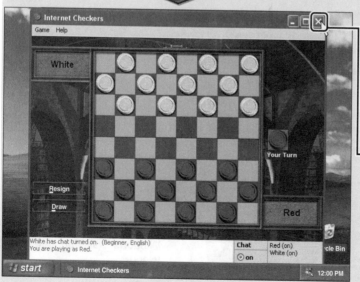

● A window appears, displaying the game. In this example, the Internet Checkers window appears.

**6** When you finish playing the game, click ▣ to close the window.

● If you are playing an Internet game, a message may appear, confirming that you want to leave the game. Click **Yes** to leave the game.

# CLOSE A MISBEHAVING PROGRAM

You can close a program that is no longer responding without having to shut down Windows. When you close a misbehaving program, you will lose any information you did not save in the program. Closing a misbehaving program should not affect other open programs.

## CLOSE A MISBEHAVING PROGRAM

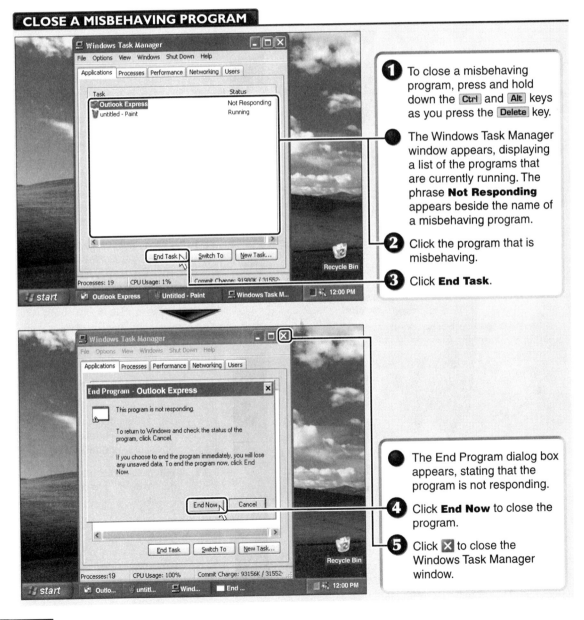

**1** To close a misbehaving program, press and hold down the `Ctrl` and `Alt` keys as you press the `Delete` key.

■ The Windows Task Manager window appears, displaying a list of the programs that are currently running. The phrase **Not Responding** appears beside the name of a misbehaving program.

**2** Click the program that is misbehaving.

**3** Click **End Task**.

■ The End Program dialog box appears, stating that the program is not responding.

**4** Click **End Now** to close the program.

**5** Click ✕ to close the Windows Task Manager window.

# SHUT DOWN WINDOWS

When you finish using your computer, you should shut down Windows before turning off the computer. Turning off your computer without shutting down properly may cause you to lose data. Before shutting down Windows, you should close all the programs you have open.

## SHUT DOWN WINDOWS

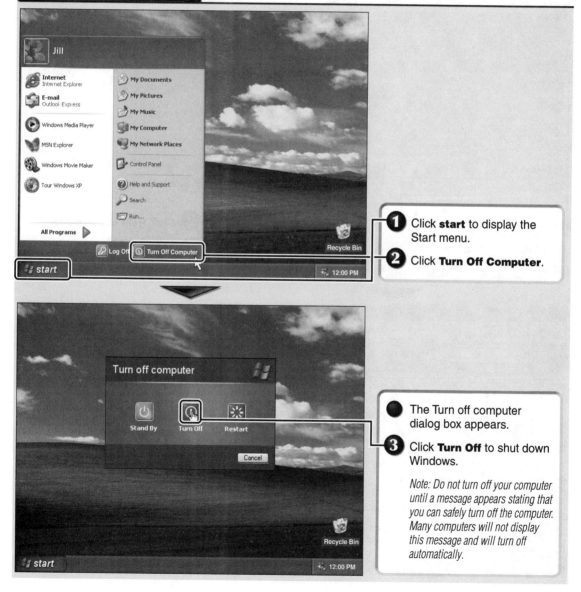

**1** Click **start** to display the Start menu.

**2** Click **Turn Off Computer**.

● The Turn off computer dialog box appears.

**3** Click **Turn Off** to shut down Windows.

*Note: Do not turn off your computer until a message appears stating that you can safely turn off the computer. Many computers will not display this message and will turn off automatically.*

15

# FIND HELP INFORMATION

If you do not know how to perform a task in Windows, you can use the Help feature to find information about the task. The Help feature provides a search tool that allows you to type one or more words and have Windows display help topics that contain the words. You can then select a help topic to display information about the topic.

## FIND HELP INFORMATION

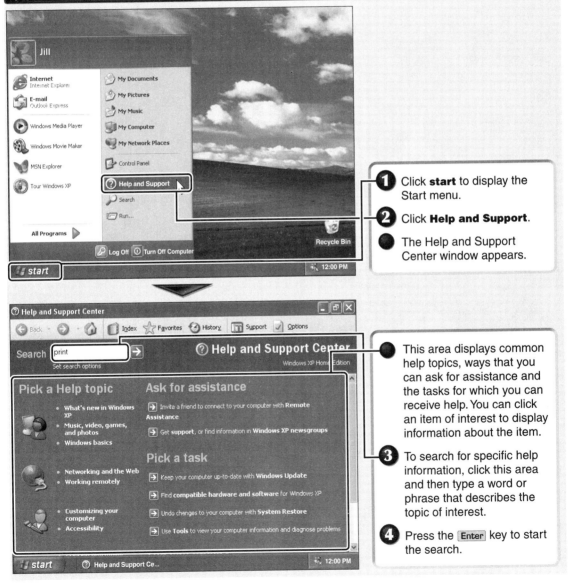

① Click **start** to display the Start menu.

② Click **Help and Support**.

● The Help and Support Center window appears.

● This area displays common help topics, ways that you can ask for assistance and the tasks for which you can receive help. You can click an item of interest to display information about the item.

③ To search for specific help information, click this area and then type a word or phrase that describes the topic of interest.

④ Press the [Enter] key to start the search.

**in an** *instant*

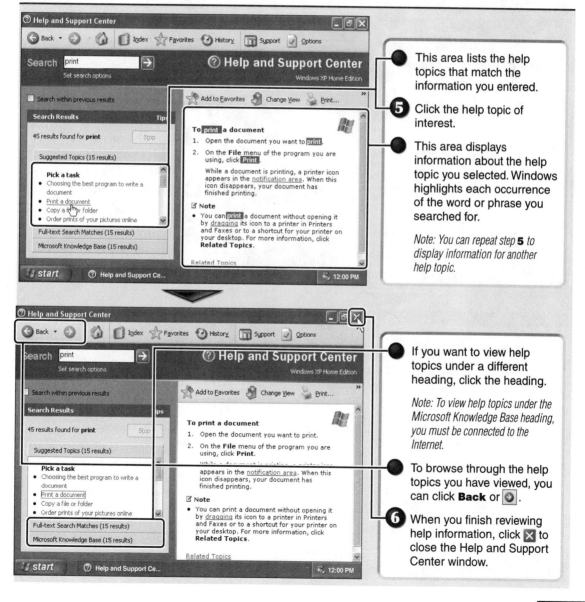

This area lists the help topics that match the information you entered.

**5** Click the help topic of interest.

This area displays information about the help topic you selected. Windows highlights each occurrence of the word or phrase you searched for.

*Note: You can repeat step **5** to display information for another help topic.*

If you want to view help topics under a different heading, click the heading.

*Note: To view help topics under the Microsoft Knowledge Base heading, you must be connected to the Internet.*

To browse through the help topics you have viewed, you can click **Back** or ⊙ .

**6** When you finish reviewing help information, click ☒ to close the Help and Support Center window.

# START WORDPAD

You can use WordPad to create and edit documents, such as letters and memos. WordPad provides features that allow you to easily make changes to the content and appearance of your document, but you may want to obtain a more sophisticated word processor, such as Microsoft Word or Corel WordPerfect, which offers more advanced features.

## START WORDPAD

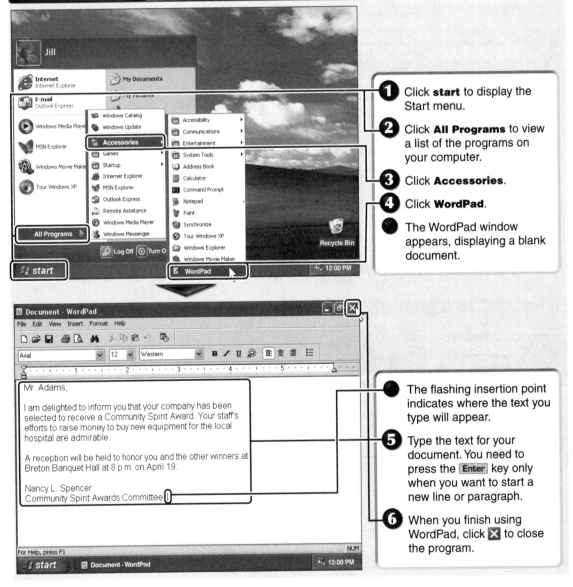

**1** Click **start** to display the Start menu.

**2** Click **All Programs** to view a list of the programs on your computer.

**3** Click **Accessories**.

**4** Click **WordPad**.

● The WordPad window appears, displaying a blank document.

● The flashing insertion point indicates where the text you type will appear.

**5** Type the text for your document. You need to press the `Enter` key only when you want to start a new line or paragraph.

**6** When you finish using WordPad, click ☒ to close the program.

# EDIT TEXT

You can easily edit the text in your document. You can
insert new text or remove text you no longer need. When
you insert new text into a document, the existing text will
shift to make room for the text you add. When you delete
text from a document, the remaining text will shift to fill
any empty spaces.

## EDIT TEXT

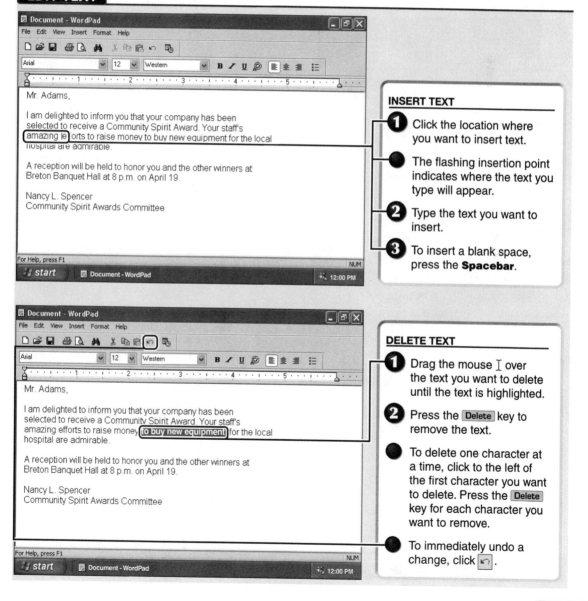

**INSERT TEXT**

**1** Click the location where
you want to insert text.

● The flashing insertion point
indicates where the text you
type will appear.

**2** Type the text you want to
insert.

**3** To insert a blank space,
press the **Spacebar**.

**DELETE TEXT**

**1** Drag the mouse I over
the text you want to delete
until the text is highlighted.

**2** Press the Delete key to
remove the text.

● To delete one character at
a time, click to the left of
the first character you want
to delete. Press the Delete
key for each character you
want to remove.

● To immediately undo a
change, click.

# CHANGE FONT OF TEXT

You can change the font of text to enhance the appearance of your document. WordPad provides a list of fonts for you to choose from. The fonts available in WordPad depend on your printer and the setup of your computer.

## CHANGE FONT OF TEXT

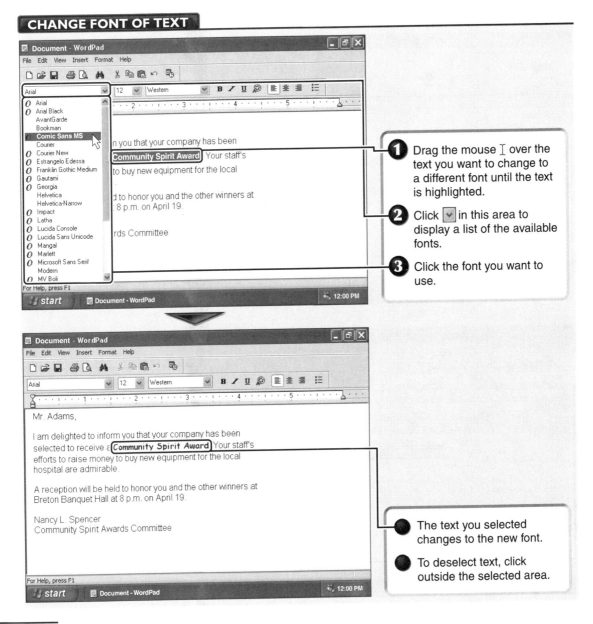

① Drag the mouse I over the text you want to change to a different font until the text is highlighted.

② Click ∨ in this area to display a list of the available fonts.

③ Click the font you want to use.

● The text you selected changes to the new font.

● To deselect text, click outside the selected area.

# CHANGE SIZE OF TEXT

You can increase or decrease the size of text in your document. Larger text is easier to read, but smaller text allows you to fit more information on a page. WordPad measures the size of text in points. There are approximately 72 points in an inch.

## CHANGE SIZE OF TEXT

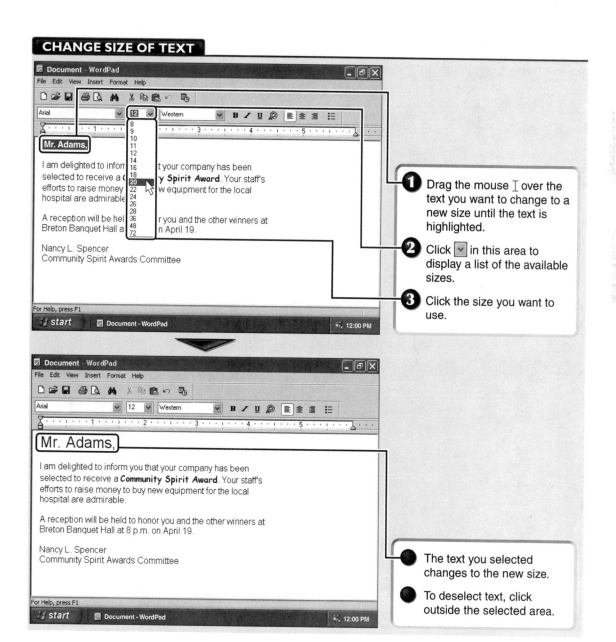

1 Drag the mouse I over the text you want to change to a new size until the text is highlighted.

2 Click ⌄ in this area to display a list of the available sizes.

3 Click the size you want to use.

● The text you selected changes to the new size.

● To deselect text, click outside the selected area.

# SAVE A DOCUMENT

You can save your document to store the document for future use. This allows you to later review and make changes to the document. To avoid losing your work due to a computer problem or power failure, you should regularly save changes you make to the document.

## SAVE A DOCUMENT

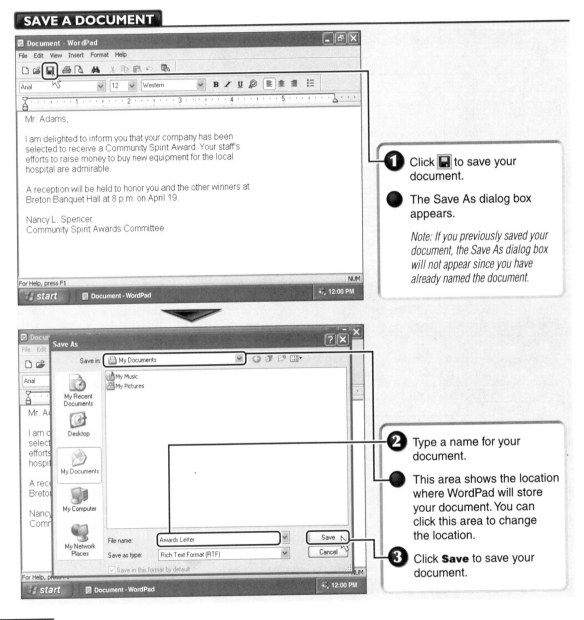

1 Click 🖫 to save your document.

● The Save As dialog box appears.

*Note: If you previously saved your document, the Save As dialog box will not appear since you have already named the document.*

2 Type a name for your document.

● This area shows the location where WordPad will store your document. You can click this area to change the location.

3 Click **Save** to save your document.

# OPEN A DOCUMENT

You can open a saved document to display the document on your screen. This allows you to review and make changes to the document. Since WordPad allows you to work with only one document at a time, you should make sure you save the document you are currently working with before opening another document.

## OPEN A DOCUMENT

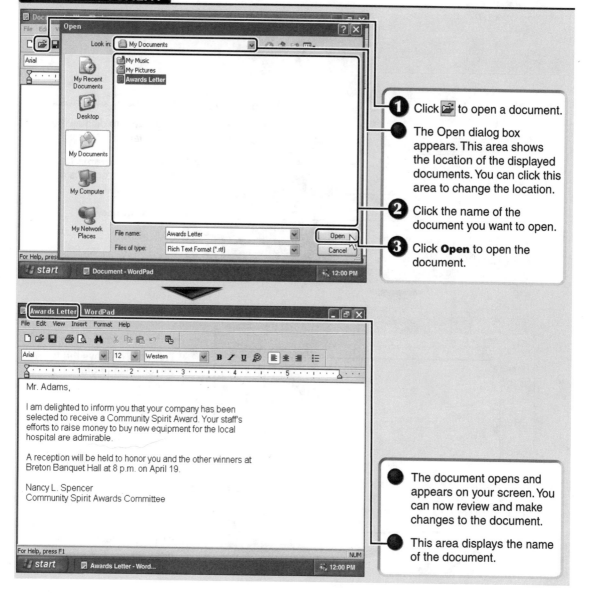

**1** Click 📂 to open a document.

The Open dialog box appears. This area shows the location of the displayed documents. You can click this area to change the location.

**2** Click the name of the document you want to open.

**3** Click **Open** to open the document.

The document opens and appears on your screen. You can now review and make changes to the document.

This area displays the name of the document.

# START PAINT

Paint is a simple program you can use to create and edit pictures on your computer. Pictures you create in Paint can be printed or inserted into other documents. Although Paint offers many features to help you create pictures, you may want to obtain an image editing program with more advanced features, such as Jasc Paint Shop Pro or Adobe Photoshop.

## START PAINT

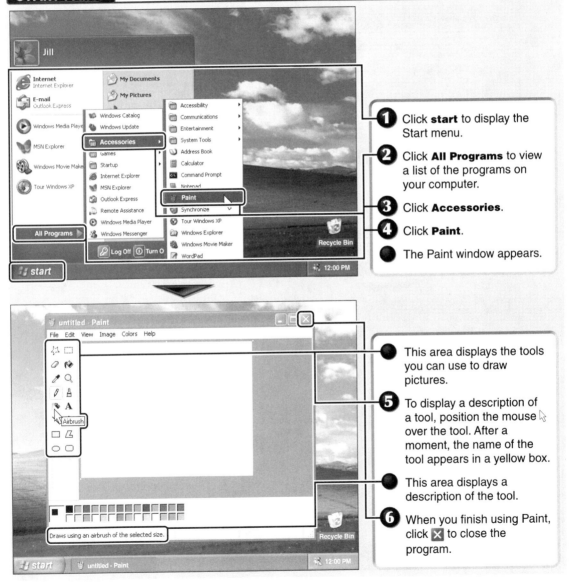

1. Click **start** to display the Start menu.

2. Click **All Programs** to view a list of the programs on your computer.

3. Click **Accessories**.

4. Click **Paint**.

● The Paint window appears.

● This area displays the tools you can use to draw pictures.

5. To display a description of a tool, position the mouse over the tool. After a moment, the name of the tool appears in a yellow box.

● This area displays a description of the tool.

6. When you finish using Paint, click ☒ to close the program.

You can use Paint's tools to draw shapes such as circles, squares and polygons in various colors. Before you draw a shape, you can specify whether you want to outline the shape, fill the shape with a color or both. You can also specify the colors you want to use for the outline and the inside of the shape.

## DRAW SHAPES

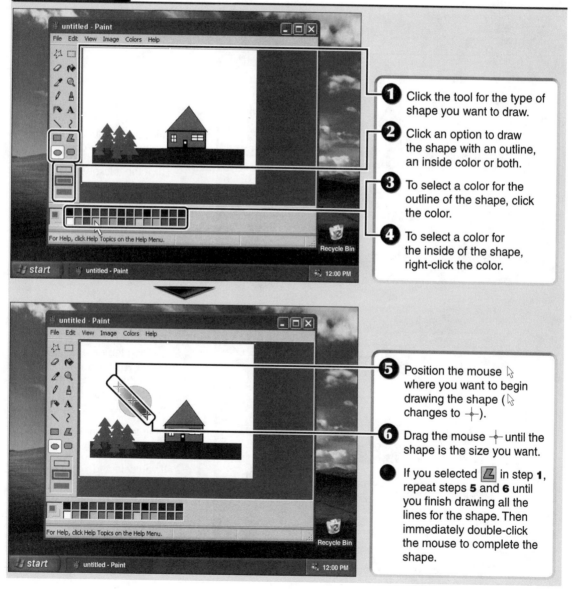

1. Click the tool for the type of shape you want to draw.

2. Click an option to draw the shape with an outline, an inside color or both.

3. To select a color for the outline of the shape, click the color.

4. To select a color for the inside of the shape, right-click the color.

5. Position the mouse where you want to begin drawing the shape ( changes to +).

6. Drag the mouse + until the shape is the size you want.

● If you selected ▣ in step 1, repeat steps 5 and 6 until you finish drawing all the lines for the shape. Then immediately double-click the mouse to complete the shape.

# DRAW LINES

Paint provides several tools that allow you to draw straight, wavy and curved lines in your pictures. The Pencil, Brush, Airbrush, Line and Curve tools can all help you obtain exactly the appearance you want for your lines. When you draw lines, you can specify the thickness and color for the lines.

DRAW LINES

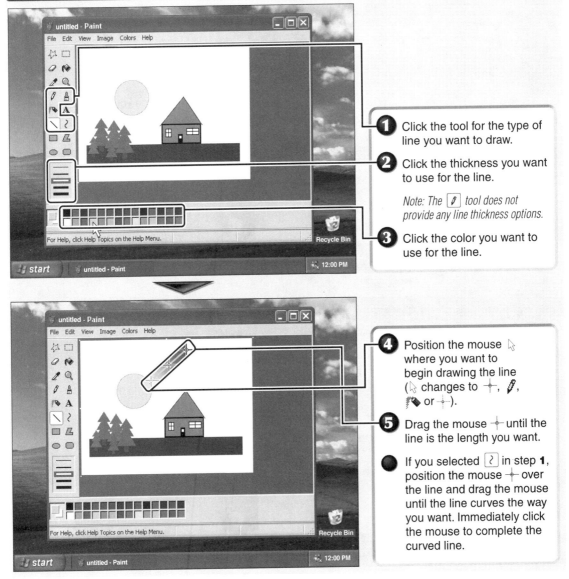

1 Click the tool for the type of line you want to draw.

2 Click the thickness you want to use for the line.

*Note: The ✐ tool does not provide any line thickness options.*

3 Click the color you want to use for the line.

4 Position the mouse ⌐ where you want to begin drawing the line (⌐ changes to ┼, ✐, 🖌 or ┉).

5 Drag the mouse ┼ until the line is the length you want.

● If you selected ⟨ in step 1, position the mouse ┼ over the line and drag the mouse until the line curves the way you want. Immediately click the mouse to complete the curved line.

# ERASE PART OF A PICTURE

You can use the Eraser tool to remove part of your picture. You can choose the size and color you want to use for the eraser. The size you should choose depends on the size of the area you want to erase. The color you choose should match the background color of the picture.

## ERASE PART OF A PICTURE

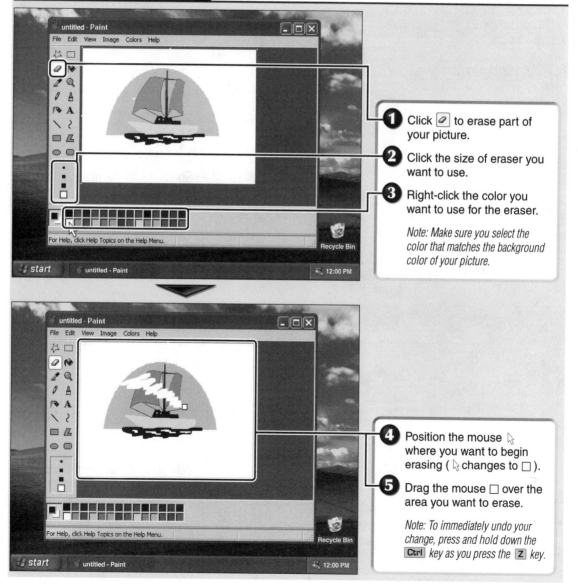

**1** Click 🖉 to erase part of your picture.

**2** Click the size of eraser you want to use.

**3** Right-click the color you want to use for the eraser.

*Note: Make sure you select the color that matches the background color of your picture.*

**4** Position the mouse ⊾ where you want to begin erasing ( ⊾ changes to ☐ ).

**5** Drag the mouse ☐ over the area you want to erase.

*Note: To immediately undo your change, press and hold down the* **Ctrl** *key as you press the* **Z** *key.*

You should save your picture to store the picture for future use. When saving a picture, Paint allows you to choose the location where you want to store the picture. To avoid losing your work due to a computer problem or power failure, you should regularly save changes you make to the picture.

## SAVE A PICTURE

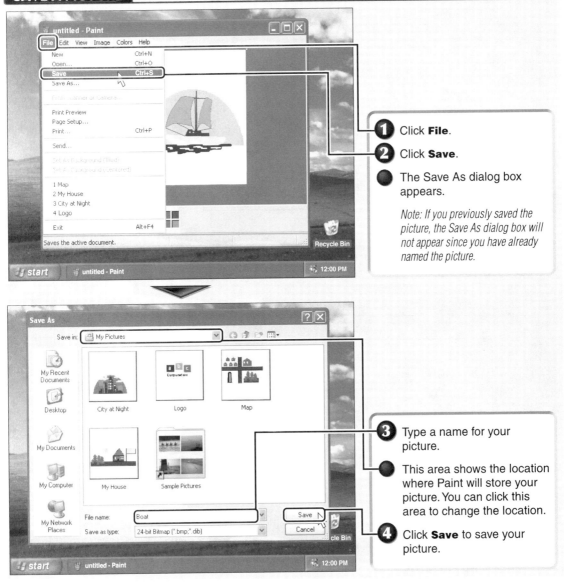

**1** Click **File**.

**2** Click **Save**.

● The Save As dialog box appears.

*Note: If you previously saved the picture, the Save As dialog box will not appear since you have already named the picture.*

**3** Type a name for your picture.

● This area shows the location where Paint will store your picture. You can click this area to change the location.

**4** Click **Save** to save your picture.

You can open a saved picture to display the picture on your screen. This allows you to review and make changes to the picture. Since Paint allows you to work with only one picture at a time, you should make sure you save the picture you are currently working with before opening another picture.

## OPEN A PICTURE

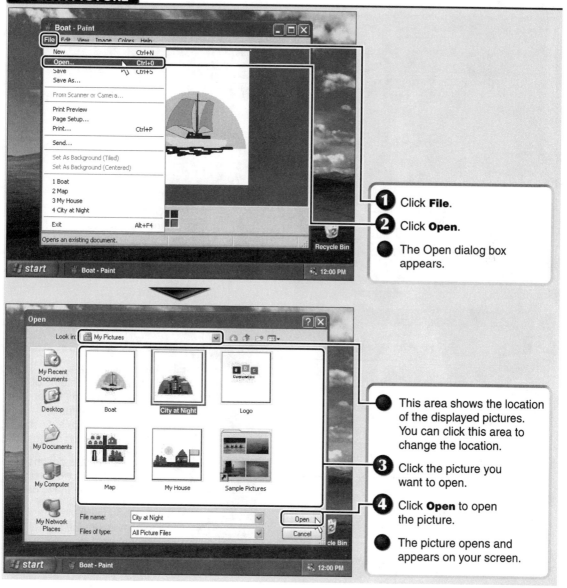

1 Click **File**.

2 Click **Open**.

● The Open dialog box appears.

● This area shows the location of the displayed pictures. You can click this area to change the location.

3 Click the picture you want to open.

4 Click **Open** to open the picture.

● The picture opens and appears on your screen.

# VIEW YOUR PERSONAL FOLDERS

Windows provides personal folders that offer a convenient place to store and manage your files. Your personal folders include the My Documents folder and its subfolders—the My Pictures and My Music folders. Many programs automatically store files in your personal folders. For example, pictures you create in Paint are automatically stored in the My Pictures folder.

## VIEW YOUR DOCUMENTS

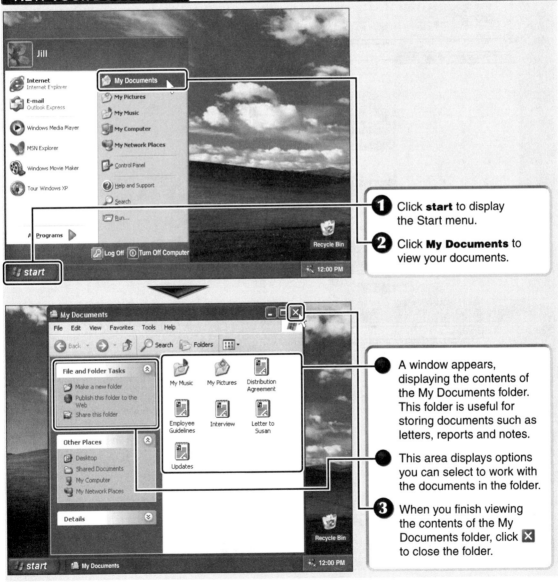

**1** Click **start** to display the Start menu.

**2** Click **My Documents** to view your documents.

■ A window appears, displaying the contents of the My Documents folder. This folder is useful for storing documents such as letters, reports and notes.

■ This area displays options you can select to work with the documents in the folder.

**3** When you finish viewing the contents of the My Documents folder, click ⊠ to close the folder.

# in an *instant*

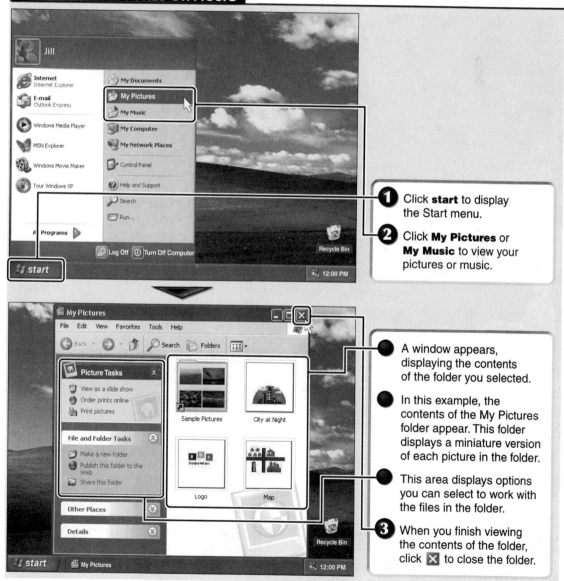

**1** Click **start** to display the Start menu.

**2** Click **My Pictures** or **My Music** to view your pictures or music.

● A window appears, displaying the contents of the folder you selected.

● In this example, the contents of the My Pictures folder appear. This folder displays a miniature version of each picture in the folder.

● This area displays options you can select to work with the files in the folder.

**3** When you finish viewing the contents of the folder, click ✕ to close the folder.

You can easily browse through the drives, folders and files on your computer. Windows uses folders to organize the information stored on your computer. A folder can contain items such as documents, programs and other folders. You can display the contents of folders and files of interest when viewing the contents of your computer.

## VIEW CONTENTS OF YOUR COMPUTER

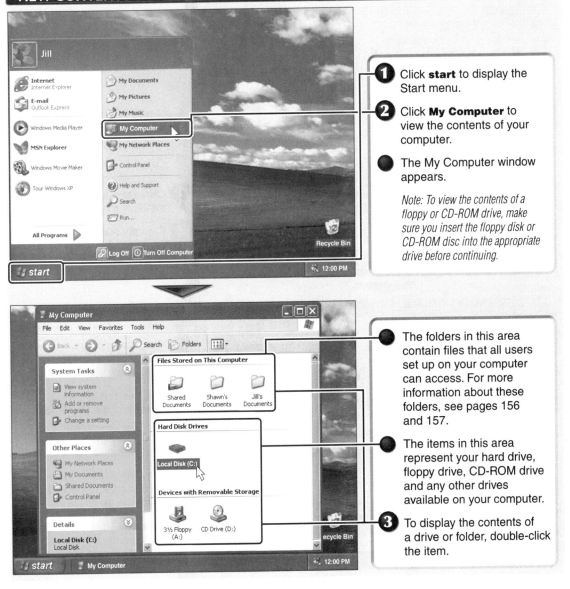

**1** Click **start** to display the Start menu.

**2** Click **My Computer** to view the contents of your computer.

● The My Computer window appears.

*Note: To view the contents of a floppy or CD-ROM drive, make sure you insert the floppy disk or CD-ROM disc into the appropriate drive before continuing.*

● The folders in this area contain files that all users set up on your computer can access. For more information about these folders, see pages 156 and 157.

● The items in this area represent your hard drive, floppy drive, CD-ROM drive and any other drives available on your computer.

**3** To display the contents of a drive or folder, double-click the item.

in an *Instant*

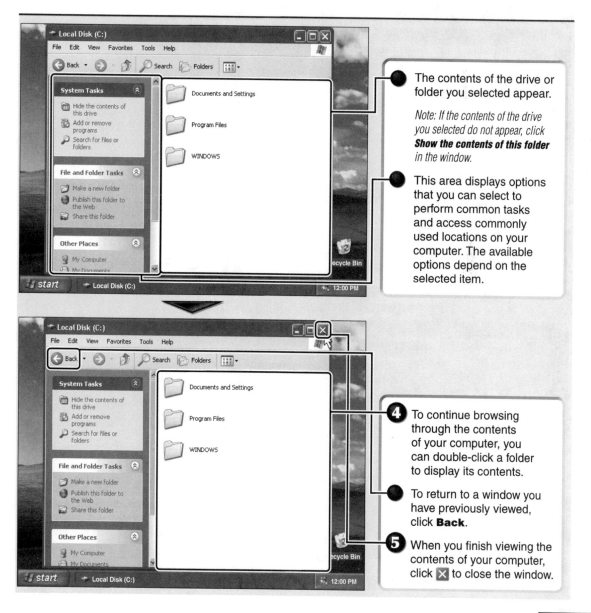

The contents of the drive or folder you selected appear.

*Note: If the contents of the drive you selected do not appear, click* **Show the contents of this folder** *in the window.*

This area displays options that you can select to perform common tasks and access commonly used locations on your computer. The available options depend on the selected item.

**4** To continue browsing through the contents of your computer, you can double-click a folder to display its contents.

To return to a window you have previously viewed, click **Back**.

**5** When you finish viewing the contents of your computer, click ☒ to close the window.

# CHANGE VIEW OF ITEMS

You can change the view of the items in a window. The view you select determines the way files and folders will appear in the window. Changing the view of items affects only the open window. Each window remembers the view you selected and displays the items in that view the next time you open the window.

CHANGE VIEW OF ITEMS

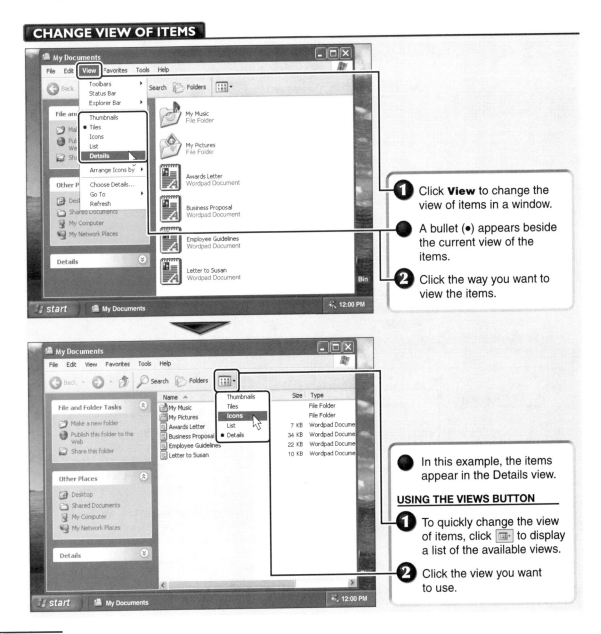

1 Click **View** to change the view of items in a window.

A bullet (•) appears beside the current view of the items.

2 Click the way you want to view the items.

In this example, the items appear in the Details view.

**USING THE VIEWS BUTTON**

1 To quickly change the view of items, click 🔲▾ to display a list of the available views.

2 Click the view you want to use.

34

# in an instant

## THE VIEWS

### FILMSTRIP

The Filmstrip view displays pictures in a single row that you can scroll through. This view is only available in some windows, such as the My Pictures window. You can click a picture to display a larger version of the picture above the other pictures.

### THUMBNAILS

The Thumbnails view displays a miniature version of each picture and some other types of files. If a miniature version of a file cannot be shown, an icon is displayed to indicate the type of file, such as a WordPad document (📄). In this view, miniature versions of a few pictures within a folder are shown on the folder's icon.

### TILES

The Tiles view displays items as large icons and displays information about each item below the item's filename. You can sort the items to change the information each item displays.

### ICONS

The Icons view displays items as small icons with the filenames appearing below each icon. This view allows you to display more items in the window at one time.

### LIST

The List view displays items as small icons arranged in a list. This view is useful if you want to find a particular item in a long list of items.

### DETAILS

The Details view displays information about each item, including the name, size, type and date the items were last changed.

# SORT ITEMS

You can sort the items displayed in a window to help you find files and folders more easily. You can sort items by name, size, type or the date the items were last changed. Some windows allow you to sort items in other ways. For example, the My Music window allows you to sort items by artist, album and track number.

## SORT ITEMS

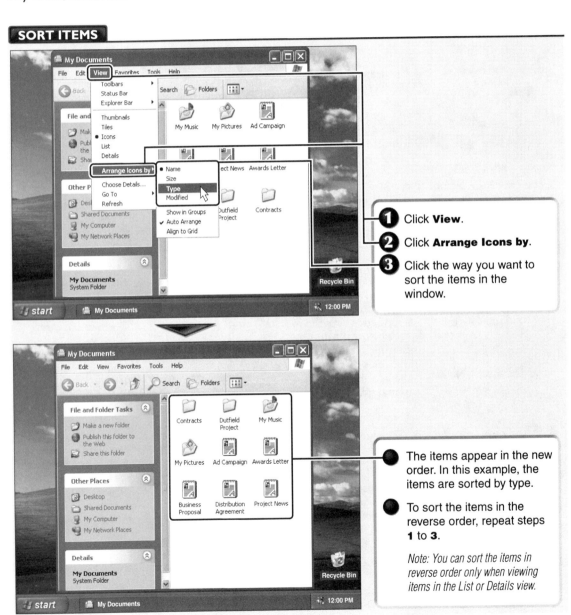

**1** Click **View**.

**2** Click **Arrange Icons by**.

**3** Click the way you want to sort the items in the window.

● The items appear in the new order. In this example, the items are sorted by type.

● To sort the items in the reverse order, repeat steps **1** to **3**.

*Note: You can sort the items in reverse order only when viewing items in the List or Details view.*

# GROUP ITEMS

You can group items to better organize the files and folders in a window. Windows will group items in most windows alphabetically by name. If you have previously sorted the items, however, Windows will group the items according to the order in which they were last sorted.

## GROUP ITEMS

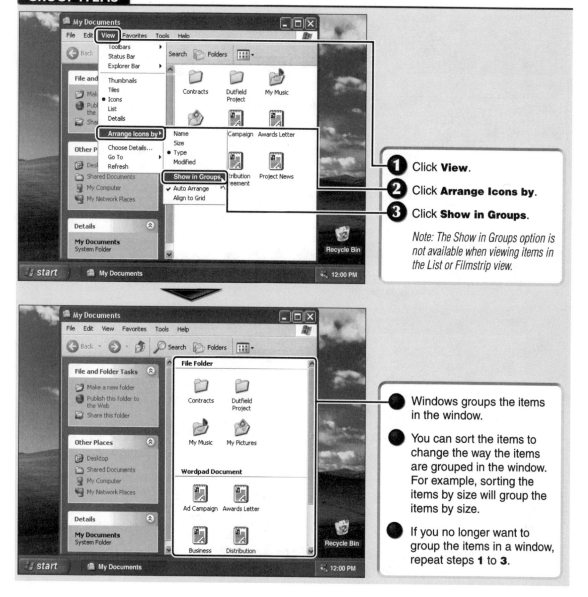

**1** Click **View**.

**2** Click **Arrange Icons by**.

**3** Click **Show in Groups**.

*Note: The Show in Groups option is not available when viewing items in the List or Filmstrip view.*

● Windows groups the items in the window.

● You can sort the items to change the way the items are grouped in the window. For example, sorting the items by size will group the items by size.

● If you no longer want to group the items in a window, repeat steps **1** to **3**.

# USING WINDOWS EXPLORER

Windows Explorer shows the organization of all the folders and files on your computer. You can work with the files in Windows Explorer as you would work with files in any window. For example, you can move, rename and delete files in Windows Explorer. This makes Windows Explorer useful for managing and organizing your files.

## USING WINDOWS EXPLORER

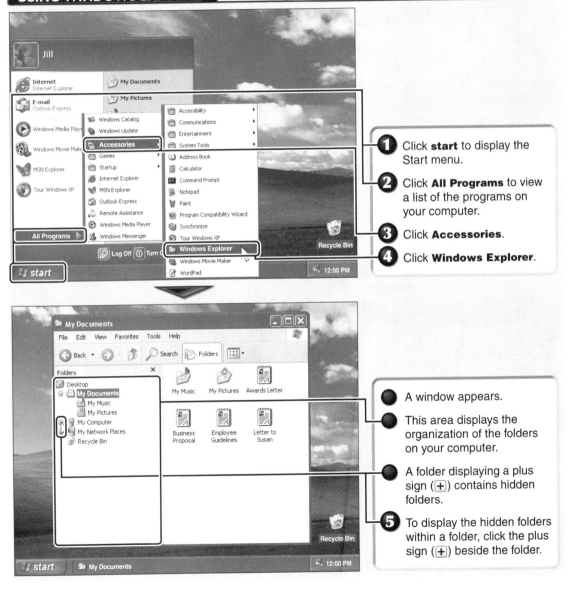

1 Click **start** to display the Start menu.

2 Click **All Programs** to view a list of the programs on your computer.

3 Click **Accessories**.

4 Click **Windows Explorer**.

● A window appears.

● This area displays the organization of the folders on your computer.

● A folder displaying a plus sign (⊞) contains hidden folders.

5 To display the hidden folders within a folder, click the plus sign (⊞) beside the folder.

# in an *instant*

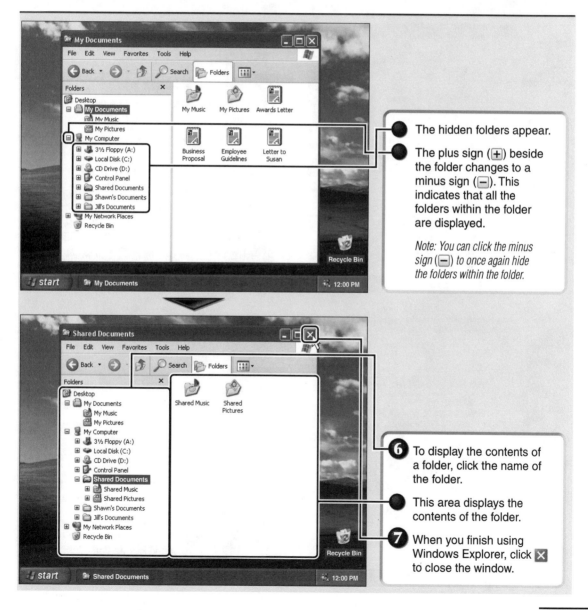

The hidden folders appear.

The plus sign (⊞) beside the folder changes to a minus sign (⊟). This indicates that all the folders within the folder are displayed.

*Note: You can click the minus sign (⊟) to once again hide the folders within the folder.*

**6** To display the contents of a folder, click the name of the folder.

This area displays the contents of the folder.

**7** When you finish using Windows Explorer, click ✕ to close the window.

# SELECT FILES

Before working with files, you often need to select the files you want to work with. Selected files appear highlighted on your screen. You can select folders the same way you select files. Selecting a folder will select all the files in the folder and any changes you make to the selected folder will affect all the files.

## SELECT FILES

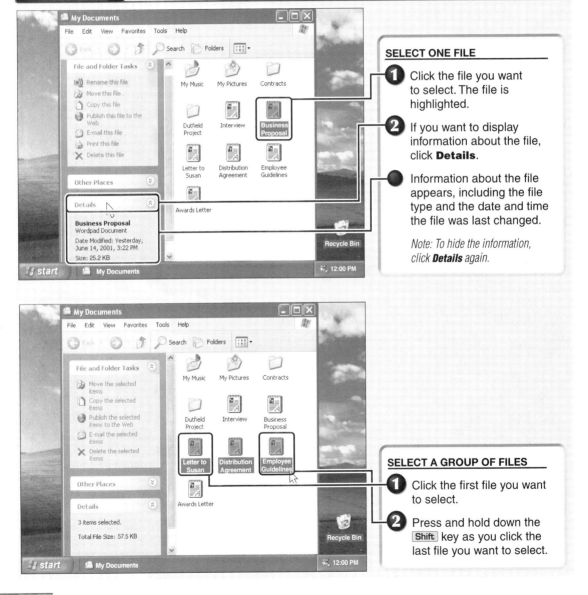

### SELECT ONE FILE

**1** Click the file you want to select. The file is highlighted.

**2** If you want to display information about the file, click **Details**.

● Information about the file appears, including the file type and the date and time the file was last changed.

*Note: To hide the information, click Details again.*

### SELECT A GROUP OF FILES

**1** Click the first file you want to select.

**2** Press and hold down the Shift key as you click the last file you want to select.

# in an instant

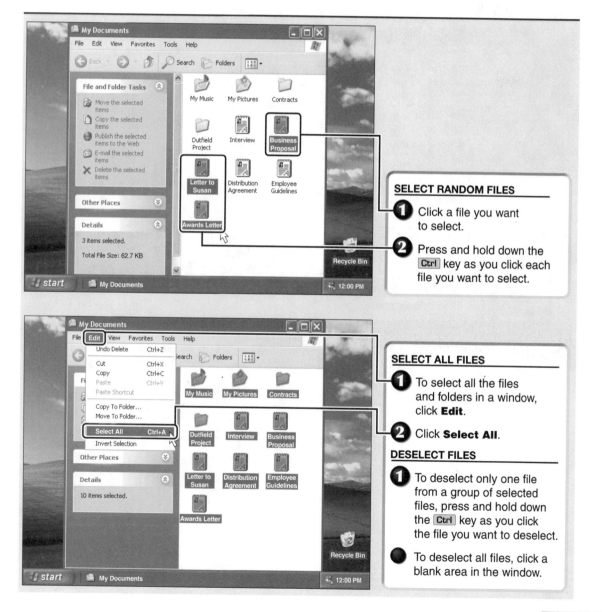

## SELECT RANDOM FILES

**1** Click a file you want to select.

**2** Press and hold down the **Ctrl** key as you click each file you want to select.

## SELECT ALL FILES

**1** To select all the files and folders in a window, click **Edit**.

**2** Click **Select All**.

## DESELECT FILES

**1** To deselect only one file from a group of selected files, press and hold down the **Ctrl** key as you click the file you want to deselect.

● To deselect all files, click a blank area in the window.

# OPEN A FILE

You can open a file to display its contents on your screen. Opening a file allows you to review and make changes to the file. Each file on your computer is associated with a specific program. When you open a file, the associated program starts automatically. You can also open a folder the same way you open a file.

## OPEN A FILE

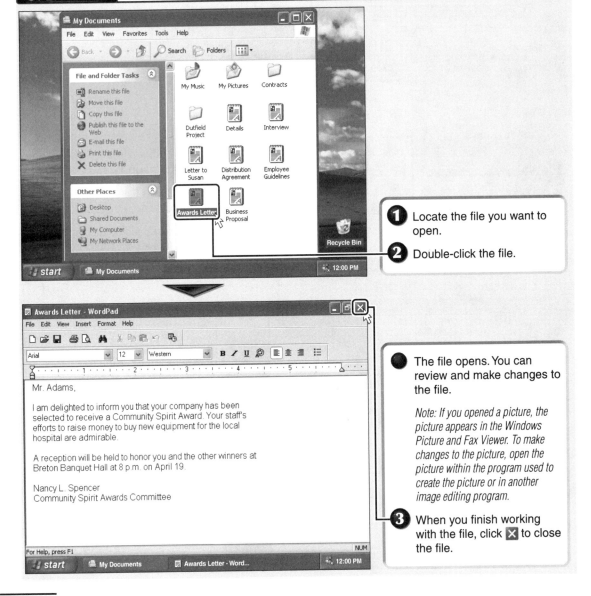

1 Locate the file you want to open.

2 Double-click the file.

● The file opens. You can review and make changes to the file.

*Note: If you opened a picture, the picture appears in the Windows Picture and Fax Viewer. To make changes to the picture, open the picture within the program used to create the picture or in another image editing program.*

3 When you finish working with the file, click ☒ to close the file.

# RENAME A FILE

You can rename a file to better describe the contents of the file. Renaming a file can help make the file easier to locate in the future. You can also rename folders the same way you rename files. You should not rename files or folders that Windows or other programs require to operate.

## RENAME A FILE

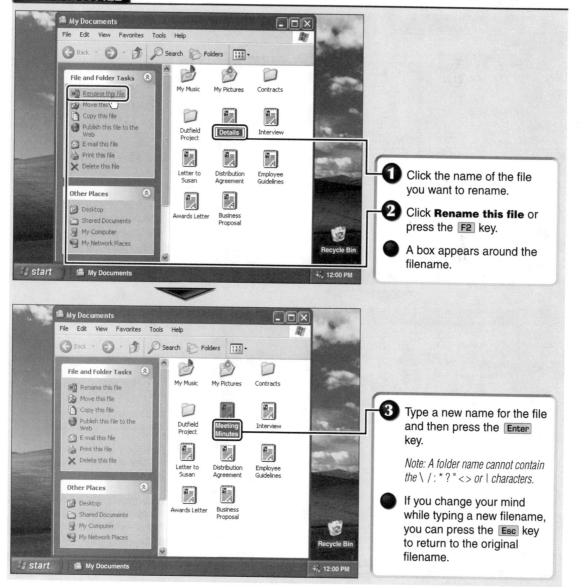

**1** Click the name of the file you want to rename.

**2** Click **Rename this file** or press the F2 key.

● A box appears around the filename.

**3** Type a new name for the file and then press the Enter key.

*Note: A folder name cannot contain the \ / : * ? " < > or | characters.*

● If you change your mind while typing a new filename, you can press the Esc key to return to the original filename.

# PRINT A FILE

You can produce a paper copy of a file stored on your computer. Windows allows you to quickly print a file from a window or the desktop. You can also stop a file from printing if you accidentally selected the wrong file or if you want to make last-minute changes to the file.

## PRINT A FILE

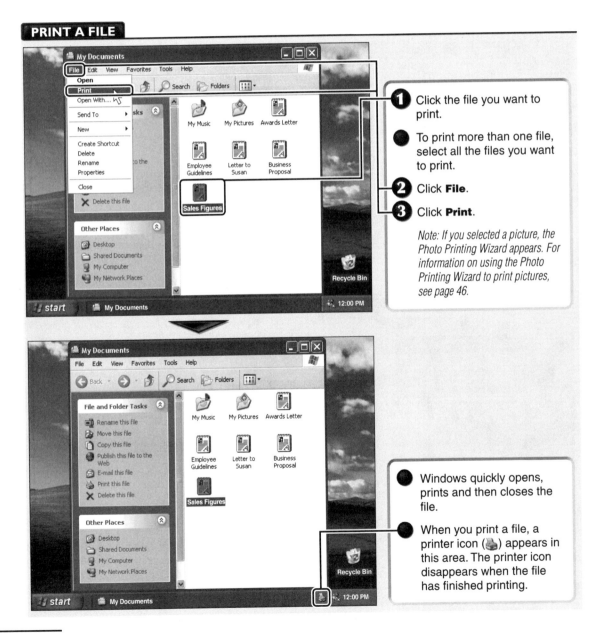

1 Click the file you want to print.

● To print more than one file, select all the files you want to print.

2 Click **File**.

3 Click **Print**.

*Note: If you selected a picture, the Photo Printing Wizard appears. For information on using the Photo Printing Wizard to print pictures, see page 46.*

● Windows quickly opens, prints and then closes the file.

● When you print a file, a printer icon (🖨) appears in this area. The printer icon disappears when the file has finished printing.

# in an *instant*

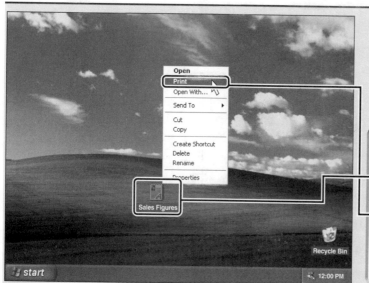

## PRINT A FILE LOCATED ON THE DESKTOP

**1** Right-click the file you want to print. A menu appears.

**2** Click **Print** to print the file.

● Windows quickly opens, prints and then closes the file.

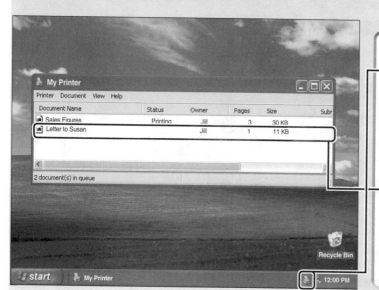

## STOP A FILE FROM PRINTING

**1** Double-click the printer icon (🖨) to display information about the files waiting to print.

*Note: If the printer icon is not displayed, the files have finished printing.*

**2** Click the file you no longer want to print and then press the Delete key.

● A confirmation dialog box will appear. Click **Yes** to stop the file from printing.

**45**

# PRINT PICTURES

You can use the Photo Printing Wizard to print a single picture or multiple pictures at once. For the best results when printing pictures, you should set your printer to the highest possible resolution and, if your printer allows, use high-quality, glossy paper specifically designed for printing pictures.

## PRINT PICTURES

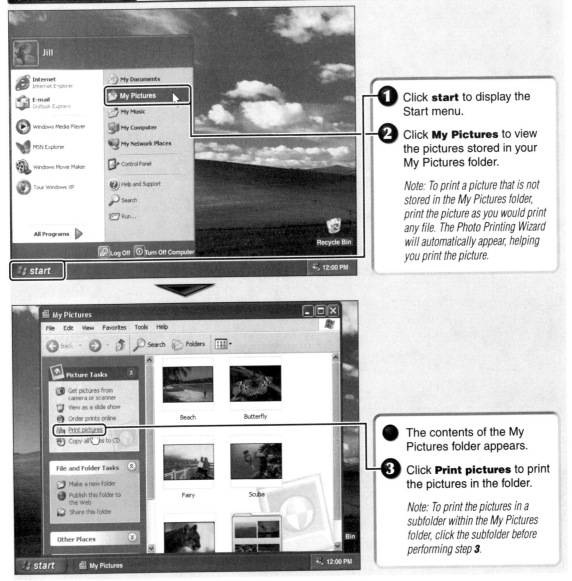

**1** Click **start** to display the Start menu.

**2** Click **My Pictures** to view the pictures stored in your My Pictures folder.

*Note: To print a picture that is not stored in the My Pictures folder, print the picture as you would print any file. The Photo Printing Wizard will automatically appear, helping you print the picture.*

■ The contents of the My Pictures folder appears.

**3** Click **Print pictures** to print the pictures in the folder.

*Note: To print the pictures in a subfolder within the My Pictures folder, click the subfolder before performing step 3.*

# in an instant

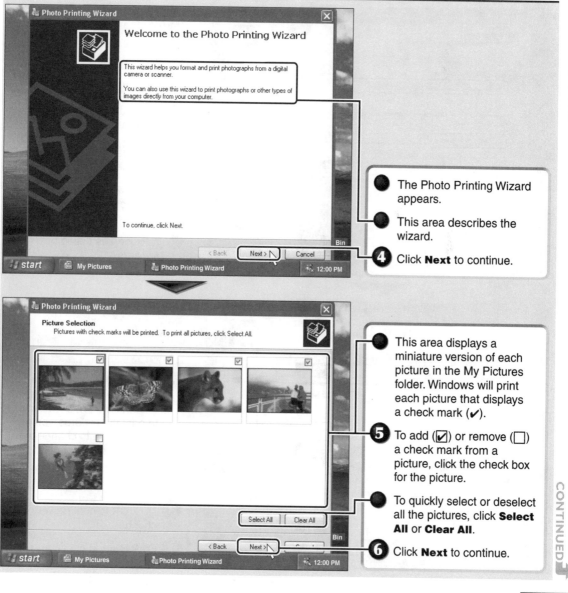

The Photo Printing Wizard appears.

This area describes the wizard.

**4** Click **Next** to continue.

This area displays a miniature version of each picture in the My Pictures folder. Windows will print each picture that displays a check mark (✔).

**5** To add (☑) or remove (☐) a check mark from a picture, click the check box for the picture.

To quickly select or deselect all the pictures, click **Select All** or **Clear All**.

**6** Click **Next** to continue.

CONTINUED

**47**

# PRINT PICTURES

The Photo Printing Wizard allows you to select the layout you want to use for the printed pictures. Some layouts may crop part of a large picture so the picture will fit better on a page. To conserve paper, you may want to choose a layout that prints more than one picture on a page.

## PRINT PICTURES (CONTINUED)

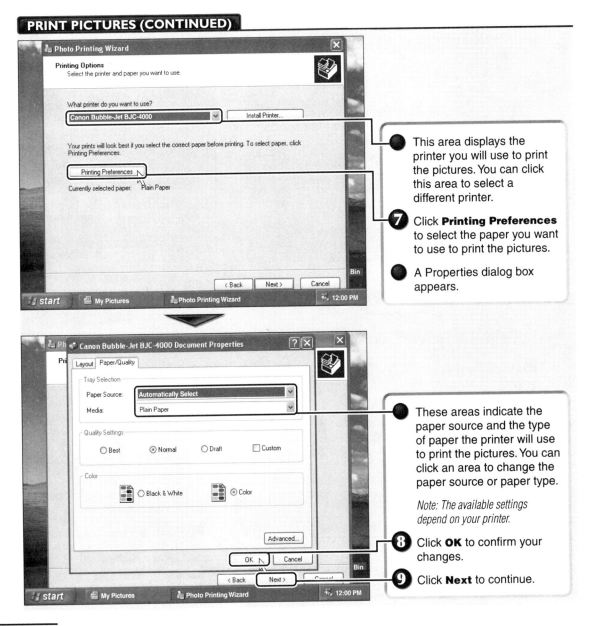

This area displays the printer you will use to print the pictures. You can click this area to select a different printer.

**7** Click **Printing Preferences** to select the paper you want to use to print the pictures.

A Properties dialog box appears.

These areas indicate the paper source and the type of paper the printer will use to print the pictures. You can click an area to change the paper source or paper type.

*Note: The available settings depend on your printer.*

**8** Click **OK** to confirm your changes.

**9** Click **Next** to continue.

in an *instant*

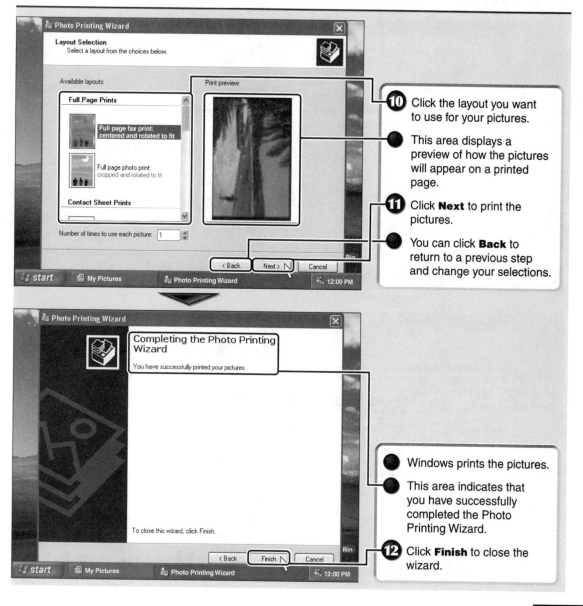

10 Click the layout you want to use for your pictures.

● This area displays a preview of how the pictures will appear on a printed page.

11 Click **Next** to print the pictures.

● You can click **Back** to return to a previous step and change your selections.

● Windows prints the pictures.

● This area indicates that you have successfully completed the Photo Printing Wizard.

12 Click **Finish** to close the wizard.

# DELETE A FILE

You can delete a file or folder you no longer need to free up space on your computer. When you delete a folder, Windows will also delete all the files and folders within the folder. To protect you from accidentally erasing important files, Windows stores deleted files in the Recycle Bin.

## DELETE A FILE

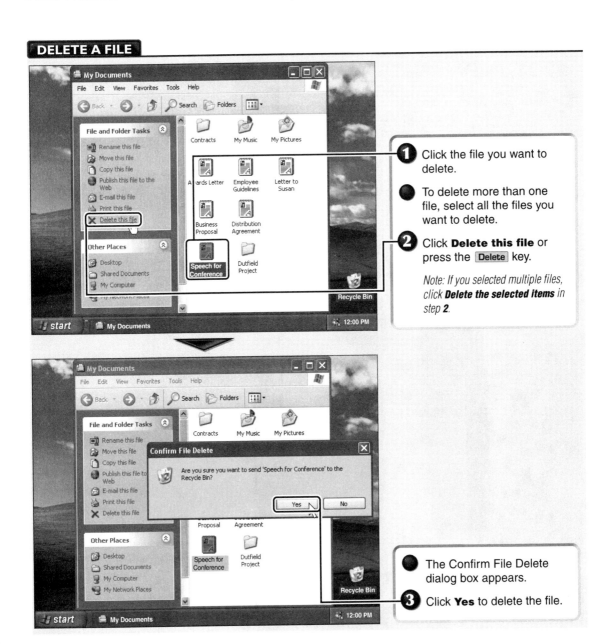

**1** Click the file you want to delete.

● To delete more than one file, select all the files you want to delete.

**2** Click **Delete this file** or press the `Delete` key.

*Note: If you selected multiple files, click **Delete the selected items** in step 2.*

● The Confirm File Delete dialog box appears.

**3** Click **Yes** to delete the file.

# in an instant

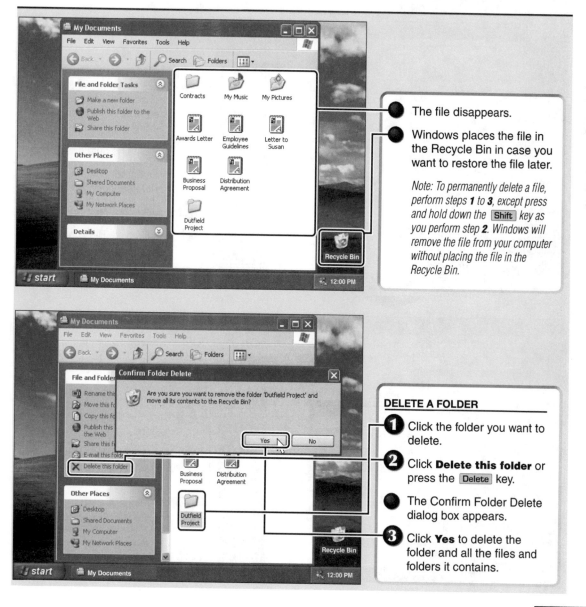

The file disappears.

Windows places the file in the Recycle Bin in case you want to restore the file later.

*Note: To permanently delete a file, perform steps 1 to 3, except press and hold down the* Shift *key as you perform step 2. Windows will remove the file from your computer without placing the file in the Recycle Bin.*

## DELETE A FOLDER

**1** Click the folder you want to delete.

**2** Click **Delete this folder** or press the Delete key.

The Confirm Folder Delete dialog box appears.

**3** Click **Yes** to delete the folder and all the files and folders it contains.

# RESTORE A DELETED FILE

The Recycle Bin stores all the files you have deleted from your computer. You can restore any file in the Recycle Bin to its original location on your computer. You cannot restore files you deleted from your network or from removable storage media, such as a floppy disk. Files deleted from these sources are permanently deleted.

## RESTORE A DELETED FILE

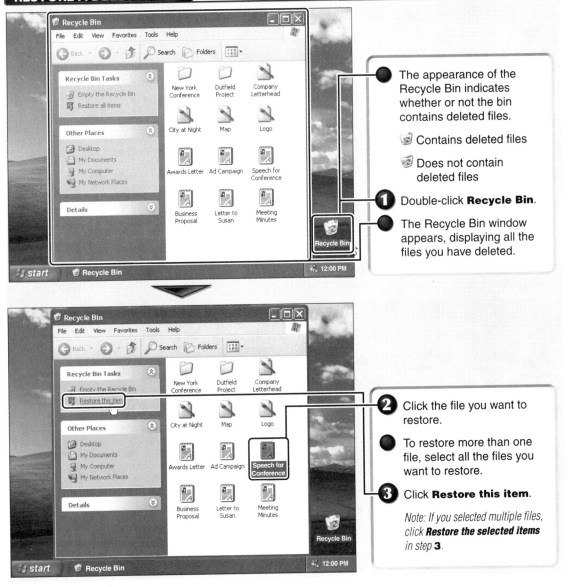

The appearance of the Recycle Bin indicates whether or not the bin contains deleted files.

🗑 Contains deleted files

🗑 Does not contain deleted files

**1** Double-click **Recycle Bin**.

The Recycle Bin window appears, displaying all the files you have deleted.

**2** Click the file you want to restore.

To restore more than one file, select all the files you want to restore.

**3** Click **Restore this item**.

*Note: If you selected multiple files, click **Restore the selected items** in step 3.*

# in an *instant*

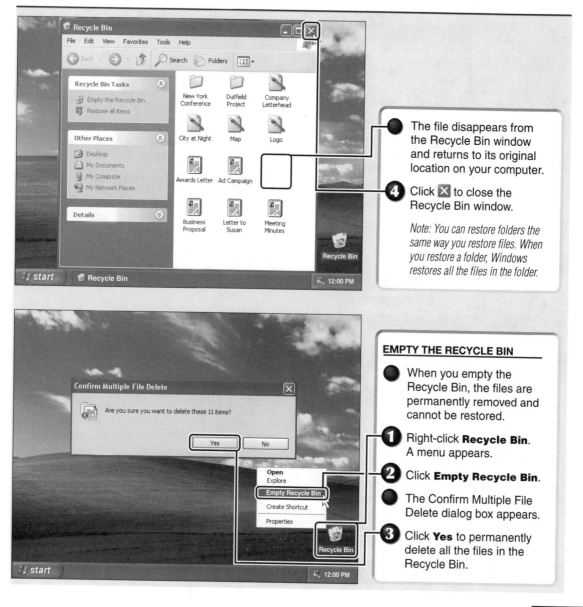

The file disappears from the Recycle Bin window and returns to its original location on your computer.

**4** Click ⊠ to close the Recycle Bin window.

*Note: You can restore folders the same way you restore files. When you restore a folder, Windows restores all the files in the folder.*

## EMPTY THE RECYCLE BIN

When you empty the Recycle Bin, the files are permanently removed and cannot be restored.

**1** Right-click **Recycle Bin**. A menu appears.

**2** Click **Empty Recycle Bin**.

The Confirm Multiple File Delete dialog box appears.

**3** Click **Yes** to permanently delete all the files in the Recycle Bin.

# MOVE A FILE

You can move a file to a new location on your computer to re-organize your files. When you move a file, the file will disappear from its original location and appear in the new location. You can move a folder the same way you move a file. When you move a folder, all the files in the folder are also moved.

MOVE A FILE

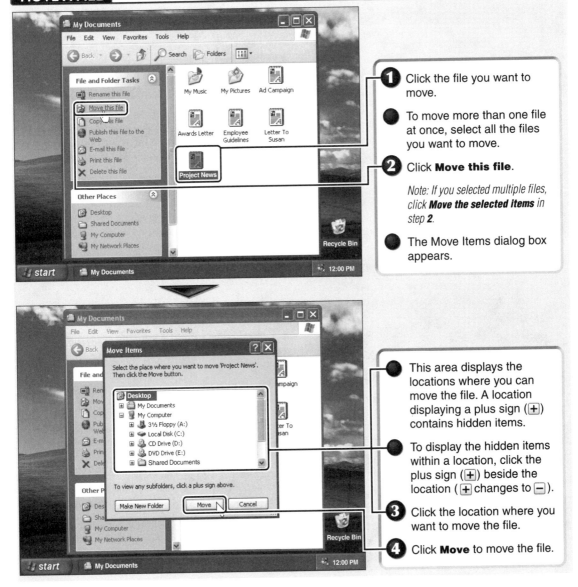

1 Click the file you want to move.

● To move more than one file at once, select all the files you want to move.

2 Click **Move this file**.

*Note: If you selected multiple files, click **Move the selected items** in step 2.*

● The Move Items dialog box appears.

● This area displays the locations where you can move the file. A location displaying a plus sign (⊞) contains hidden items.

● To display the hidden items within a location, click the plus sign (⊞) beside the location (⊞ changes to ⊟).

3 Click the location where you want to move the file.

4 Click **Move** to move the file.

# in an *instant*

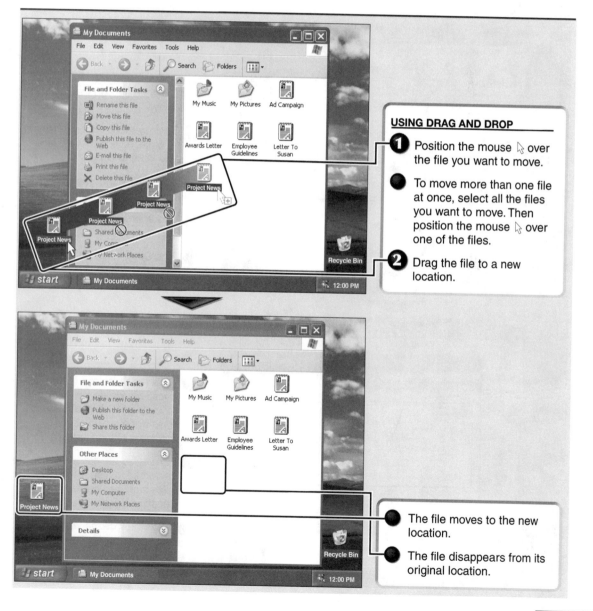

### USING DRAG AND DROP

**1** Position the mouse ⅄ over the file you want to move.

● To move more than one file at once, select all the files you want to move. Then position the mouse ⅄ over one of the files.

**2** Drag the file to a new location.

● The file moves to the new location.

● The file disappears from its original location.

# COPY A FILE

You can copy a file to a new location on your computer. When you copy a file, the file appears in both the original and new locations. You can copy a folder the same way you copy a file. When you copy a folder, all the files in the folder are also copied.

## COPY A FILE

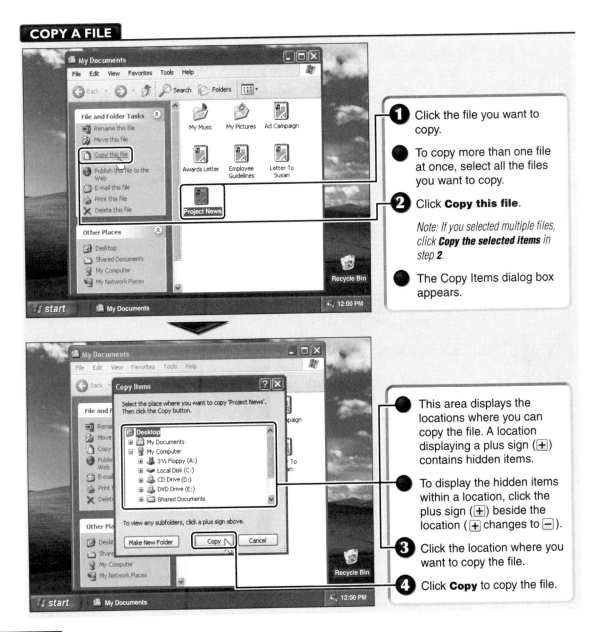

**1** Click the file you want to copy.

● To copy more than one file at once, select all the files you want to copy.

**2** Click **Copy this file**.

*Note: If you selected multiple files, click **Copy the selected items** in step 2.*

● The Copy Items dialog box appears.

● This area displays the locations where you can copy the file. A location displaying a plus sign (⊞) contains hidden items.

● To display the hidden items within a location, click the plus sign (⊞) beside the location (⊞ changes to ⊟).

**3** Click the location where you want to copy the file.

**4** Click **Copy** to copy the file.

# in an *instant*

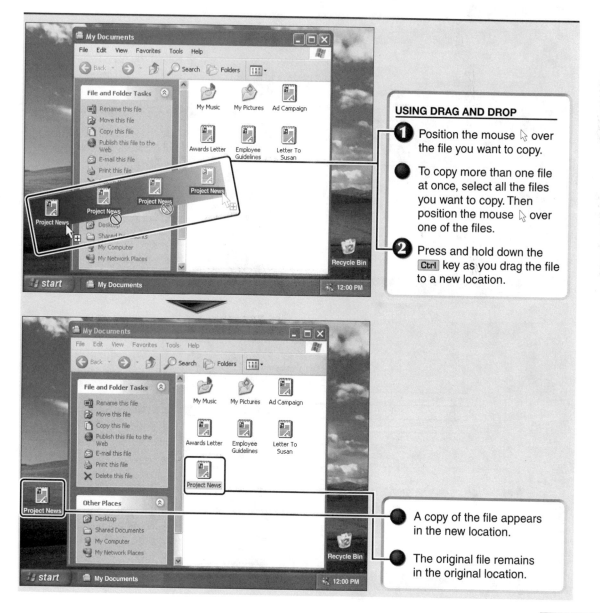

**USING DRAG AND DROP**

**1** Position the mouse ⬚ over the file you want to copy.

● To copy more than one file at once, select all the files you want to copy. Then position the mouse ⬚ over one of the files.

**2** Press and hold down the `Ctrl` key as you drag the file to a new location.

● A copy of the file appears in the new location.

● The original file remains in the original location.

# E-MAIL A FILE

If you have an e-mail account set up on your computer, you can e-mail a file to another person who has an e-mail account. You can e-mail many types of files, including documents, pictures, videos and sounds. The computer receiving the file must have the necessary hardware and software installed to display or play the file.

## E-MAIL A FILE

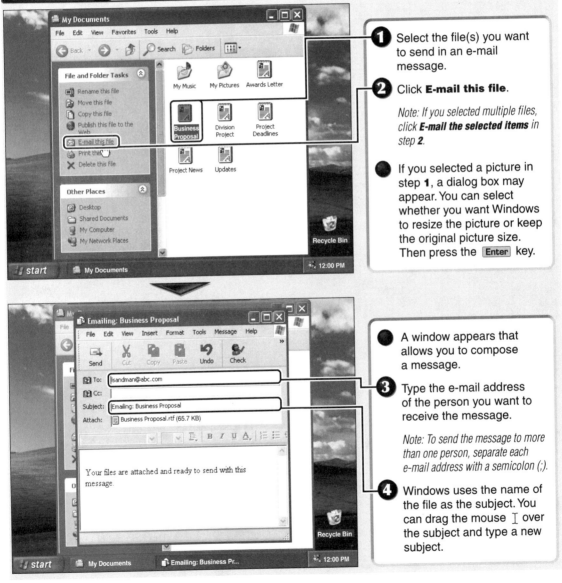

① Select the file(s) you want to send in an e-mail message.

② Click **E-mail this file**.

*Note: If you selected multiple files, click **E-mail the selected items** in step 2.*

● If you selected a picture in step 1, a dialog box may appear. You can select whether you want Windows to resize the picture or keep the original picture size. Then press the Enter key.

● A window appears that allows you to compose a message.

③ Type the e-mail address of the person you want to receive the message.

*Note: To send the message to more than one person, separate each e-mail address with a semicolon (;).*

④ Windows uses the name of the file as the subject. You can drag the mouse I over the subject and type a new subject.

# in an instant

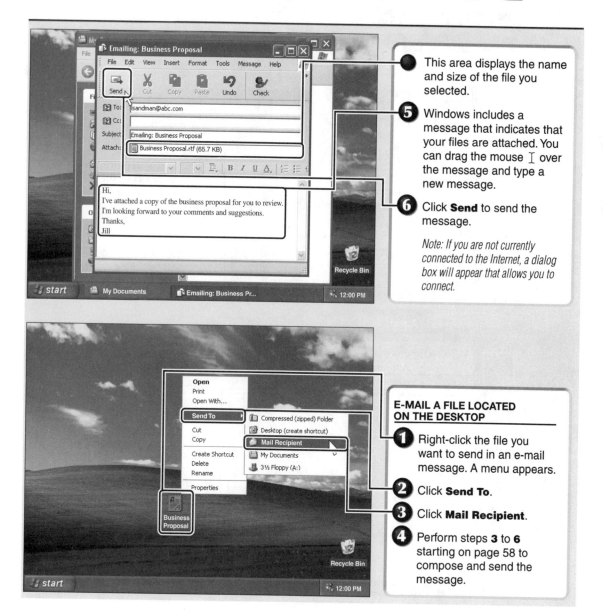

This area displays the name and size of the file you selected.

**5** Windows includes a message that indicates that your files are attached. You can drag the mouse I over the message and type a new message.

**6** Click **Send** to send the message.

*Note: If you are not currently connected to the Internet, a dialog box will appear that allows you to connect.*

**E-MAIL A FILE LOCATED ON THE DESKTOP**

**1** Right-click the file you want to send in an e-mail message. A menu appears.

**2** Click **Send To**.

**3** Click **Mail Recipient**.

**4** Perform steps **3** to **6** starting on page 58 to compose and send the message.

# PUBLISH A FILE TO THE WEB

You can publish files, such as documents and pictures, to the Web to allow friends, family and colleagues to view the files from many locations. The first time you publish a file to the Web, you will need to set up an account with a service provider. If you have previously set up an account, you may be asked to log in to your account.

## PUBLISH A FILE TO THE WEB

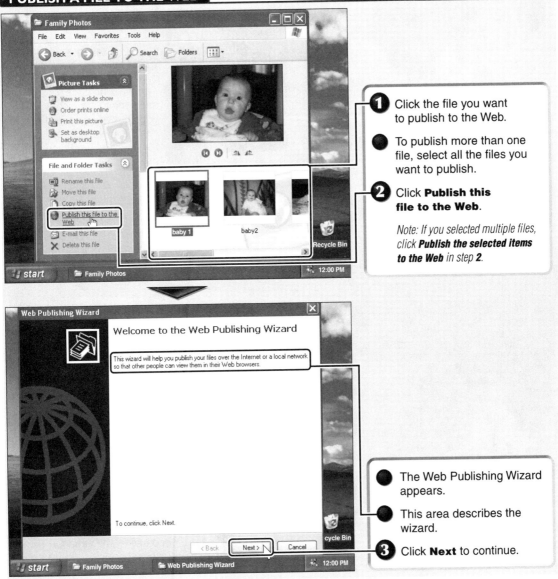

**1** Click the file you want to publish to the Web.

To publish more than one file, select all the files you want to publish.

**2** Click **Publish this file to the Web**.

*Note: If you selected multiple files, click Publish the selected items to the Web in step 2.*

The Web Publishing Wizard appears.

This area describes the wizard.

**3** Click **Next** to continue.

# in an *instant*

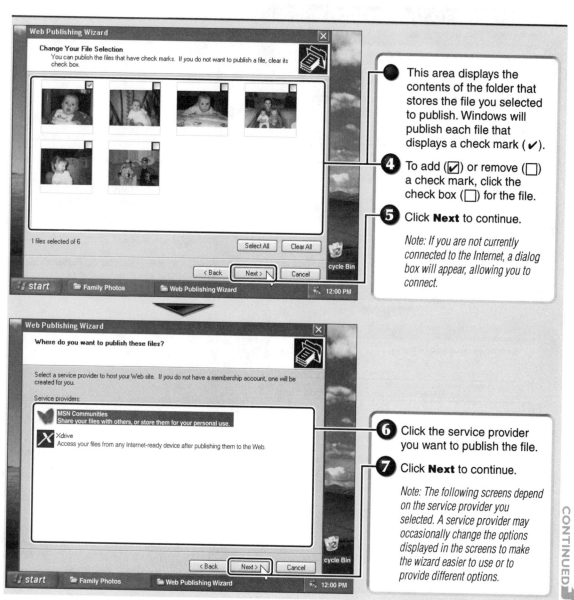

This area displays the contents of the folder that stores the file you selected to publish. Windows will publish each file that displays a check mark (✔).

④ To add (☑) or remove (☐) a check mark, click the check box (☐) for the file.

⑤ Click **Next** to continue.

*Note: If you are not currently connected to the Internet, a dialog box will appear, allowing you to connect.*

⑥ Click the service provider you want to publish the file.

⑦ Click **Next** to continue.

*Note: The following screens depend on the service provider you selected. A service provider may occasionally change the options displayed in the screens to make the wizard easier to use or to provide different options.*

CONTINUED

**61**

# PUBLISH A FILE TO THE WEB

If you selected the MSN service provider to publish your file, you can share the file with other people or publish the file for your own private use. Publishing a file for private use allows you to access the file from many locations or store a backup copy of an important file.

## PUBLISH A FILE TO THE WEB (CONTINUED)

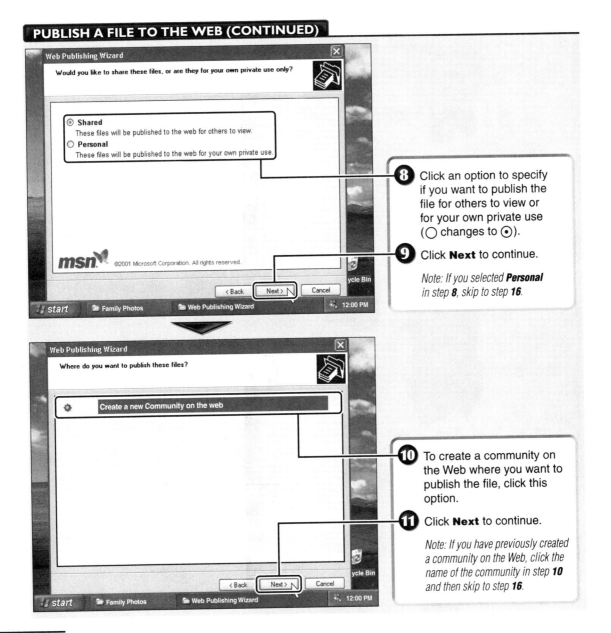

**8** Click an option to specify if you want to publish the file for others to view or for your own private use (○ changes to ⊙).

**9** Click **Next** to continue.

*Note: If you selected Personal in step 8, skip to step 16.*

**10** To create a community on the Web where you want to publish the file, click this option.

**11** Click **Next** to continue.

*Note: If you have previously created a community on the Web, click the name of the community in step 10 and then skip to step 16.*

# in an instant

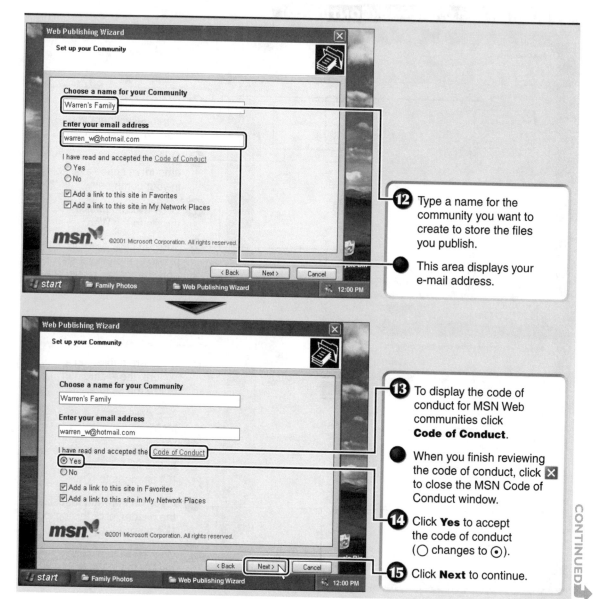

**Web Publishing Wizard**

**Set up your Community**

Choose a name for your Community

Warren's Family

Enter your email address

warren_w@hotmail.com

I have read and accepted the Code of Conduct
○ Yes
○ No

☑ Add a link to this site in Favorites
☑ Add a link to this site in My Network Places

msn @2001 Microsoft Corporation. All rights reserved.

< Back    Next >    Cancel

start    Family Photos    Web Publishing Wizard    12:00 PM

**12** Type a name for the community you want to create to store the files you publish.

● This area displays your e-mail address.

**Web Publishing Wizard**

**Set up your Community**

Choose a name for your Community

Warren's Family

Enter your email address

warren_w@hotmail.com

I have read and accepted the Code of Conduct
⊙ Yes
○ No

☑ Add a link to this site in Favorites
☑ Add a link to this site in My Network Places

msn @2001 Microsoft Corporation. All rights reserved.

< Back    Next >    Cancel

start    Family Photos    Web Publishing Wizard    12:00 PM

**13** To display the code of conduct for MSN Web communities click **Code of Conduct**.

● When you finish reviewing the code of conduct, click ☒ to close the MSN Code of Conduct window.

**14** Click **Yes** to accept the code of conduct (○ changes to ⊙).

**15** Click **Next** to continue.

CONTINUED

# PUBLISH A FILE TO THE WEB

After you publish files to the Web, the My Network Places window may contain a folder that stores links to the files you have published. Your list of favorite Web pages may also display a link to the Web site where you published the files.

## PUBLISH A FILE TO THE WEB (CONTINUED)

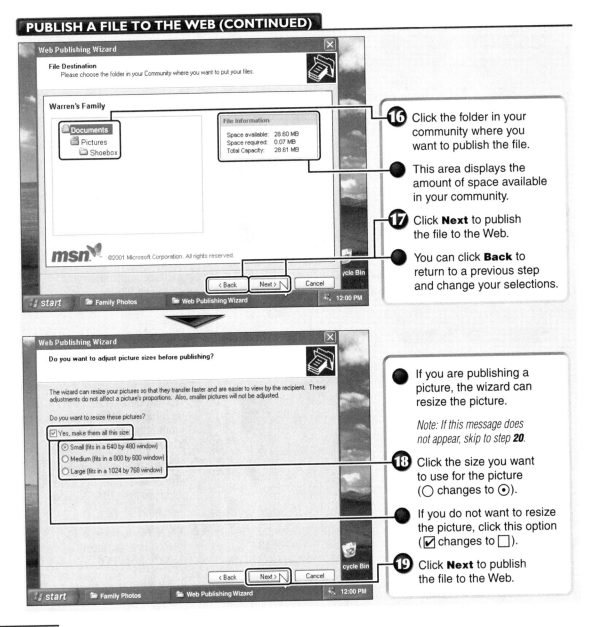

**16** Click the folder in your community where you want to publish the file.

● This area displays the amount of space available in your community.

**17** Click **Next** to publish the file to the Web.

● You can click **Back** to return to a previous step and change your selections.

● If you are publishing a picture, the wizard can resize the picture.

*Note: If this message does not appear, skip to step **20**.*

**18** Click the size you want to use for the picture (○ changes to ◉).

● If you do not want to resize the picture, click this option (☑ changes to ☐).

**19** Click **Next** to publish the file to the Web.

# in an *instant*

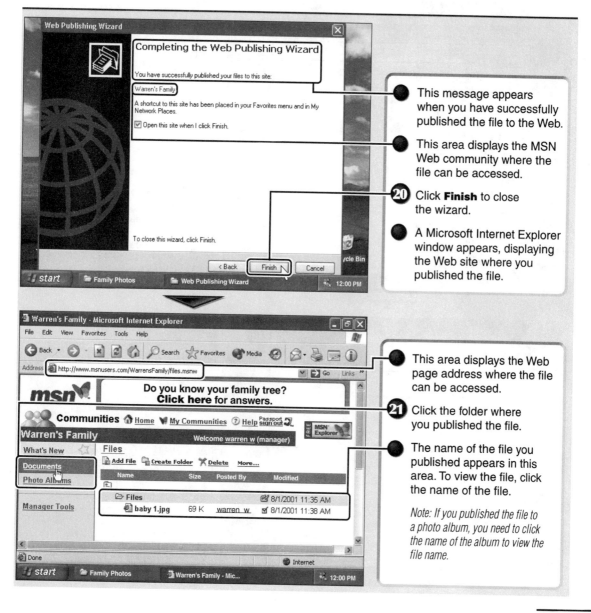

This message appears when you have successfully published the file to the Web.

This area displays the MSN Web community where the file can be accessed.

**20** Click **Finish** to close the wizard.

A Microsoft Internet Explorer window appears, displaying the Web site where you published the file.

This area displays the Web page address where the file can be accessed.

**21** Click the folder where you published the file.

The name of the file you published appears in this area. To view the file, click the name of the file.

*Note: If you published the file to a photo album, you need to click the name of the album to view the file name.*

# CREATE A NEW FILE

You can instantly create, name and store a new file in the location you want without starting a program. Creating a new file without starting a program allows you to focus on the organization of your files rather than the programs you need to accomplish your tasks.

CREATE A NEW FILE

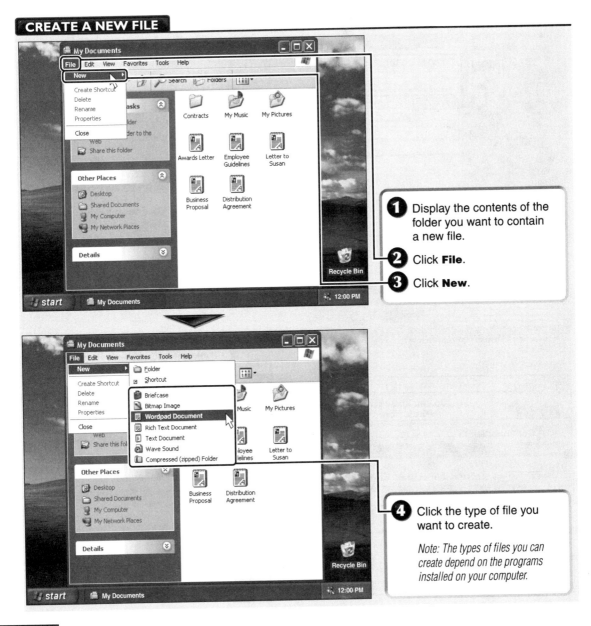

1 Display the contents of the folder you want to contain a new file.

2 Click **File**.

3 Click **New**.

4 Click the type of file you want to create.

*Note: The types of files you can create depend on the programs installed on your computer.*

# in an instant

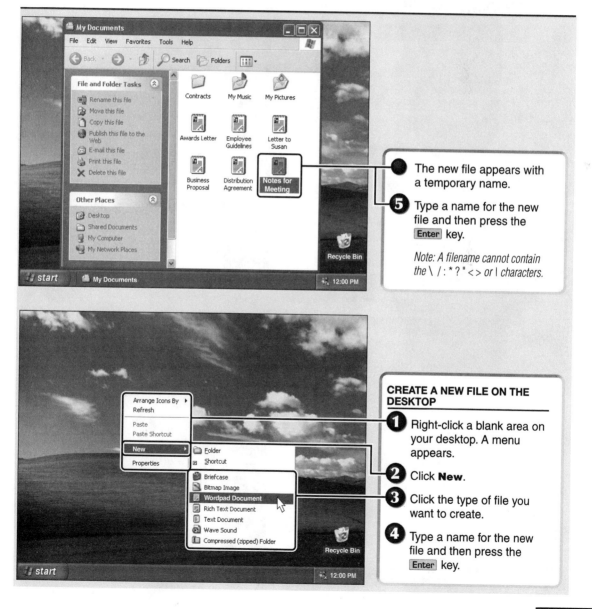

The new file appears with a temporary name.

**5** Type a name for the new file and then press the **Enter** key.

*Note: A filename cannot contain the \ / : * ? " < > or | characters.*

**CREATE A NEW FILE ON THE DESKTOP**

**1** Right-click a blank area on your desktop. A menu appears.

**2** Click **New**.

**3** Click the type of file you want to create.

**4** Type a name for the new file and then press the **Enter** key.

# CREATE A NEW FOLDER

You can create a new folder to help you organize the files stored on your computer. Creating a folder is like placing a new folder in a filing cabinet. You can create a new folder to store files you want to keep together, such as files for a particular project. For example, you can create a folder named "Reports" to store all of your reports.

## CREATE A NEW FOLDER

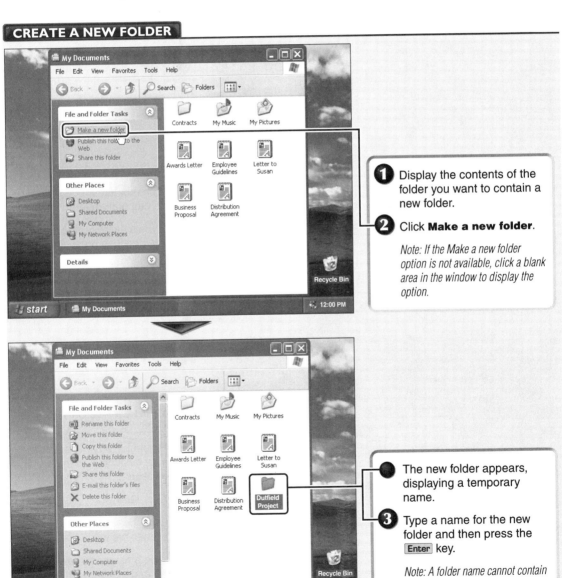

**1** Display the contents of the folder you want to contain a new folder.

**2** Click **Make a new folder**.

*Note: If the Make a new folder option is not available, click a blank area in the window to display the option.*

■ The new folder appears, displaying a temporary name.

**3** Type a name for the new folder and then press the **Enter** key.

*Note: A folder name cannot contain the \ / : * ? " < > or | characters.*

in an *instant*

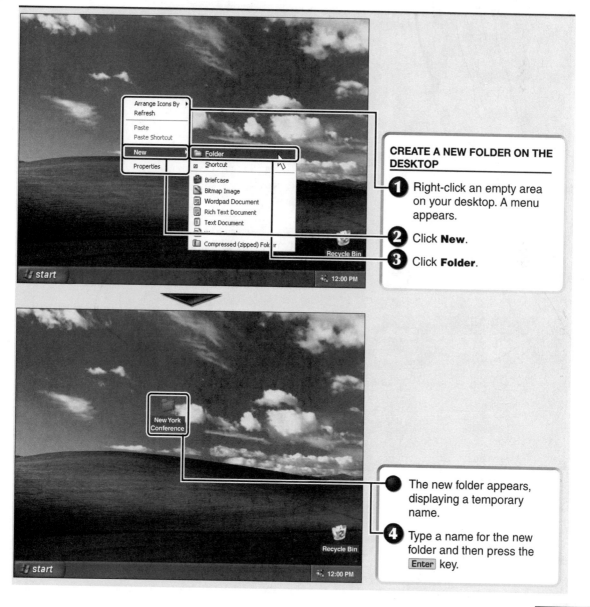

**CREATE A NEW FOLDER ON THE DESKTOP**

**1** Right-click an empty area on your desktop. A menu appears.

**2** Click **New**.

**3** Click **Folder**.

● The new folder appears, displaying a temporary name.

**4** Type a name for the new folder and then press the Enter key.

# SEARCH FOR FILES

If you cannot remember the exact name or location of a file you want to work with, you can have Windows search for the file on your computer. When you specify the type of file you want to find, Windows offers different options to help you find the file.

## SEARCH FOR FILES

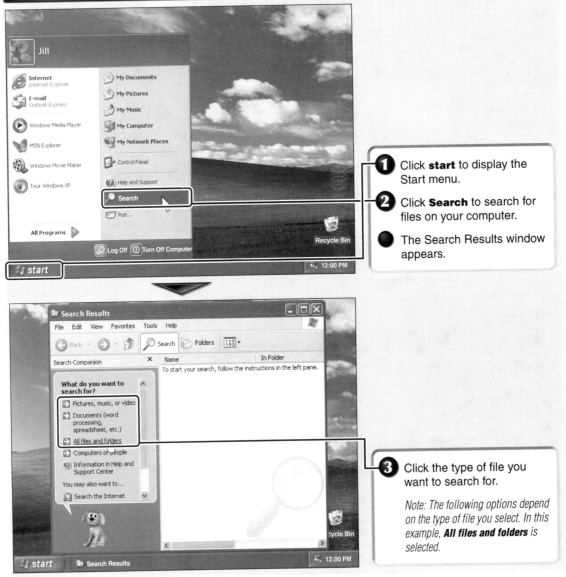

1. Click **start** to display the Start menu.

2. Click **Search** to search for files on your computer.

● The Search Results window appears.

3. Click the type of file you want to search for.

   *Note: The following options depend on the type of file you select. In this example, **All files and folders** is selected.*

# in an instant

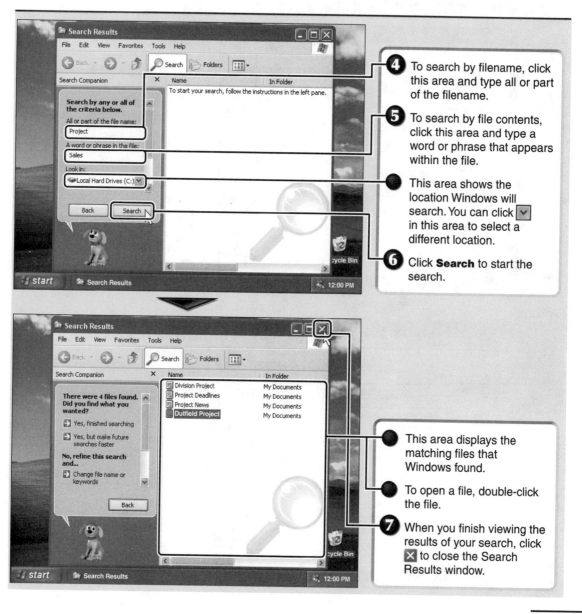

**4** To search by filename, click this area and type all or part of the filename.

**5** To search by file contents, click this area and type a word or phrase that appears within the file.

This area shows the location Windows will search. You can click ⌄ in this area to select a different location.

**6** Click **Search** to start the search.

This area displays the matching files that Windows found.

To open a file, double-click the file.

**7** When you finish viewing the results of your search, click ✕ to close the Search Results window.

# ADD A SHORTCUT TO THE DESKTOP

You can add a shortcut to the desktop to provide a quick way of opening a file you use regularly. A shortcut is a link to the original file. After creating a shortcut, you can rename, delete or move the shortcut the same way you would rename, delete or move any file.

## ADD A SHORTCUT TO THE DESKTOP

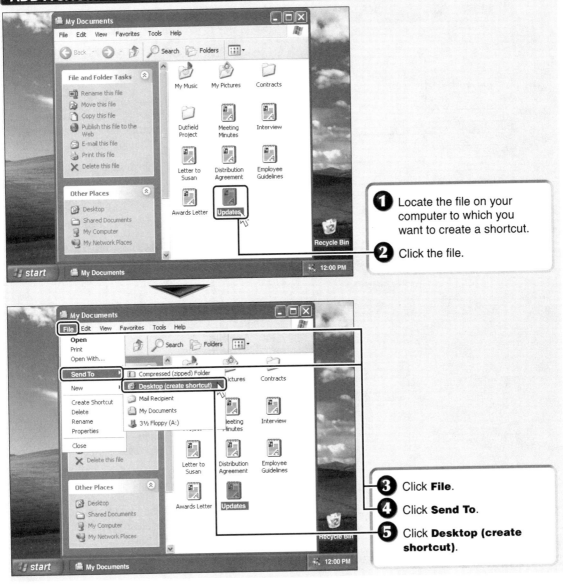

**1** Locate the file on your computer to which you want to create a shortcut.

**2** Click the file.

**3** Click **File**.

**4** Click **Send To**.

**5** Click **Desktop (create shortcut)**.

# in an instant

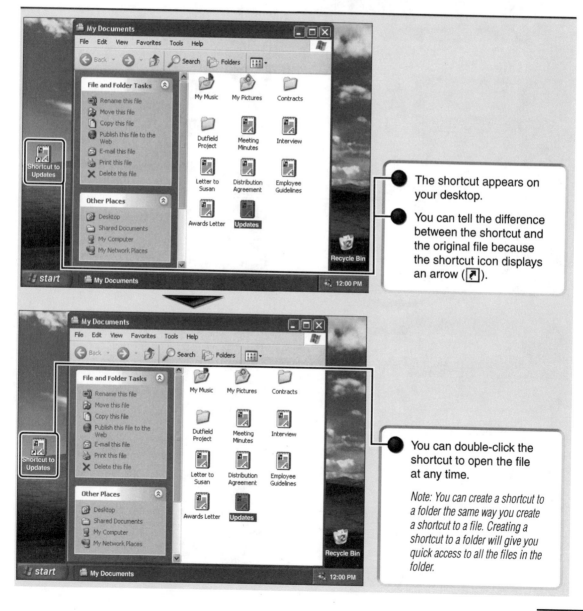

The shortcut appears on your desktop.

You can tell the difference between the shortcut and the original file because the shortcut icon displays an arrow ( ).

You can double-click the shortcut to open the file at any time.

*Note: You can create a shortcut to a folder the same way you create a shortcut to a file. Creating a shortcut to a folder will give you quick access to all the files in the folder.*

# COPY A FILE TO A FLOPPY DISK

You can copy a file stored on your computer to a floppy disk. Copying files to a floppy disk is useful when you want to share files with a colleague or make backup copies of your files. You can protect the information stored on a floppy disk by keeping the disk away from moisture, heat and magnets, which can damage the information.

COPY A FILE TO A FLOPPY DISK

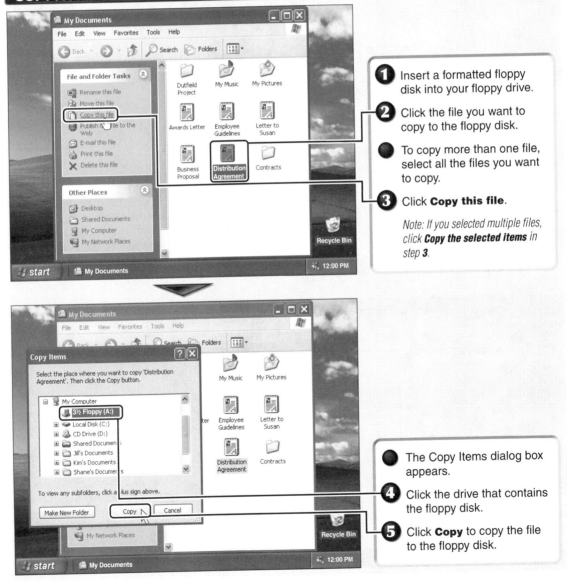

1. Insert a formatted floppy disk into your floppy drive.

2. Click the file you want to copy to the floppy disk.

● To copy more than one file, select all the files you want to copy.

3. Click **Copy this file**.

*Note: If you selected multiple files, click **Copy the selected items** in step **3**.*

● The Copy Items dialog box appears.

4. Click the drive that contains the floppy disk.

5. Click **Copy** to copy the file to the floppy disk.

# in an *instant*

Windows places a copy of the file on the floppy disk.

*Note: You can copy a folder to a floppy disk the same way you copy a file. When you copy a folder, Windows copies all the files in the folder.*

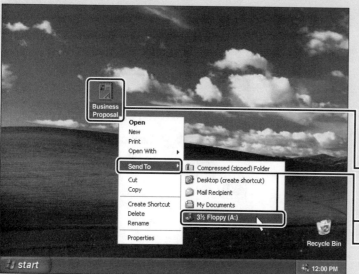

## COPY A FILE ON YOUR DESKTOP

**1** Insert a floppy disk into your floppy drive.

**2** Right-click the file you want to copy to the floppy disk. A menu appears.

**3** Click **Send To**.

**4** Click the drive that contains the floppy disk.

# COPY FILES TO A CD

You can copy files, such as documents and pictures, from your computer to a CD. Copying files to a CD allows you to transfer large amounts of information between computers or make backup copies of the files stored on your computer. A CD can typically store 650 MB of information. You will need a recordable CD drive to copy files to a CD.

## COPY FILES TO A CD

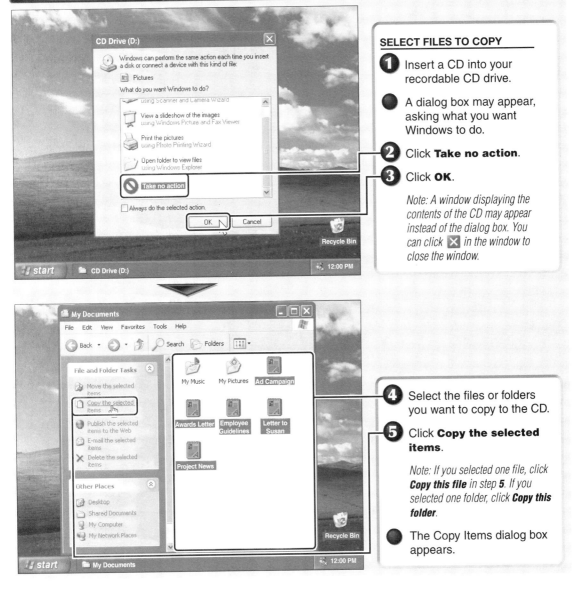

### SELECT FILES TO COPY

**1** Insert a CD into your recordable CD drive.

● A dialog box may appear, asking what you want Windows to do.

**2** Click **Take no action**.

**3** Click **OK**.

*Note: A window displaying the contents of the CD may appear instead of the dialog box. You can click ☒ in the window to close the window.*

**4** Select the files or folders you want to copy to the CD.

**5** Click **Copy the selected items**.

*Note: If you selected one file, click Copy this file in step 5. If you selected one folder, click Copy this folder.*

● The Copy Items dialog box appears.

in an *Instant*

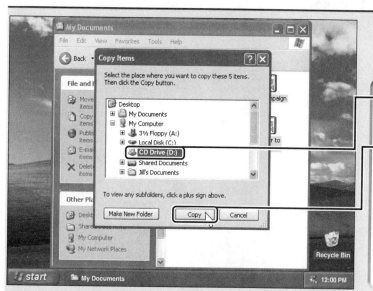

**6** Click the recordable CD drive that contains the CD you want to copy the files to.

**7** Click **Copy** to place a copy of the files in a temporary storage area on your computer where the files will be held until you copy them to the CD.

● You can repeat steps **4** to **7** for each set of files you want to copy to the CD.

**COPY SELECTED FILES TO A CD**

**1** Click **start** to display the Start menu.

**2** Click **My Computer** to view the contents of your computer.

CONTINUED

# COPY FILES TO A CD

Windows stores the files you selected in a temporary storage area on your computer. This allows you to review the files before copying them to a CD. Extra information is stored on a CD each time you copy files to the CD. To make the best use of the CD's storage space, you should copy all the files you intend to store on the CD at the same time.

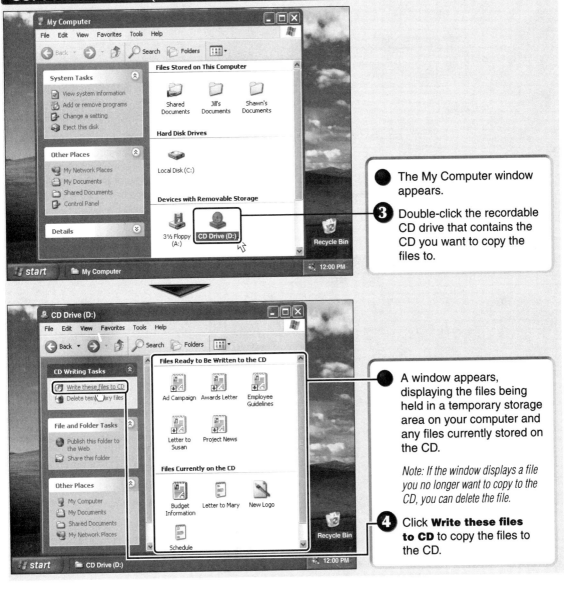

The My Computer window appears.

**3** Double-click the recordable CD drive that contains the CD you want to copy the files to.

A window appears, displaying the files being held in a temporary storage area on your computer and any files currently stored on the CD.

*Note: If the window displays a file you no longer want to copy to the CD, you can delete the file.*

**4** Click **Write these files to CD** to copy the files to the CD.

# in an instant

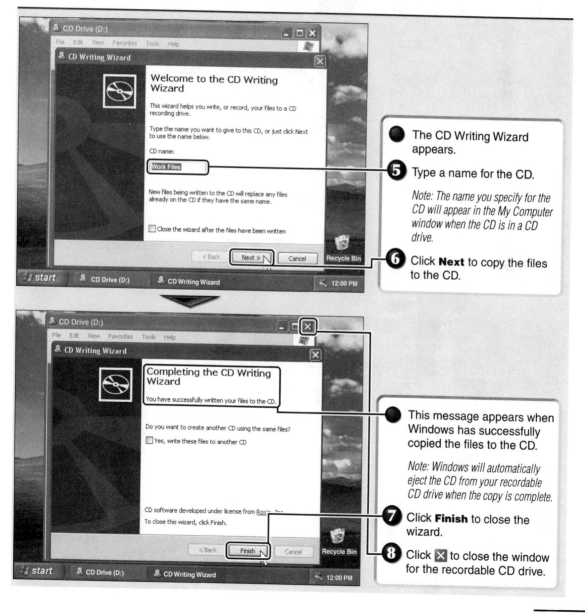

The CD Writing Wizard appears.

**5** Type a name for the CD.

*Note: The name you specify for the CD will appear in the My Computer window when the CD is in a CD drive.*

**6** Click **Next** to copy the files to the CD.

This message appears when Windows has successfully copied the files to the CD.

*Note: Windows will automatically eject the CD from your recordable CD drive when the copy is complete.*

**7** Click **Finish** to close the wizard.

**8** Click ✕ to close the window for the recordable CD drive.

You can use the Scanner and Camera Wizard to copy pictures stored on a digital camera to your computer. To copy pictures from a digital camera, the camera must be installed, connected to your computer and turned on. You may also need to set your camera to a specific mode, such as the Connect mode.

## COPY PICTURES FROM A DIGITAL CAMERA

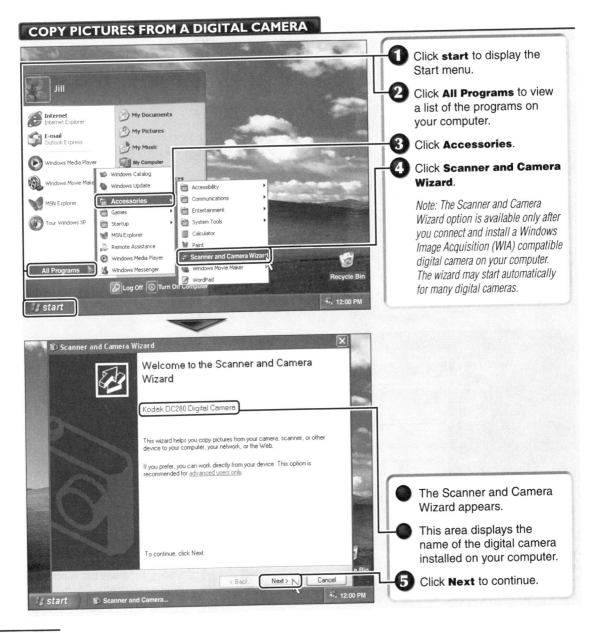

**1** Click **start** to display the Start menu.

**2** Click **All Programs** to view a list of the programs on your computer.

**3** Click **Accessories**.

**4** Click **Scanner and Camera Wizard**.

*Note: The Scanner and Camera Wizard option is available only after you connect and install a Windows Image Acquisition (WIA) compatible digital camera on your computer. The wizard may start automatically for many digital cameras.*

● The Scanner and Camera Wizard appears.

● This area displays the name of the digital camera installed on your computer.

**5** Click **Next** to continue.

# in an instant

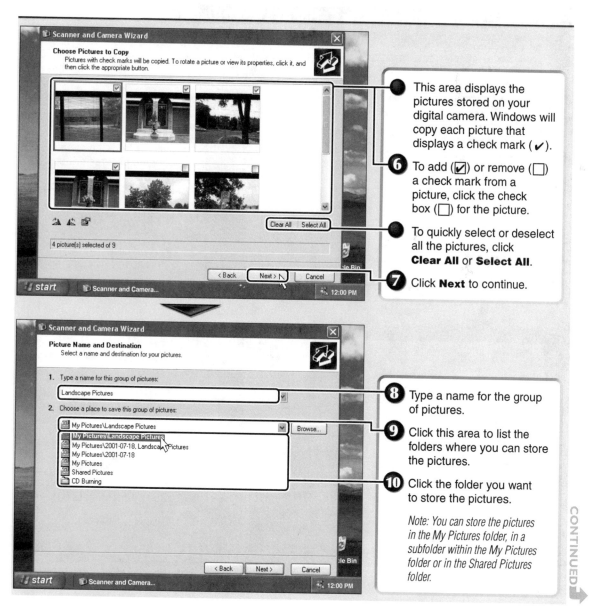

This area displays the pictures stored on your digital camera. Windows will copy each picture that displays a check mark (✔).

**6** To add (☑) or remove (☐) a check mark from a picture, click the check box (☐) for the picture.

To quickly select or deselect all the pictures, click **Clear All** or **Select All**.

**7** Click **Next** to continue.

**8** Type a name for the group of pictures.

**9** Click this area to list the folders where you can store the pictures.

**10** Click the folder you want to store the pictures.

*Note: You can store the pictures in the My Pictures folder, in a subfolder within the My Pictures folder or in the Shared Pictures folder.*

CONTINUED➡

You can choose to delete the pictures stored on your digital camera after the pictures are copied to your computer. If you choose to delete the pictures stored on your digital camera, you will not be able to recover the pictures.

## COPY PICTURES FROM A DIGITAL CAMERA (CONTINUED)

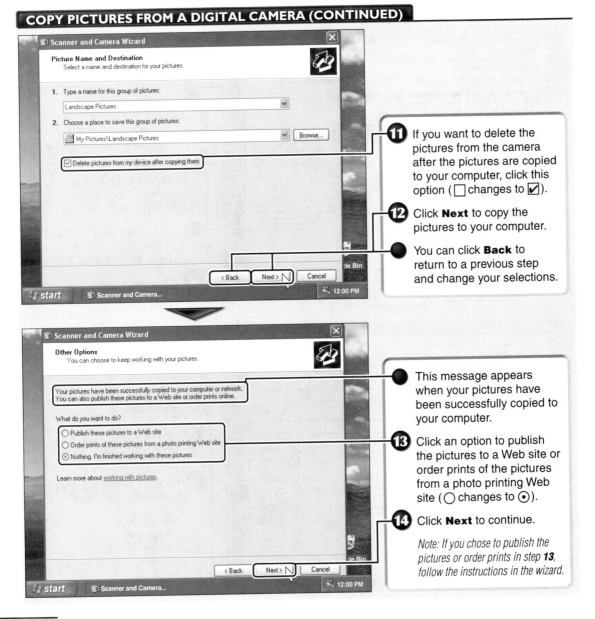

**11** If you want to delete the pictures from the camera after the pictures are copied to your computer, click this option (☐ changes to ☑).

**12** Click **Next** to copy the pictures to your computer.

● You can click **Back** to return to a previous step and change your selections.

● This message appears when your pictures have been successfully copied to your computer.

**13** Click an option to publish the pictures to a Web site or order prints of the pictures from a photo printing Web site (○ changes to ⊙).

**14** Click **Next** to continue.

*Note: If you chose to publish the pictures or order prints in step 13, follow the instructions in the wizard.*

# in an *instant*

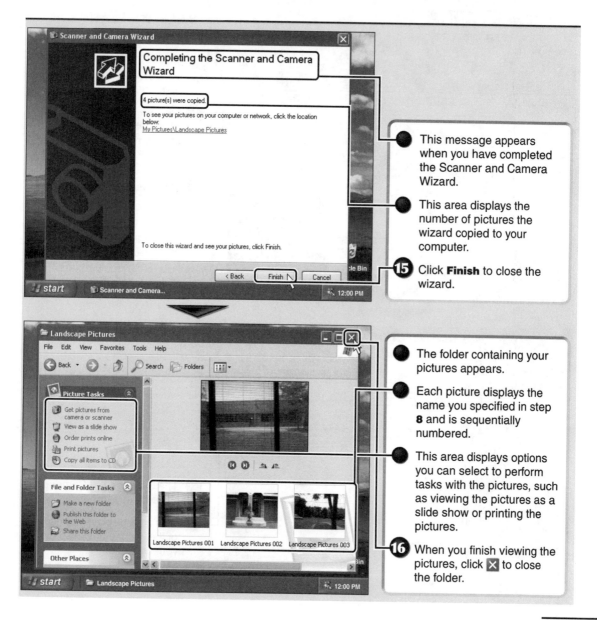

This message appears when you have completed the Scanner and Camera Wizard.

This area displays the number of pictures the wizard copied to your computer.

**15** Click **Finish** to close the wizard.

The folder containing your pictures appears.

Each picture displays the name you specified in step **8** and is sequentially numbered.

This area displays options you can select to perform tasks with the pictures, such as viewing the pictures as a slide show or printing the pictures.

**16** When you finish viewing the pictures, click ⊠ to close the folder.

# SCAN A DOCUMENT

You can use the Scanner and Camera Wizard to scan paper documents into your computer. You can scan documents such as photographs, drawings, newspaper articles and forms into your computer. When scanning a document, you can specify whether the document is a color, grayscale, black and white or text document.

## SCAN A DOCUMENT

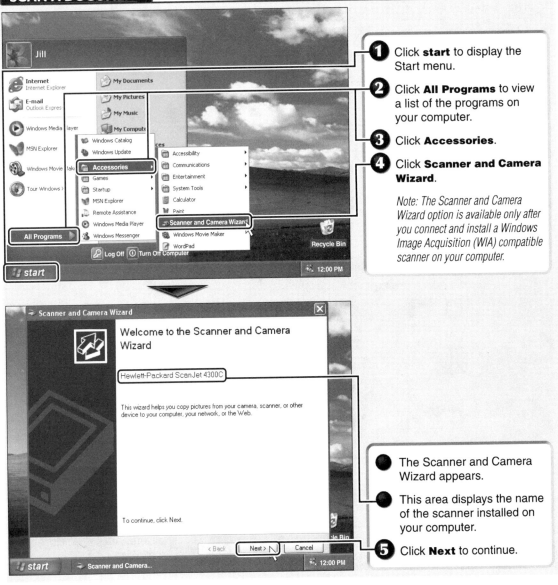

**1** Click **start** to display the Start menu.

**2** Click **All Programs** to view a list of the programs on your computer.

**3** Click **Accessories**.

**4** Click **Scanner and Camera Wizard**.

*Note: The Scanner and Camera Wizard option is available only after you connect and install a Windows Image Acquisition (WIA) compatible scanner on your computer.*

● The Scanner and Camera Wizard appears.

● This area displays the name of the scanner installed on your computer.

**5** Click **Next** to continue.

# in an instant

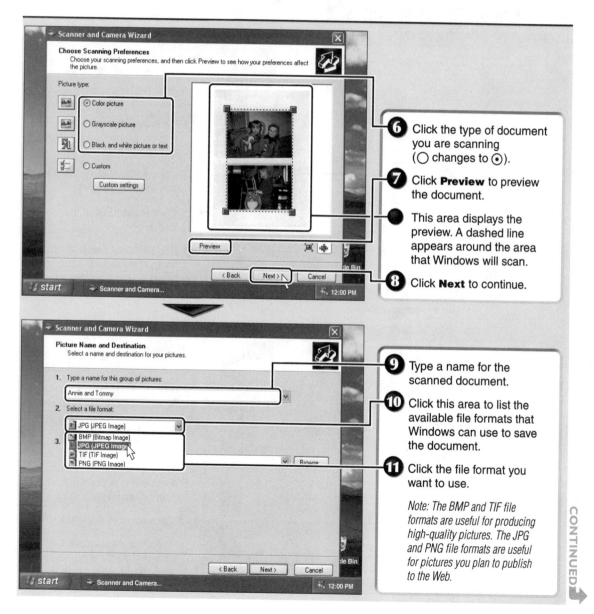

**Scanner and Camera Wizard**

**Choose Scanning Preferences**
Choose your scanning preferences, and then click Preview to see how your preferences affect the picture.

Picture type:
- ⊙ Color picture
- ○ Grayscale picture
- ○ Black and white picture or text
- ○ Custom
  - Custom settings

Preview

< Back   Next >   Cancel

start   Scanner and Camera...   12:00 PM

**6** Click the type of document you are scanning (○ changes to ⊙).

**7** Click **Preview** to preview the document.

● This area displays the preview. A dashed line appears around the area that Windows will scan.

**8** Click **Next** to continue.

**Scanner and Camera Wizard**

**Picture Name and Destination**
Select a name and destination for your pictures.

1. Type a name for this group of pictures:
   Annie and Tommy

2. Select a file format:
   JPG (JPEG Image)
   - BMP (Bitmap Image)
   - JPG (JPEG Image)
   - TIF (TIF Image)
   - PNG (PNG Image)

3.

Browse

< Back   Next >   Cancel

start   Scanner and Camera...   12:00 PM

**9** Type a name for the scanned document.

**10** Click this area to list the available file formats that Windows can use to save the document.

**11** Click the file format you want to use.

*Note: The BMP and TIF file formats are useful for producing high-quality pictures. The JPG and PNG file formats are useful for pictures you plan to publish to the Web.*

CONTINUED

# SCAN A DOCUMENT

You can store your scanned document in one of the convenient folders Windows provides, such as the My Pictures folder or one of its subfolders. You can also store the document in the Shared Pictures folder to allow other users set up on your computer access to the scanned document.

## SCAN A DOCUMENT (CONTINUED)

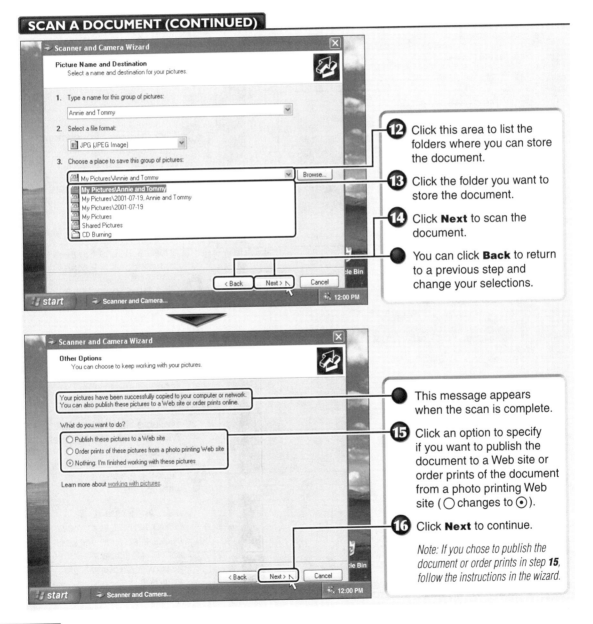

**12** Click this area to list the folders where you can store the document.

**13** Click the folder you want to store the document.

**14** Click **Next** to scan the document.

● You can click **Back** to return to a previous step and change your selections.

● This message appears when the scan is complete.

**15** Click an option to specify if you want to publish the document to a Web site or order prints of the document from a photo printing Web site ( ○ changes to ⊙ ).

**16** Click **Next** to continue.

*Note: If you chose to publish the document or order prints in step 15, follow the instructions in the wizard.*

in an *instant*

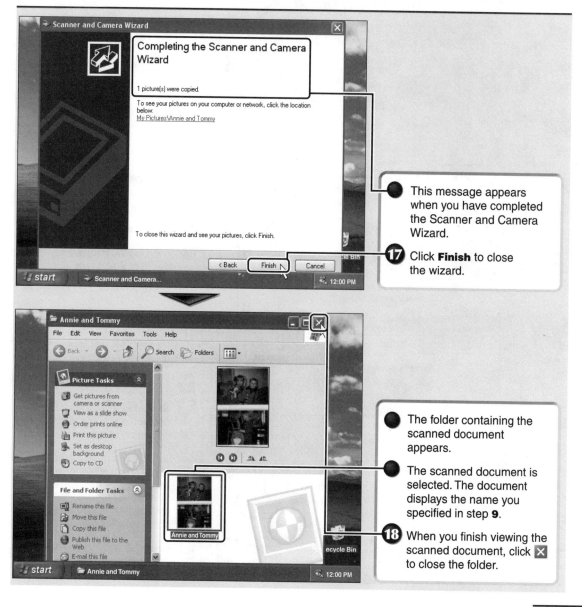

This message appears when you have completed the Scanner and Camera Wizard.

**17** Click **Finish** to close the wizard.

The folder containing the scanned document appears.

The scanned document is selected. The document displays the name you specified in step **9**.

**18** When you finish viewing the scanned document, click ☒ to close the folder.

# CHANGE THE DESKTOP BACKGROUND

You can select a picture, background color or both to decorate your desktop. You can center a picture to display the picture in the middle of your desktop, tile a picture to repeat the picture until it fills the desktop or stretch a picture to cover the entire desktop.

## CHANGE THE DESKTOP BACKGROUND

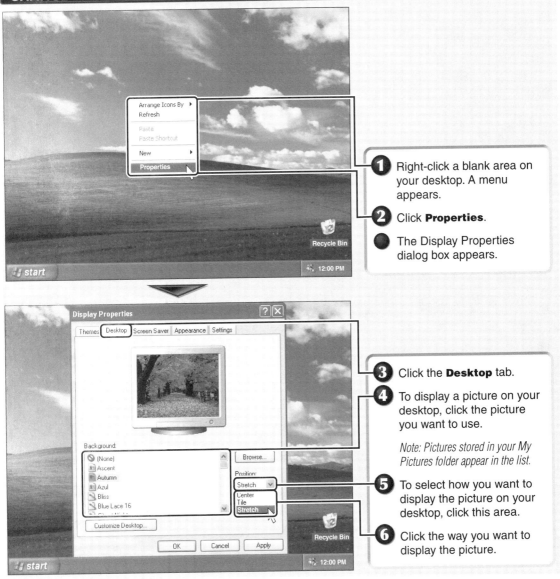

**1** Right-click a blank area on your desktop. A menu appears.

**2** Click **Properties**.

● The Display Properties dialog box appears.

**3** Click the **Desktop** tab.

**4** To display a picture on your desktop, click the picture you want to use.

*Note: Pictures stored in your My Pictures folder appear in the list.*

**5** To select how you want to display the picture on your desktop, click this area.

**6** Click the way you want to display the picture.

88

# in an *Instant*

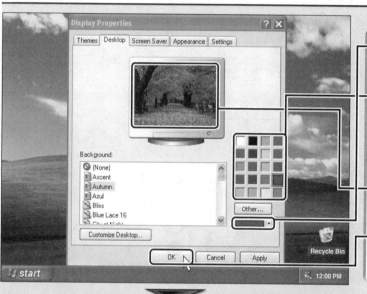

**7** To select a color for your desktop, click this area to display a list of colors.

**8** Click the color you want to use.

*Note: If you selected a picture in step 4, the color will fill any space not covered by the picture.*

● This area displays how the picture and/or color will appear on your desktop.

**9** Click **OK** to add the picture and/or color to your desktop.

● The picture and/or color appear on your desktop.

● To remove a picture from your desktop, perform steps **1** to **4**, selecting **(None)** in step **4**. Then perform step **9**.

# CHANGE THE SCREEN SAVER

A screen saver is a moving picture or pattern that appears on the screen when you do not use your computer for a period of time. You can use a screen saver to hide your work while you are away from your desk. By default, Windows displays a screen saver when you do not use your computer for 10 minutes.

CHANGE THE SCREEN SAVER

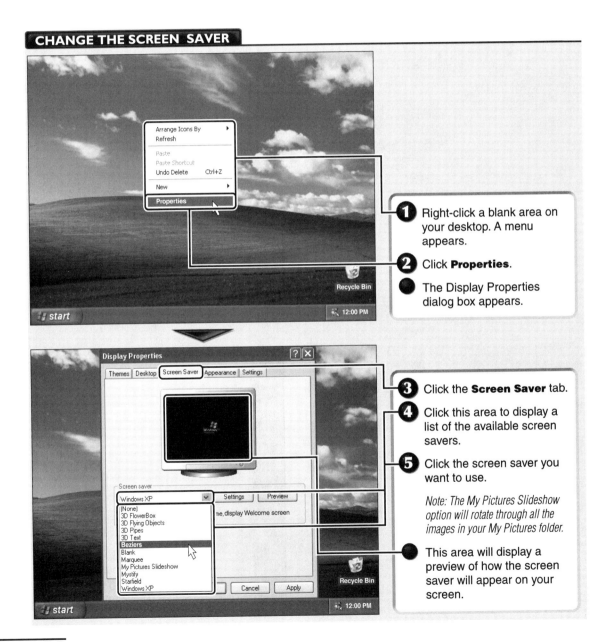

**1** Right-click a blank area on your desktop. A menu appears.

**2** Click **Properties**.

● The Display Properties dialog box appears.

**3** Click the **Screen Saver** tab.

**4** Click this area to display a list of the available screen savers.

**5** Click the screen saver you want to use.

*Note: The My Pictures Slideshow option will rotate through all the images in your My Pictures folder.*

● This area will display a preview of how the screen saver will appear on your screen.

# in an instant

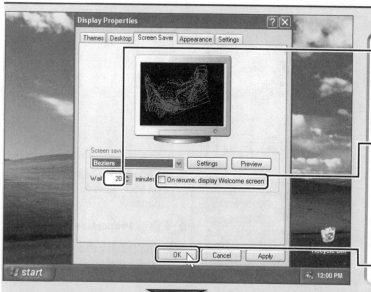

**6** To specify the number of minutes your computer must be inactive before the screen saver will appear, double-click this area. Then type the number of minutes.

**7** If multiple users are set up on your computer, this option requires you to log on to Windows each time you remove the screen saver. Click this option to turn the option off (☑ changes to ☐).

**8** Click **OK**.

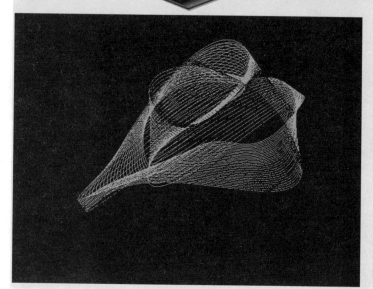

● The screen saver appears when you do not use your computer for the number of minutes you specified.

● You can move the mouse or press a key on the keyboard to remove the screen saver from your screen.

● To stop a screen saver from appearing, perform steps **1** to **5**, selecting **(None)** in step **5**. Then perform step **8**.

# CHANGE THE SCREEN APPEARANCE

You can change the style and colors that Windows uses to display items on your screen. You can choose the default Windows XP style or the Windows Classic style. You can also specify the colors you want to use in items such as dialog boxes and change the size of text shown in items such as menus.

CHANGE THE SCREEN APPEARANCE

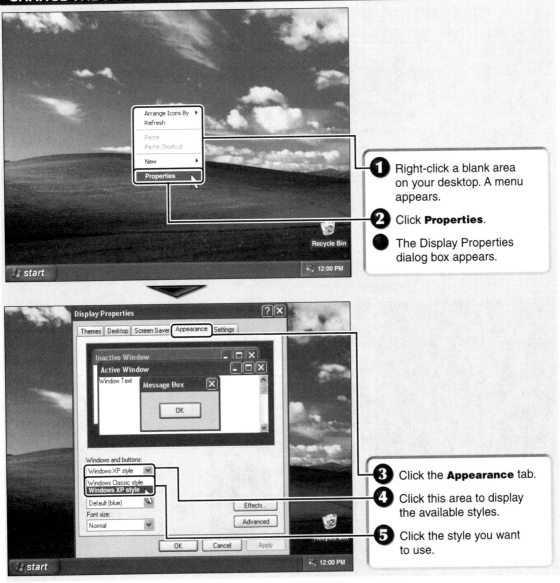

**1** Right-click a blank area on your desktop. A menu appears.

**2** Click **Properties**.

● The Display Properties dialog box appears.

**3** Click the **Appearance** tab.

**4** Click this area to display the available styles.

**5** Click the style you want to use.

# in an instant

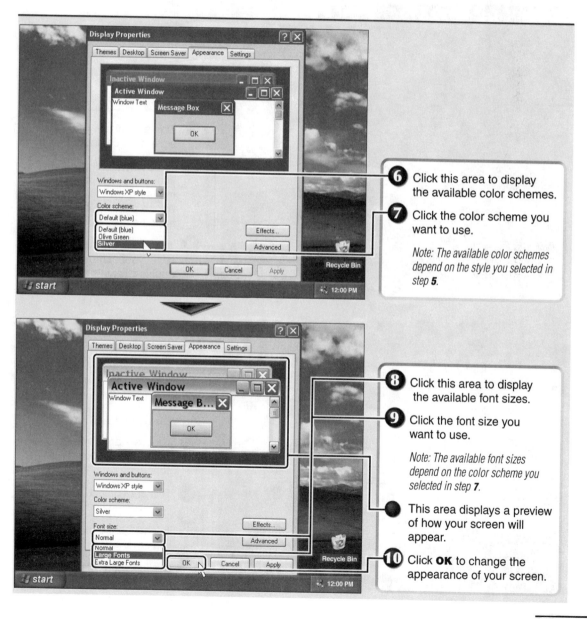

**6** Click this area to display the available color schemes.

**7** Click the color scheme you want to use.

*Note: The available color schemes depend on the style you selected in step 5.*

**8** Click this area to display the available font sizes.

**9** Click the font size you want to use.

*Note: The available font sizes depend on the color scheme you selected in step 7.*

This area displays a preview of how your screen will appear.

**10** Click **OK** to change the appearance of your screen.

# CHANGE THE DATE AND TIME

You should make sure the correct date and time are set in
your computer. Windows uses the date and time to determine
when you create and update your files. Your computer has a
built-in clock that keeps track of the date and time even when
you turn off your computer. Windows will also change the time
automatically to compensate for daylight saving time.

## CHANGE THE DATE AND TIME

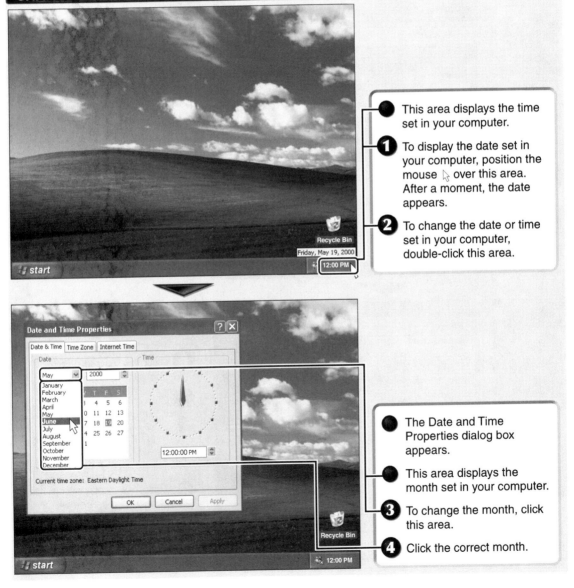

This area displays the time
set in your computer.

**1** To display the date set in
your computer, position the
mouse ⌐ over this area.
After a moment, the date
appears.

**2** To change the date or time
set in your computer,
double-click this area.

The Date and Time
Properties dialog box
appears.

This area displays the
month set in your computer.

**3** To change the month, click
this area.

**4** Click the correct month.

# in an instant

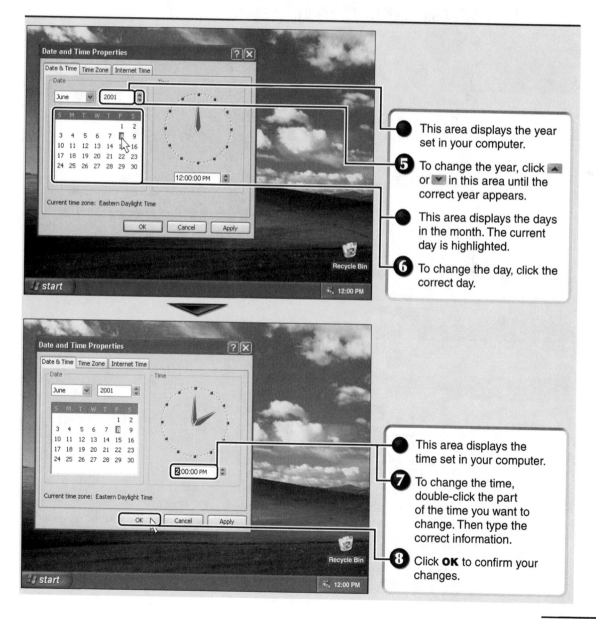

This area displays the year set in your computer.

**5** To change the year, click ▲ or ▼ in this area until the correct year appears.

This area displays the days in the month. The current day is highlighted.

**6** To change the day, click the correct day.

This area displays the time set in your computer.

**7** To change the time, double-click the part of the time you want to change. Then type the correct information.

**8** Click **OK** to confirm your changes.

95

Windows can play sound effects when certain program events occur on your computer. For example, you can hear a short tune when you start Windows. You can change the sounds assigned to many events at once by selecting a sound scheme. A sound scheme consists of a set of related sounds.

## ASSIGN SOUNDS TO PROGRAM EVENTS

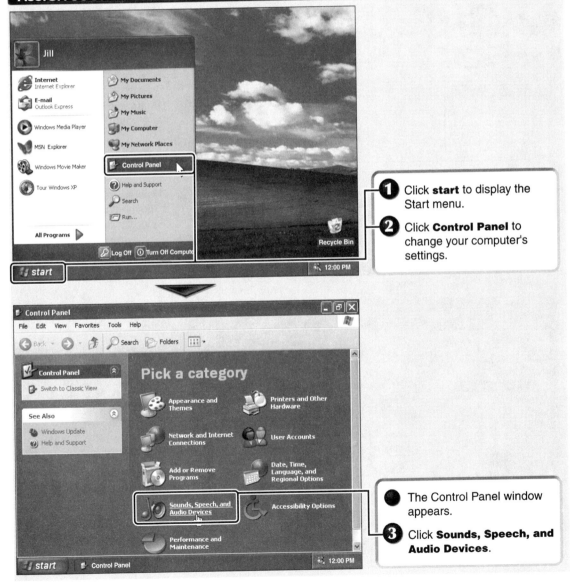

**1** Click **start** to display the Start menu.

**2** Click **Control Panel** to change your computer's settings.

● The Control Panel window appears.

**3** Click **Sounds, Speech, and Audio Devices**.

in an *instant*

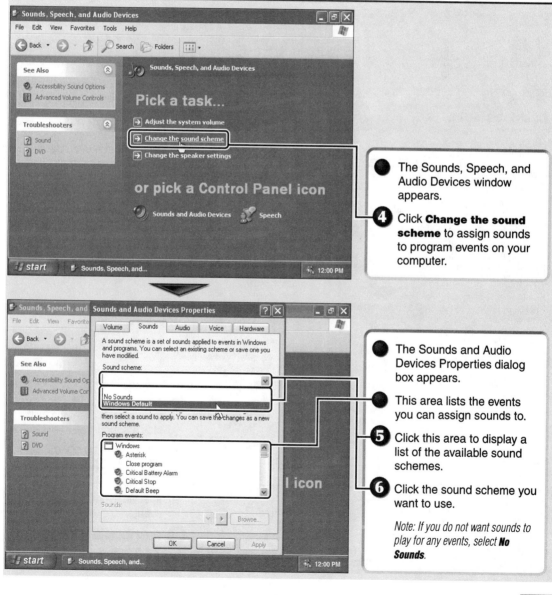

The Sounds, Speech, and Audio Devices window appears.

④ Click **Change the sound scheme** to assign sounds to program events on your computer.

The Sounds and Audio Devices Properties dialog box appears.

This area lists the events you can assign sounds to.

⑤ Click this area to display a list of the available sound schemes.

⑥ Click the sound scheme you want to use.

*Note: If you do not want sounds to play for any events, select **No Sounds**.*

CONTINUED

# ASSIGN SOUNDS TO PROGRAM EVENTS

You can use the sounds included with Windows, purchase collections of sounds at computer stores or obtain sounds on the Internet. For example, you can obtain sounds at the www.favewavs.com and www.wavlist.com Web sites. The sounds you use must be in the Wave format. Wave files have the .wav extension.

## ASSIGN SOUNDS TO PROGRAM EVENTS (CONTINUED)

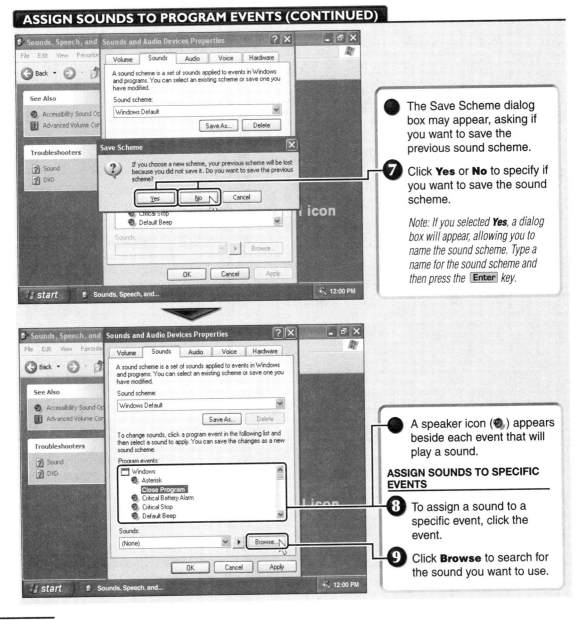

● The Save Scheme dialog box may appear, asking if you want to save the previous sound scheme.

⑦ Click **Yes** or **No** to specify if you want to save the sound scheme.

*Note: If you selected **Yes**, a dialog box will appear, allowing you to name the sound scheme. Type a name for the sound scheme and then press the Enter key.*

● A speaker icon (🔊) appears beside each event that will play a sound.

**ASSIGN SOUNDS TO SPECIFIC EVENTS**

⑧ To assign a sound to a specific event, click the event.

⑨ Click **Browse** to search for the sound you want to use.

# in an *instant*

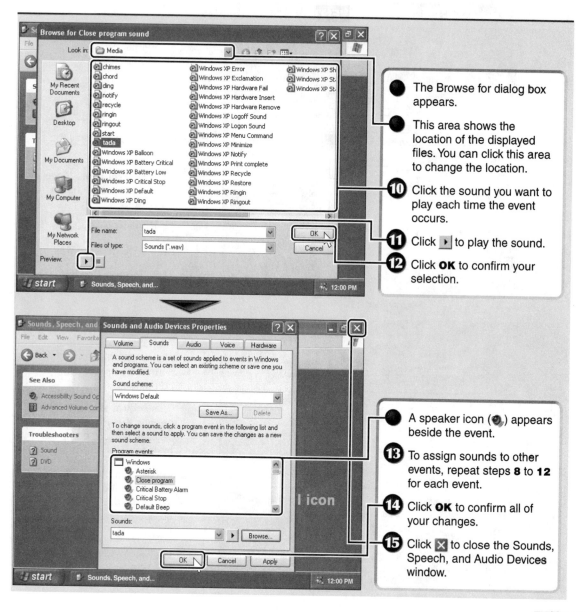

- The Browse for dialog box appears.

- This area shows the location of the displayed files. You can click this area to change the location.

**10** Click the sound you want to play each time the event occurs.

**11** Click ▶ to play the sound.

**12** Click **OK** to confirm your selection.

- A speaker icon (🔊) appears beside the event.

**13** To assign sounds to other events, repeat steps **8** to **12** for each event.

**14** Click **OK** to confirm all of your changes.

**15** Click ✖ to close the Sounds, Speech, and Audio Devices window.

# ADJUST THE VOLUME

You can adjust the volume of sound on your computer. You may want to adjust the volume of all the devices on your computer at once or adjust the volume of specific devices without affecting the volume of other devices.

## ADJUST THE VOLUME

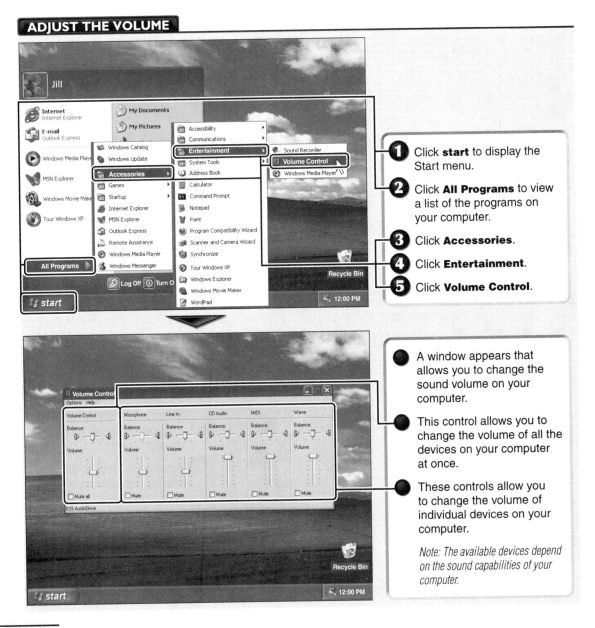

**1** Click **start** to display the Start menu.

**2** Click **All Programs** to view a list of the programs on your computer.

**3** Click **Accessories**.

**4** Click **Entertainment**.

**5** Click **Volume Control**.

● A window appears that allows you to change the sound volume on your computer.

● This control allows you to change the volume of all the devices on your computer at once.

● These controls allow you to change the volume of individual devices on your computer.

*Note: The available devices depend on the sound capabilities of your computer.*

# in an *instant*

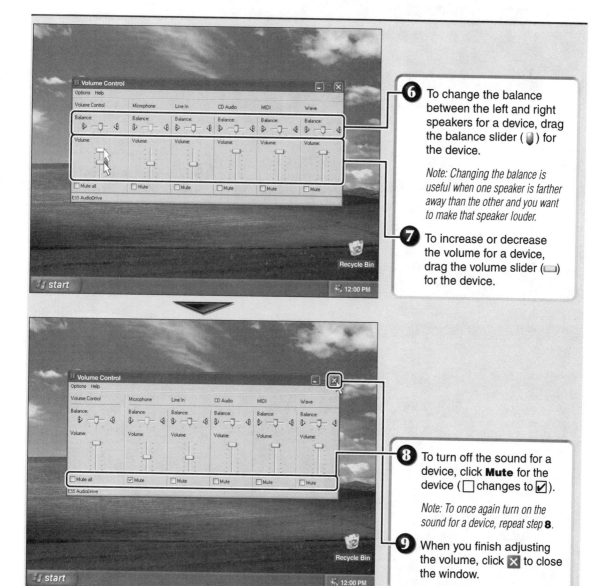

**6** To change the balance between the left and right speakers for a device, drag the balance slider ( ) for the device.

*Note: Changing the balance is useful when one speaker is farther away than the other and you want to make that speaker louder.*

**7** To increase or decrease the volume for a device, drag the volume slider ( ) for the device.

**8** To turn off the sound for a device, click **Mute** for the device ( changes to ).

*Note: To once again turn on the sound for a device, repeat step **8**.*

**9** When you finish adjusting the volume, click to close the window.

# CHANGE THE MOUSE SETTINGS

You can change the way your mouse works to make the mouse easier to use. For example, you can switch the functions of the left and right mouse buttons if you are left-handed. Your mouse may offer settings in addition to those described below.

## CHANGE THE MOUSE SETTINGS

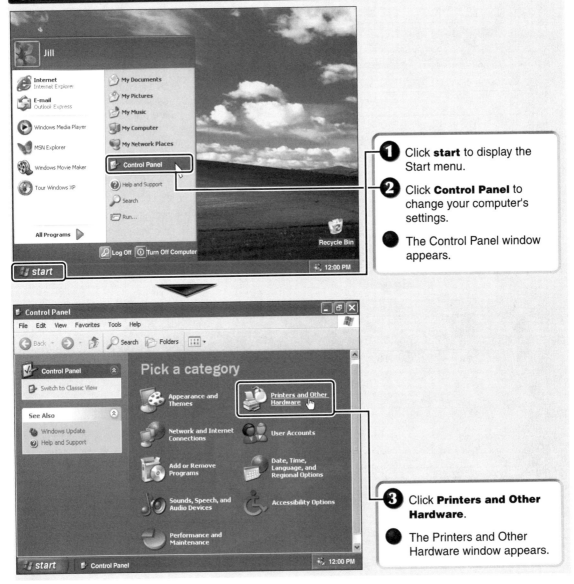

**1** Click **start** to display the Start menu.

**2** Click **Control Panel** to change your computer's settings.

● The Control Panel window appears.

**3** Click **Printers and Other Hardware**.

● The Printers and Other Hardware window appears.

# in an *instant*

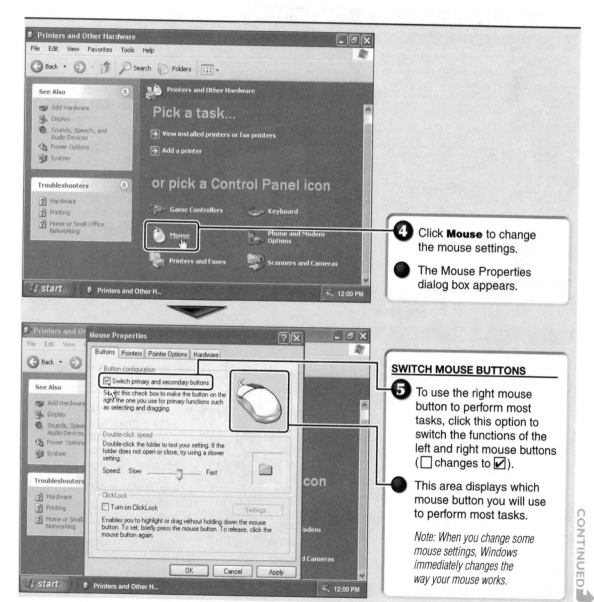

**4** Click **Mouse** to change the mouse settings.

● The Mouse Properties dialog box appears.

## SWITCH MOUSE BUTTONS

**5** To use the right mouse button to perform most tasks, click this option to switch the functions of the left and right mouse buttons (□ changes to ☑).

● This area displays which mouse button you will use to perform most tasks.

*Note: When you change some mouse settings, Windows immediately changes the way your mouse works.*

CONTINUED➡

# CHANGE THE MOUSE SETTINGS

You can personalize the way your mouse works by changing the double-click speed. If you are a new mouse user or you have difficulty double-clicking the mouse, you may find a slower double-click speed easier to use. You can also change the appearance of the mouse pointers that Windows displays.

## CHANGE THE MOUSE SETTINGS (CONTINUED)

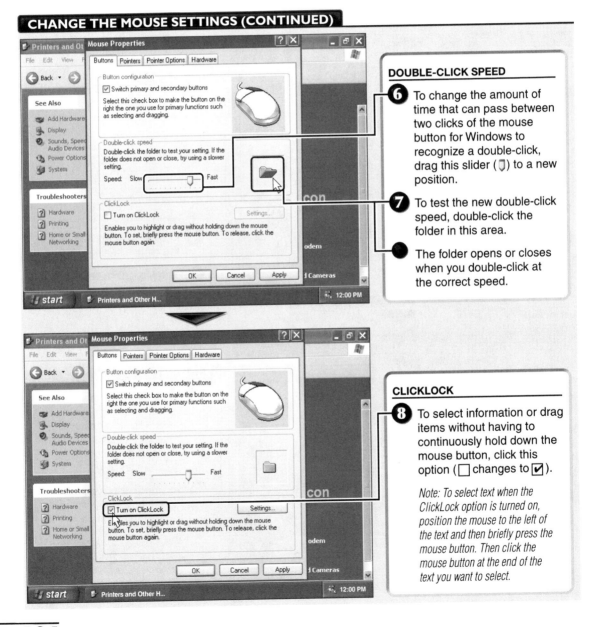

### DOUBLE-CLICK SPEED

**6** To change the amount of time that can pass between two clicks of the mouse button for Windows to recognize a double-click, drag this slider ( ) to a new position.

**7** To test the new double-click speed, double-click the folder in this area.

● The folder opens or closes when you double-click at the correct speed.

### CLICKLOCK

**8** To select information or drag items without having to continuously hold down the mouse button, click this option ( changes to ).

*Note: To select text when the ClickLock option is turned on, position the mouse to the left of the text and then briefly press the mouse button. Then click the mouse button at the end of the text you want to select.*

in an *instant*

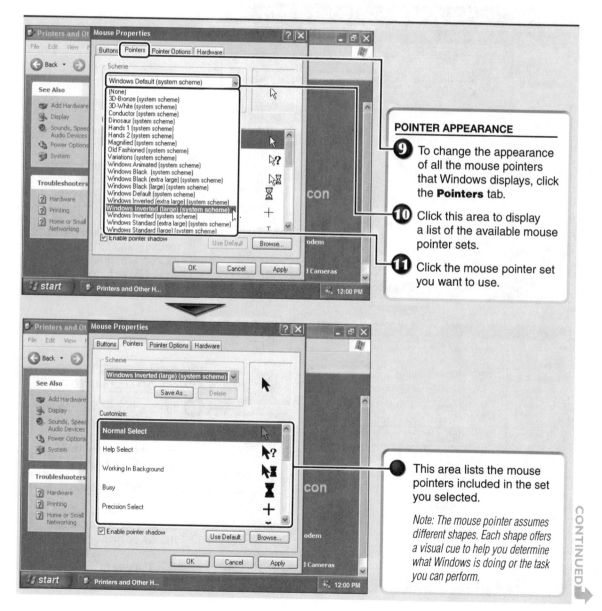

## POINTER APPEARANCE

**9** To change the appearance of all the mouse pointers that Windows displays, click the **Pointers** tab.

**10** Click this area to display a list of the available mouse pointer sets.

**11** Click the mouse pointer set you want to use.

● This area lists the mouse pointers included in the set you selected.

*Note: The mouse pointer assumes different shapes. Each shape offers a visual cue to help you determine what Windows is doing or the task you can perform.*

CONTINUED

# CHANGE THE MOUSE SETTINGS

You can change how fast the mouse pointer moves on your screen or have the mouse pointer automatically appear over the default button in most dialog boxes. Windows also allows you to display mouse pointer trails and show the location of the mouse pointer when the `Ctrl` key is pressed. These options can help you more clearly see the mouse pointer on your screen.

## CHANGE THE MOUSE SETTINGS (CONTINUED)

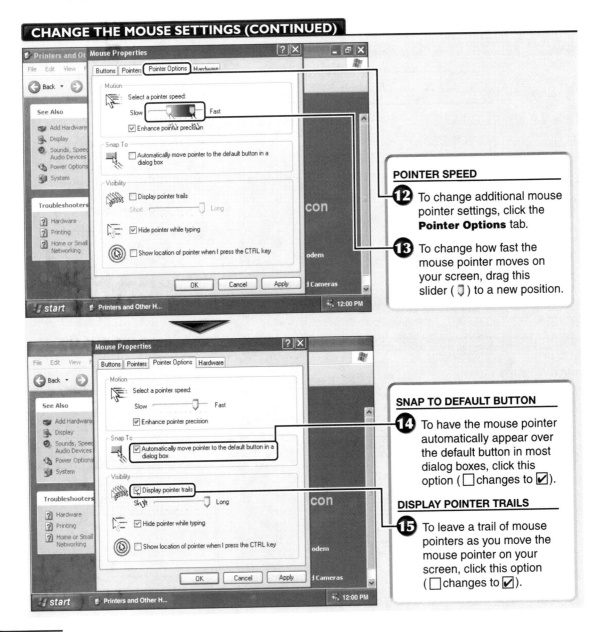

**POINTER SPEED**

⑫ To change additional mouse pointer settings, click the **Pointer Options** tab.

⑬ To change how fast the mouse pointer moves on your screen, drag this slider ( ) to a new position.

**SNAP TO DEFAULT BUTTON**

⑭ To have the mouse pointer automatically appear over the default button in most dialog boxes, click this option ( ☐ changes to ☑ ).

**DISPLAY POINTER TRAILS**

⑮ To leave a trail of mouse pointers as you move the mouse pointer on your screen, click this option ( ☐ changes to ☑ ).

# in an *instant*

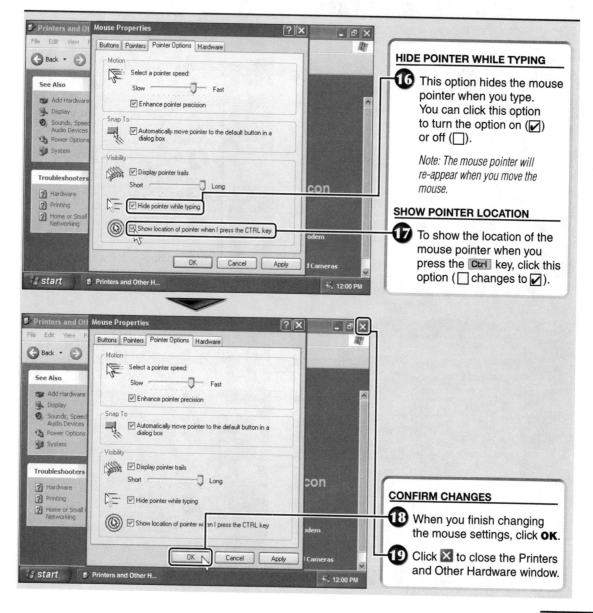

**HIDE POINTER WHILE TYPING**

**16** This option hides the mouse pointer when you type. You can click this option to turn the option on (☑) or off (☐).

*Note: The mouse pointer will re-appear when you move the mouse.*

**SHOW POINTER LOCATION**

**17** To show the location of the mouse pointer when you press the `Ctrl` key, click this option (☐ changes to ☑).

**CONFIRM CHANGES**

**18** When you finish changing the mouse settings, click **OK**.

**19** Click ☒ to close the Printers and Other Hardware window.

# START A PROGRAM AUTOMATICALLY

If you use the same program every day, you can have the program start automatically each time you turn on your computer. To have a program start automatically, you need to place a shortcut for the program in the Startup folder. A shortcut is a link to the program.

## START A PROGRAM AUTOMATICALLY

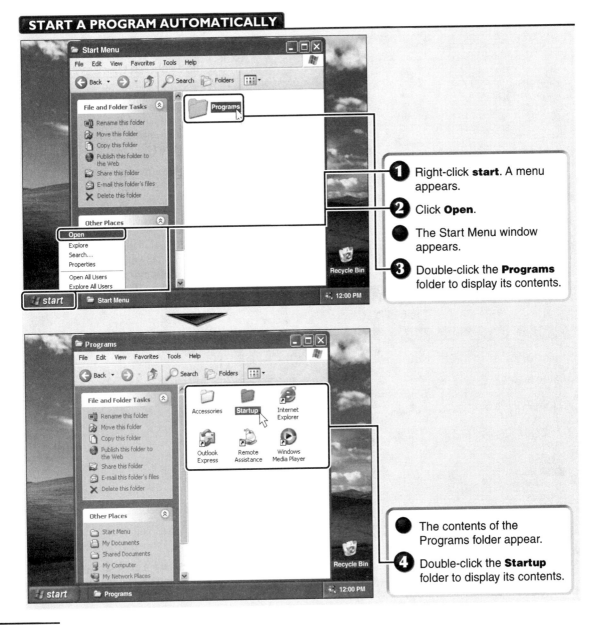

**1** Right-click **start**. A menu appears.

**2** Click **Open**.

● The Start Menu window appears.

**3** Double-click the **Programs** folder to display its contents.

● The contents of the Programs folder appear.

**4** Double-click the **Startup** folder to display its contents.

in an *instant*

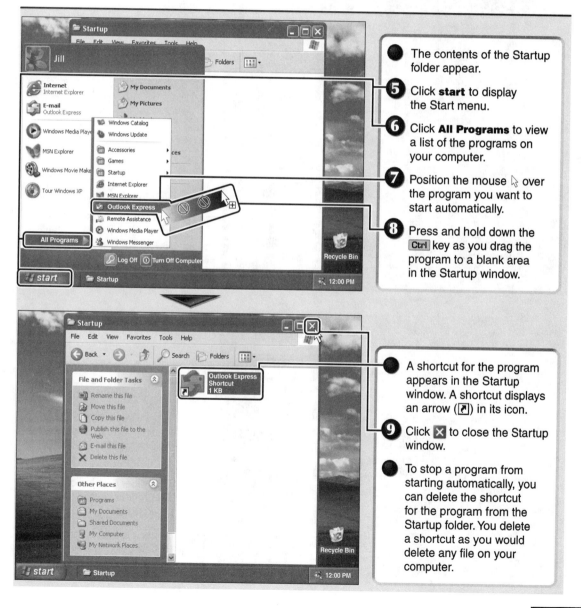

The contents of the Startup folder appear.

**5** Click **start** to display the Start menu.

**6** Click **All Programs** to view a list of the programs on your computer.

**7** Position the mouse ▷ over the program you want to start automatically.

**8** Press and hold down the `Ctrl` key as you drag the program to a blank area in the Startup window.

A shortcut for the program appears in the Startup window. A shortcut displays an arrow (↗) in its icon.

**9** Click ✕ to close the Startup window.

To stop a program from starting automatically, you can delete the shortcut for the program from the Startup folder. You delete a shortcut as you would delete any file on your computer.

# PLAY A SOUND OR VIDEO

Windows Media Player allows you to play sound and video files on your computer. You need a sound card and speakers to play sound on your computer. You can obtain sound and video files on the Internet or at computer stores. Windows also includes a few sample sounds and a video that you can play.

PLAY A SOUND OR VIDEO

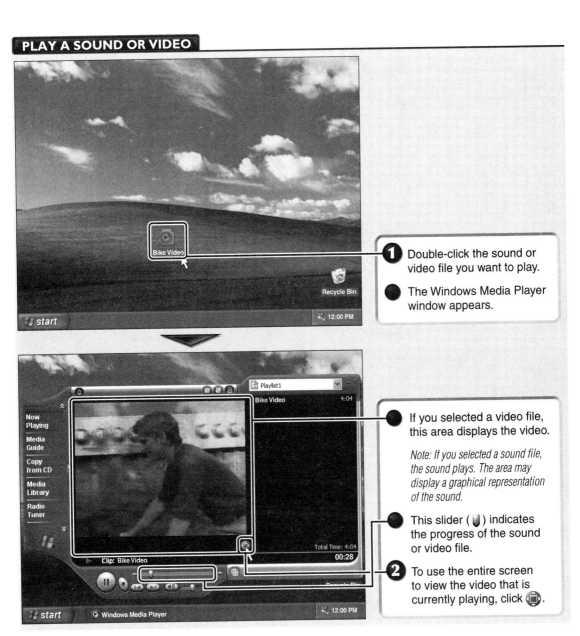

**1** Double-click the sound or video file you want to play.

● The Windows Media Player window appears.

● If you selected a video file, this area displays the video.

*Note: If you selected a sound file, the sound plays. The area may display a graphical representation of the sound.*

● This slider ( 🔘 ) indicates the progress of the sound or video file.

**2** To use the entire screen to view the video that is currently playing, click 🔲.

# in an *instant*

The video continues to play using the entire screen.

**3** To once again display the video in a window, press the Esc key.

**4** To adjust the volume, drag this slider (⬤) left or right to decrease or increase the volume.

**5** To pause or stop the play of the sound or video file, click ⏸ or ⏹ (⏸ changes to ▶).

You can click ▶ to resume the play of the sound or video file.

**6** When you finish playing the sound or video file, click ✕ to close the Windows Media Player window.

# PLAY A MUSIC CD

If your computer has sound capabilities and a CD-ROM drive, you can use the computer to play a music CD while you work. You can adjust the volume of the music or even turn off the sound temporarily. If you want to listen to a music CD privately, you can plug headphones into the jack at the front of your CD-ROM drive or into your speakers.

## PLAY A MUSIC CD

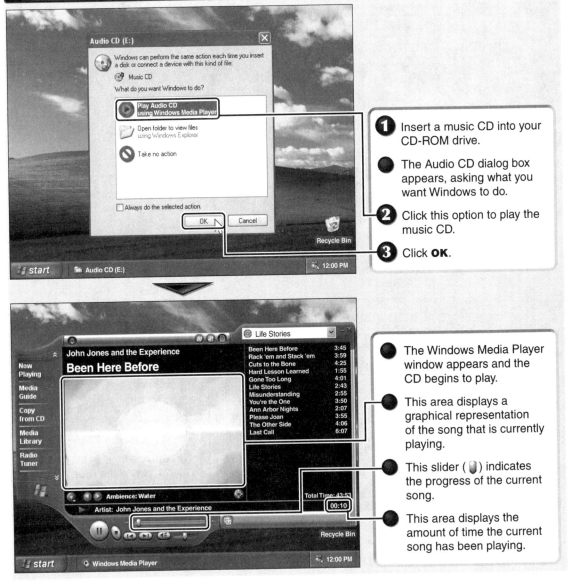

**1** Insert a music CD into your CD-ROM drive.

● The Audio CD dialog box appears, asking what you want Windows to do.

**2** Click this option to play the music CD.

**3** Click **OK**.

● The Windows Media Player window appears and the CD begins to play.

● This area displays a graphical representation of the song that is currently playing.

● This slider ( ) indicates the progress of the current song.

● This area displays the amount of time the current song has been playing.

# in an *instant*

This area displays a list of the songs on the CD and the amount of time each song will play.

*Note: If you are connected to the Internet, Windows Media Player may be able to obtain and display information about the CD, such as the name of each song. If the information is unavailable, the track number of each song appears instead.*

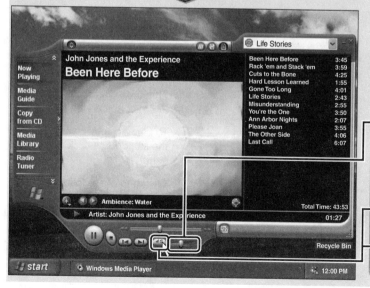

## ADJUST THE VOLUME

**4** To adjust the volume, drag this slider ( ) left or right to decrease or increase the volume.

## TURN OFF SOUND

**5** Click  to turn off the sound ( changes to ).

You can click  to once again turn on the sound.

CONTINUED

When playing a music CD, you can pause or stop the play of the CD at any time. You can also play a specific song or play the songs in random order. Once a CD has started playing, you can minimize the Windows Media Player window to temporarily remove the window from your screen so you can continue to work on your computer.

## PLAY A MUSIC CD (CONTINUED)

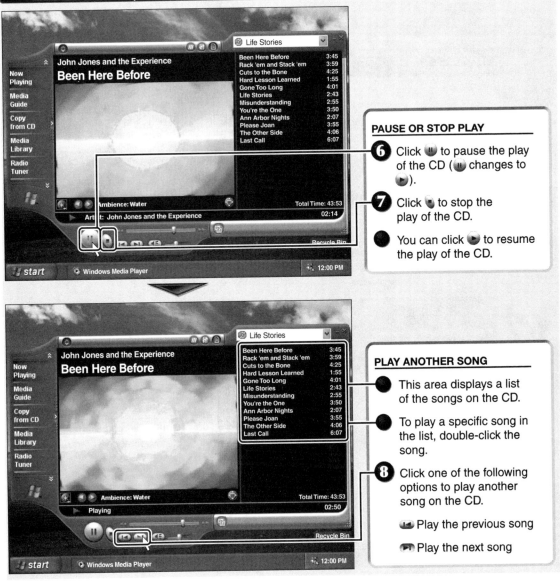

**PAUSE OR STOP PLAY**

**6** Click ⏸ to pause the play of the CD (⏸ changes to ▶).

**7** Click ⏹ to stop the play of the CD.

● You can click ▶ to resume the play of the CD.

**PLAY ANOTHER SONG**

● This area displays a list of the songs on the CD.

● To play a specific song in the list, double-click the song.

**8** Click one of the following options to play another song on the CD.

⏮ Play the previous song

⏭ Play the next song

# in an instant

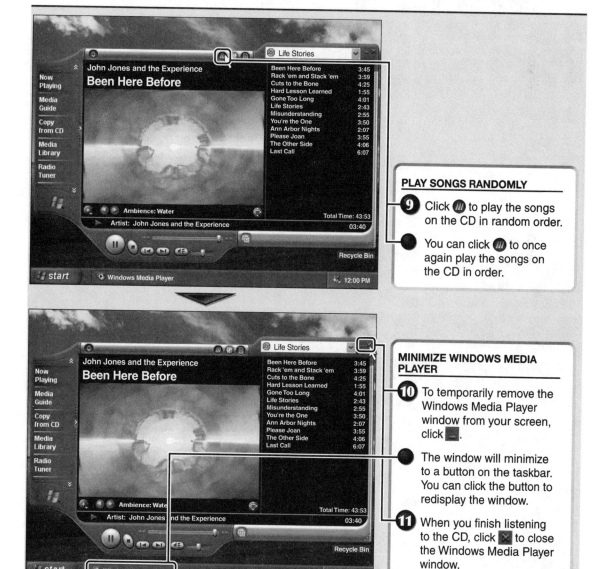

**PLAY SONGS RANDOMLY**

**9** Click 🎵 to play the songs on the CD in random order.

● You can click 🎵 to once again play the songs on the CD in order.

**MINIMIZE WINDOWS MEDIA PLAYER**

**10** To temporarily remove the Windows Media Player window from your screen, click ▬.

● The window will minimize to a button on the taskbar. You can click the button to redisplay the window.

**11** When you finish listening to the CD, click ✕ to close the Windows Media Player window.

# USING THE MEDIA GUIDE

The Media Guide is like an electronic magazine that allows you to access the latest music and movies on the Internet. You can also use the Media Guide to obtain information on various topics such as news, sports and entertainment. You must have a connection to the Internet to use the Media Guide.

USING THE MEDIA GUIDE

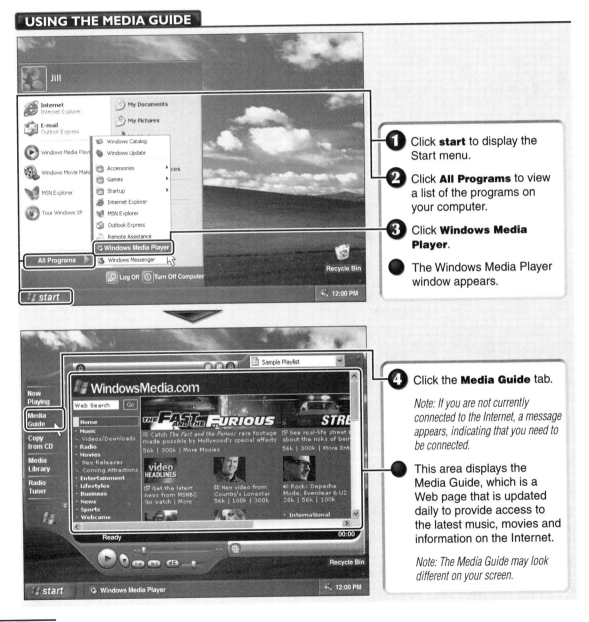

**1** Click **start** to display the Start menu.

**2** Click **All Programs** to view a list of the programs on your computer.

**3** Click **Windows Media Player**.

● The Windows Media Player window appears.

**4** Click the **Media Guide** tab.

*Note: If you are not currently connected to the Internet, a message appears, indicating that you need to be connected.*

● This area displays the Media Guide, which is a Web page that is updated daily to provide access to the latest music, movies and information on the Internet.

*Note: The Media Guide may look different on your screen.*

# in an instant

The Media Guide contains links that you can click to display additional information or play media files such as music videos or movie clips. When you position the mouse 🔓 over a link, the mouse 🔓 changes to 🖑.

**5** Click a link of interest.

In this example, information on the topic you selected appears.

You can repeat step **5** to browse through additional information or play other media files.

**6** When you finish using the Media Guide, click ✖ to close the Windows Media Player window.

# USING THE MEDIA LIBRARY

You can use the Media Library to organize and work with all the sound and video files on your computer. Many Web sites, such as earthstation1.com and www.videoclipart.com, offer sound and video files that you can transfer and play on your computer. You can also purchase collections of sound and video files at many computer stores.

## USING THE MEDIA LIBRARY

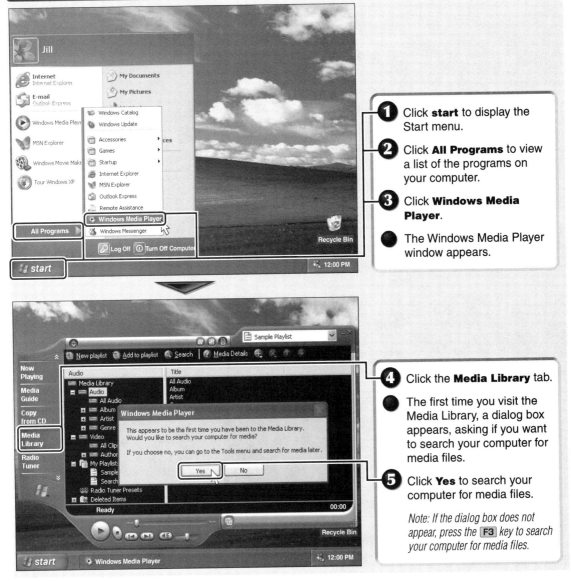

1. Click **start** to display the Start menu.

2. Click **All Programs** to view a list of the programs on your computer.

3. Click **Windows Media Player**.

■ The Windows Media Player window appears.

4. Click the **Media Library** tab.

■ The first time you visit the Media Library, a dialog box appears, asking if you want to search your computer for media files.

5. Click **Yes** to search your computer for media files.

*Note: If the dialog box does not appear, press the [F3] key to search your computer for media files.*

# in an instant

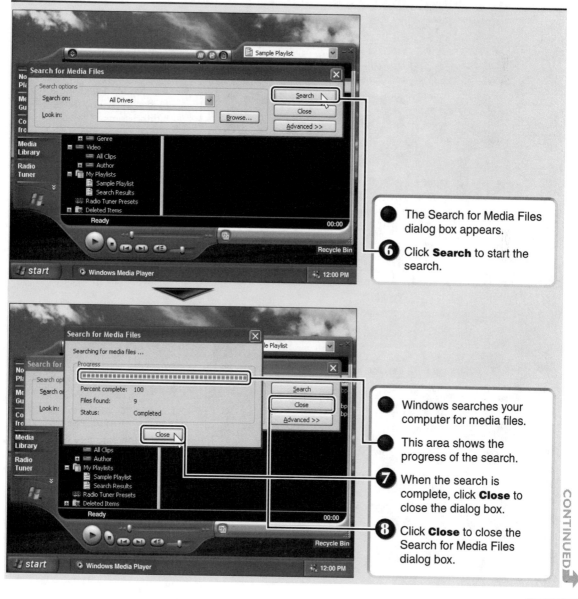

The Search for Media Files dialog box appears.

⑥ Click **Search** to start the search.

Windows searches your computer for media files.

This area shows the progress of the search.

⑦ When the search is complete, click **Close** to close the dialog box.

⑧ Click **Close** to close the Search for Media Files dialog box.

CONTINUED

**119**

# USING THE MEDIA LIBRARY

You can play sound and video files that are listed in the Media Library. The Media Library organizes your sound and video files into categories. The All Audio category lists all your sound files, while the All Clips category lists all your video files.

## USING THE MEDIA LIBRARY (CONTINUED)

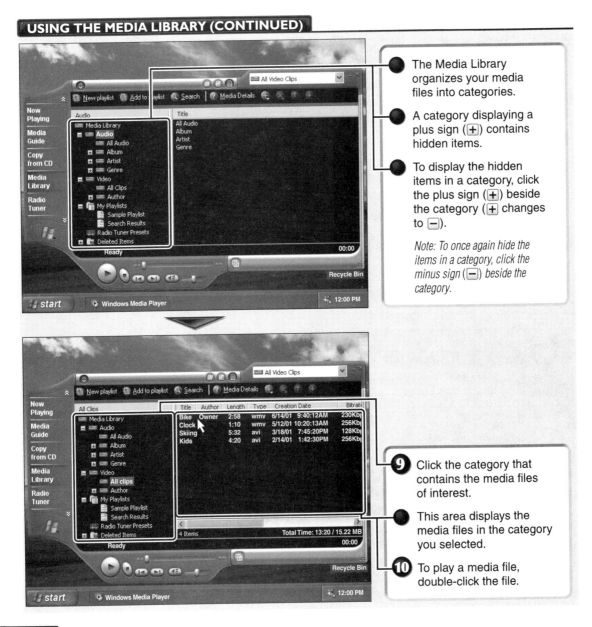

The Media Library organizes your media files into categories.

A category displaying a plus sign (⊞) contains hidden items.

To display the hidden items in a category, click the plus sign (⊞) beside the category (⊞ changes to ⊟).

*Note: To once again hide the items in a category, click the minus sign (⊟) beside the category.*

**9** Click the category that contains the media files of interest.

This area displays the media files in the category you selected.

**10** To play a media file, double-click the file.

# in an instant

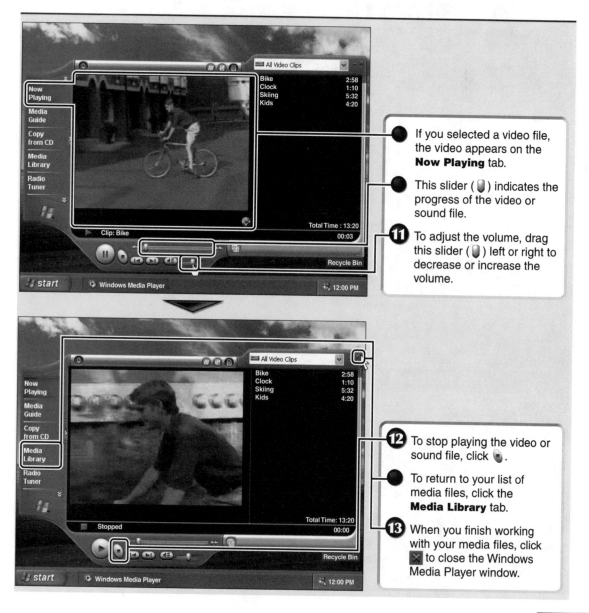

If you selected a video file, the video appears on the **Now Playing** tab.

This slider ( ) indicates the progress of the video or sound file.

**11** To adjust the volume, drag this slider ( ) left or right to decrease or increase the volume.

**12** To stop playing the video or sound file, click .

To return to your list of media files, click the **Media Library** tab.

**13** When you finish working with your media files, click ☒ to close the Windows Media Player window.

# LISTEN TO RADIO STATIONS

You can use Windows Media Player to listen to radio
stations from around the world that broadcast on the
Internet. You need a computer with sound capabilities
and an Internet connection to listen to radio stations
that broadcast on the Internet.

LISTEN TO RADIO STATIONS

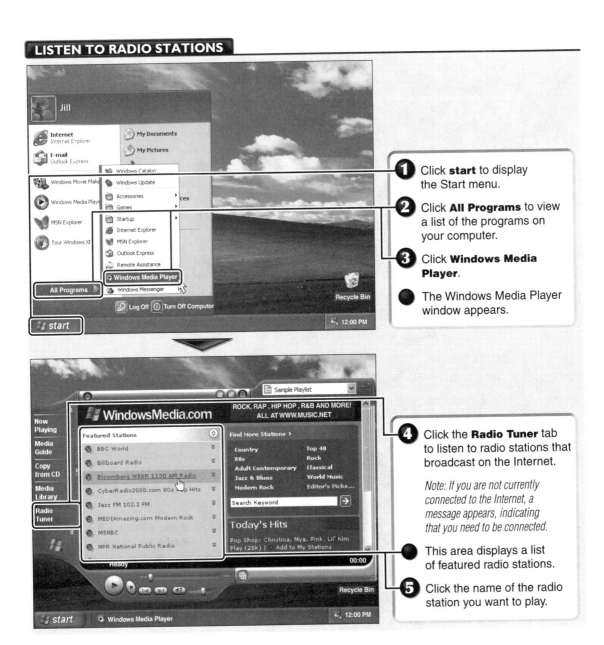

**1** Click **start** to display
the Start menu.

**2** Click **All Programs** to view
a list of the programs on
your computer.

**3** Click **Windows Media
Player**.

● The Windows Media Player
window appears.

**4** Click the **Radio Tuner** tab
to listen to radio stations that
broadcast on the Internet.

*Note: If you are not currently
connected to the Internet, a
message appears, indicating
that you need to be connected.*

● This area displays a list
of featured radio stations.

**5** Click the name of the radio
station you want to play.

# in an *instant*

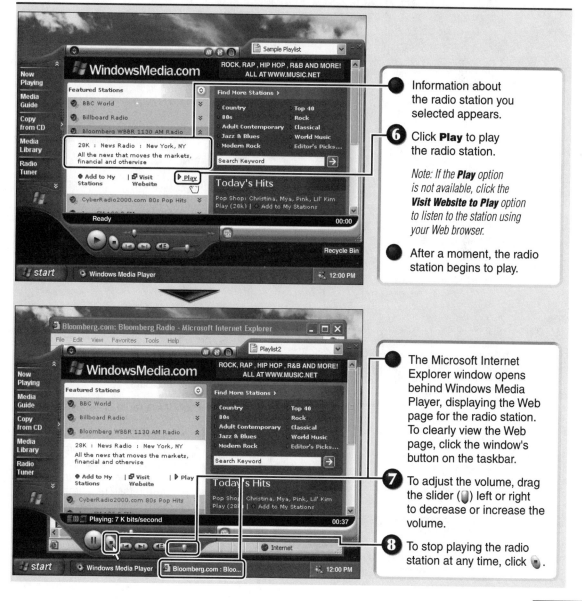

Information about the radio station you selected appears.

**6** Click **Play** to play the radio station.

*Note: If the **Play** option is not available, click the **Visit Website to Play** option to listen to the station using your Web browser.*

After a moment, the radio station begins to play.

The Microsoft Internet Explorer window opens behind Windows Media Player, displaying the Web page for the radio station. To clearly view the Web page, click the window's button on the taskbar.

**7** To adjust the volume, drag the slider (🔘) left or right to decrease or increase the volume.

**8** To stop playing the radio station at any time, click 🔘.

# LISTEN TO RADIO STATIONS

You can find specific radio stations that broadcast on the Internet. You can browse for a radio station by category, such as Country, Modern Rock or Classical. You can also enter a keyword, such as a language, location or call letters, to search for the radio station you want to listen to.

## LISTEN TO RADIO STATIONS (CONTINUED)

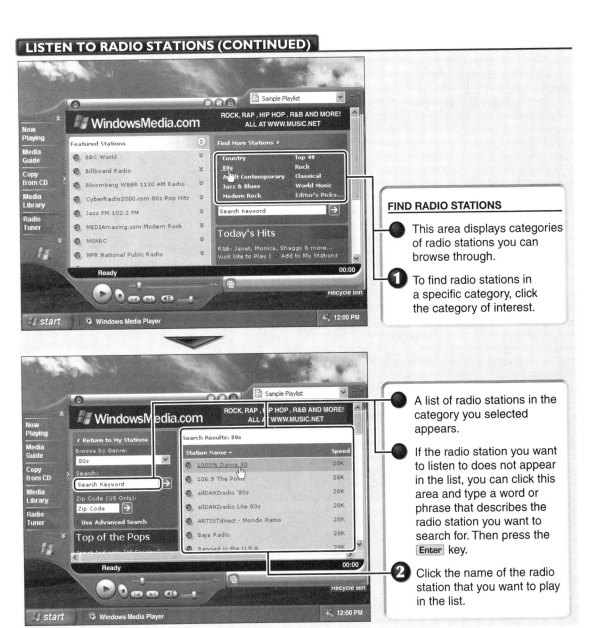

**FIND RADIO STATIONS**

● This area displays categories of radio stations you can browse through.

❶ To find radio stations in a specific category, click the category of interest.

● A list of radio stations in the category you selected appears.

● If the radio station you want to listen to does not appear in the list, you can click this area and type a word or phrase that describes the radio station you want to search for. Then press the Enter key.

❷ Click the name of the radio station that you want to play in the list.

**124**

# in an instant

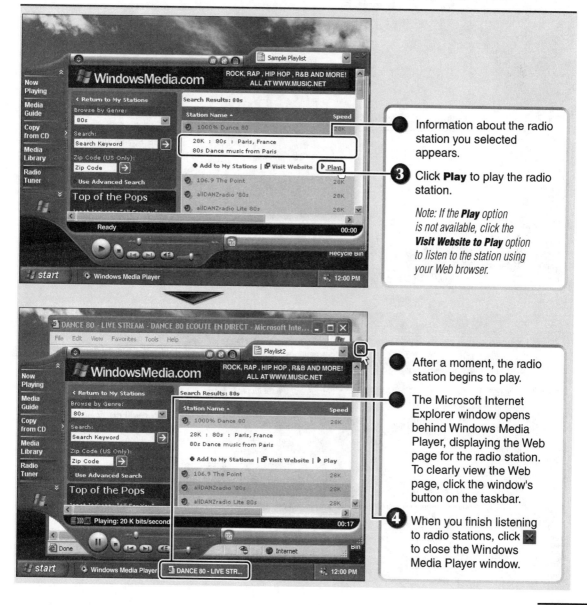

● Information about the radio station you selected appears.

❸ Click **Play** to play the radio station.

*Note: If the **Play** option is not available, click the **Visit Website to Play** option to listen to the station using your Web browser.*

● After a moment, the radio station begins to play.

● The Microsoft Internet Explorer window opens behind Windows Media Player, displaying the Web page for the radio station. To clearly view the Web page, click the window's button on the taskbar.

❹ When you finish listening to radio stations, click ▣ to close the Windows Media Player window.

# COPY SONGS FROM A MUSIC CD

You can copy songs from a music CD onto your computer. Copying songs from a music CD allows you to play the songs at any time without having to insert the CD into your computer. Copying songs from a music CD also allows you to later copy the songs to a recordable CD or portable device.

COPY SONGS FROM A MUSIC CD

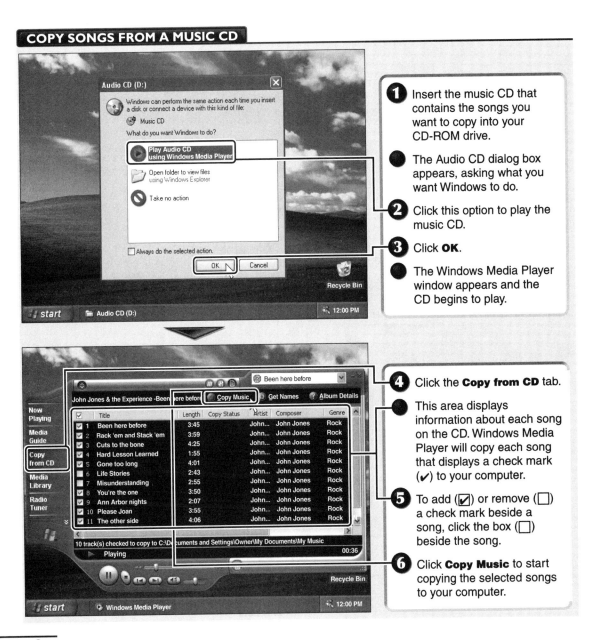

**1** Insert the music CD that contains the songs you want to copy into your CD-ROM drive.

● The Audio CD dialog box appears, asking what you want Windows to do.

**2** Click this option to play the music CD.

**3** Click **OK**.

● The Windows Media Player window appears and the CD begins to play.

**4** Click the **Copy from CD** tab.

● This area displays information about each song on the CD. Windows Media Player will copy each song that displays a check mark (✔) to your computer.

**5** To add (☑) or remove (☐) a check mark beside a song, click the box (☐) beside the song.

**6** Click **Copy Music** to start copying the selected songs to your computer.

# in an instant

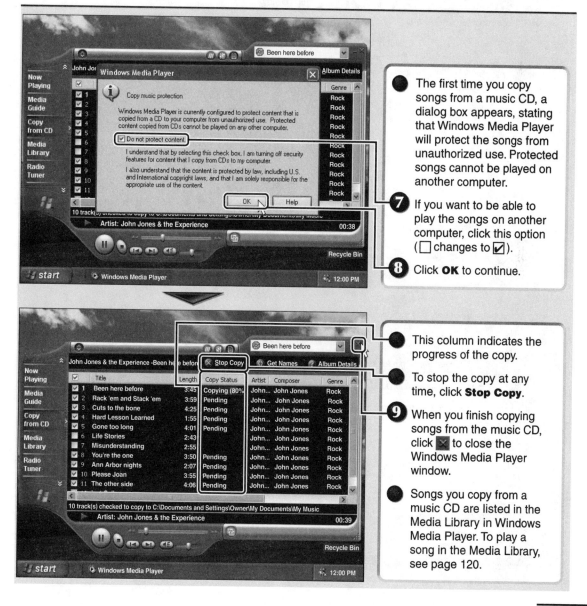

The first time you copy songs from a music CD, a dialog box appears, stating that Windows Media Player will protect the songs from unauthorized use. Protected songs cannot be played on another computer.

7 If you want to be able to play the songs on another computer, click this option (☐ changes to ☑).

8 Click **OK** to continue.

● This column indicates the progress of the copy.

● To stop the copy at any time, click **Stop Copy**.

9 When you finish copying songs from the music CD, click ✖ to close the Windows Media Player window.

● Songs you copy from a music CD are listed in the Media Library in Windows Media Player. To play a song in the Media Library, see page 120.

# COPY SONGS TO A CD OR PORTABLE DEVICE

You can copy songs that appear in the Media Library to a CD or to a portable device such as an MP3 player. You can copy songs to a CD only once using Windows Media Player, so you should be sure to carefully select all the songs you want to copy. You will need a recordable CD drive to copy songs to a CD.

## COPY SONGS TO A CD OR PORTABLE DEVICE

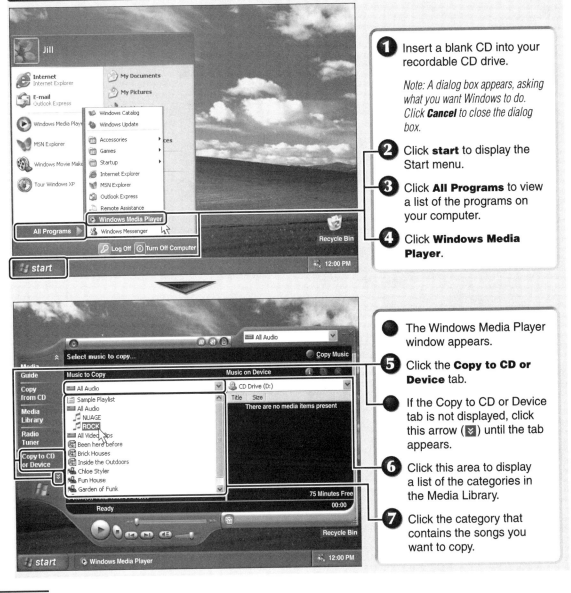

**1** Insert a blank CD into your recordable CD drive.

*Note: A dialog box appears, asking what you want Windows to do. Click **Cancel** to close the dialog box.*

**2** Click **start** to display the Start menu.

**3** Click **All Programs** to view a list of the programs on your computer.

**4** Click **Windows Media Player**.

■ The Windows Media Player window appears.

**5** Click the **Copy to CD or Device** tab.

■ If the Copy to CD or Device tab is not displayed, click this arrow (⊻) until the tab appears.

**6** Click this area to display a list of the categories in the Media Library.

**7** Click the category that contains the songs you want to copy.

**128**

# in an *instant*

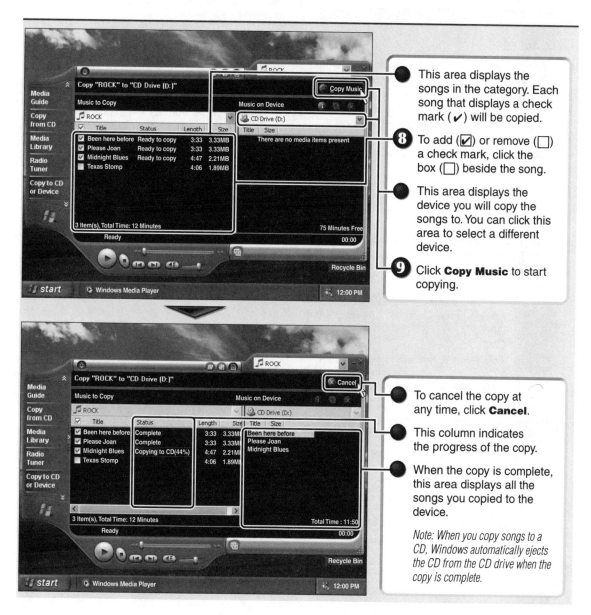

- This area displays the songs in the category. Each song that displays a check mark (✔) will be copied.

**8** To add (☑) or remove (☐) a check mark, click the box (☐) beside the song.

- This area displays the device you will copy the songs to. You can click this area to select a different device.

**9** Click **Copy Music** to start copying.

- To cancel the copy at any time, click **Cancel**.

- This column indicates the progress of the copy.

- When the copy is complete, this area displays all the songs you copied to the device.

*Note: When you copy songs to a CD, Windows automatically ejects the CD from the CD drive when the copy is complete.*

You can use Windows Movie Maker to transfer movies from a video camera, Web camera, television broadcast, VCR or DVD player to your computer. You can then organize and edit the movies before sharing them with friends and family. Before using Windows Movie Maker, you need to connect and install the equipment needed to transfer your home movies to your computer.

## HARDWARE REQUIREMENTS

### CABLES

You will need one or more cables to connect the video camera or other video source to your computer. The video source or the card you use to connect the video source to your computer may come with the cables you need. If you do not have the required cables, you can purchase the cables at a computer store.

### MINIMUM COMPUTER REQUIREMENTS

Your computer must have the following minimum requirements for Windows Movie Maker to work properly.

* 300 MHz Pentium II or equivalent
* 64 MB of RAM
* 2 GB of free hard disk space
* Sound capabilities

### CONNECTOR

You need a specific type of connector to be able to connect a video camera or other video source to your computer. If your computer does not already have the appropriate type of connector, you can purchase the connector at a computer store.

| VIDEO SOURCE | TYPE OF CONNECTOR COMMONLY REQUIRED |
|---|---|
| Analog Video Camera | Video Capture Card |
| Digital Video Camera | FireWire Port or FireWire Card |
| DVD | TV Tuner Card |
| Television Broadcast | TV Tuner Card |
| VCR | TV Tuner Card |
| Web Camera | USB Port or USB Card |

## TIPS FOR CREATING HIGH-QUALITY MOVIES

The quality of the movies you create using Windows Movie Maker directly depends on the quality of the video you record. Keep the following tips in mind when recording video.

* Use a still background whenever possible.

* If using a background that moves in your video, place your subject close to the camera lens to blur the background slightly.

* Use soft, diffuse light to avoid shadows.

* Have your subjects wear clothing that complements their skin tones, avoiding bright colors and stripes.

* Reduce background noise by turning off fans, computers and heating systems.

* When using a microphone, remind the speaker not to tap anything against the microphone or play with the cable.

You can start Windows Movie Maker to create and work with movies on your computer. After starting Windows Movie Maker, you can record video from a video camera, Web camera, television broadcast, VCR or DVD player onto your computer.

## START WINDOWS MOVIE MAKER

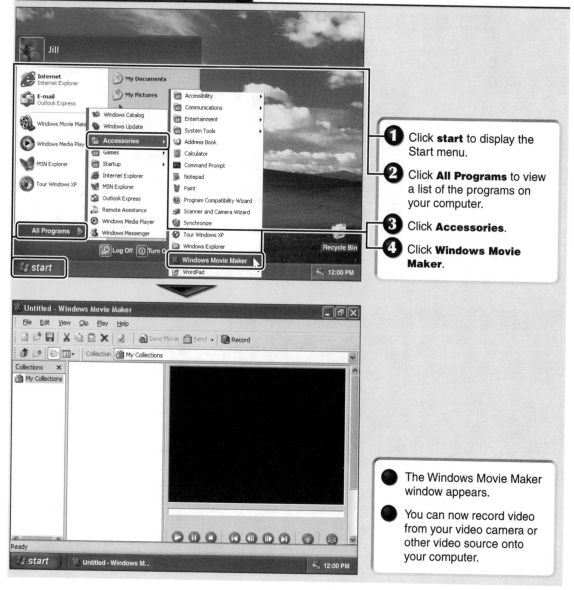

1 Click **start** to display the Start menu.

2 Click **All Programs** to view a list of the programs on your computer.

3 Click **Accessories**.

4 Click **Windows Movie Maker**.

● The Windows Movie Maker window appears.

● You can now record video from your video camera or other video source onto your computer.

# RECORD A VIDEO

You can record video from your video camera or other video source onto your computer. Before you start recording video, make sure your video camera or other video source is properly connected to your computer and turned on. Also make sure the tape or other media is at the point where you want to begin recording.

## RECORD A VIDEO

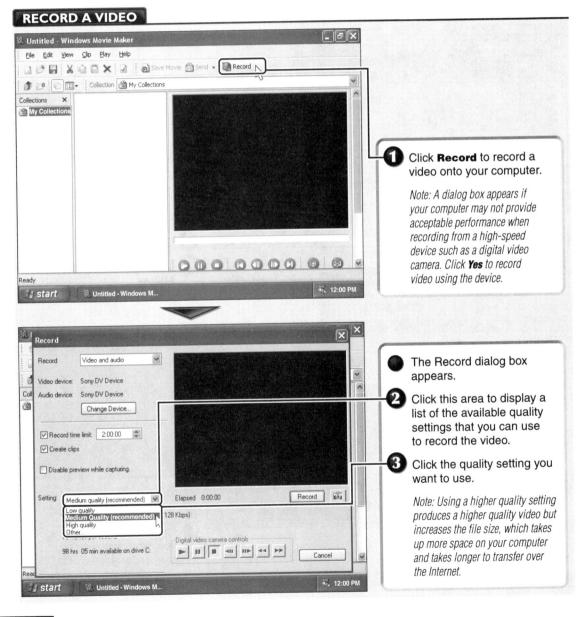

**1** Click **Record** to record a video onto your computer.

*Note: A dialog box appears if your computer may not provide acceptable performance when recording from a high-speed device such as a digital video camera. Click **Yes** to record video using the device.*

■ The Record dialog box appears.

**2** Click this area to display a list of the available quality settings that you can use to record the video.

**3** Click the quality setting you want to use.

*Note: Using a higher quality setting produces a higher quality video but increases the file size, which takes up more space on your computer and takes longer to transfer over the Internet.*

132

in an **instant**

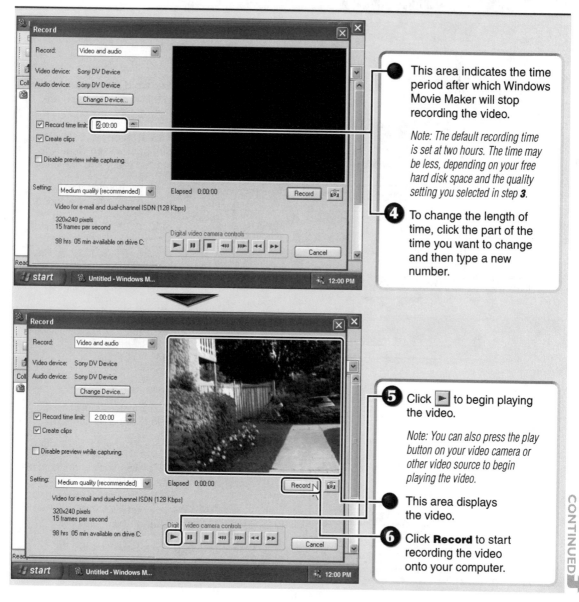

This area indicates the time period after which Windows Movie Maker will stop recording the video.

*Note: The default recording time is set at two hours. The time may be less, depending on your free hard disk space and the quality setting you selected in step 3.*

**4** To change the length of time, click the part of the time you want to change and then type a new number.

**5** Click ▶ to begin playing the video.

*Note: You can also press the play button on your video camera or other video source to begin playing the video.*

This area displays the video.

**6** Click **Record** to start recording the video onto your computer.

CONTINUED

# RECORD A VIDEO

When you record a video, Windows Movie Maker creates a collection to store the video. Collections help keep your videos organized. Windows also automatically stores each video you record in the My Videos folder on your computer. Windows creates the My Videos folder within the My Documents folder the first time you start Windows Movie Maker.

## RECORD A VIDEO (CONTINUED)

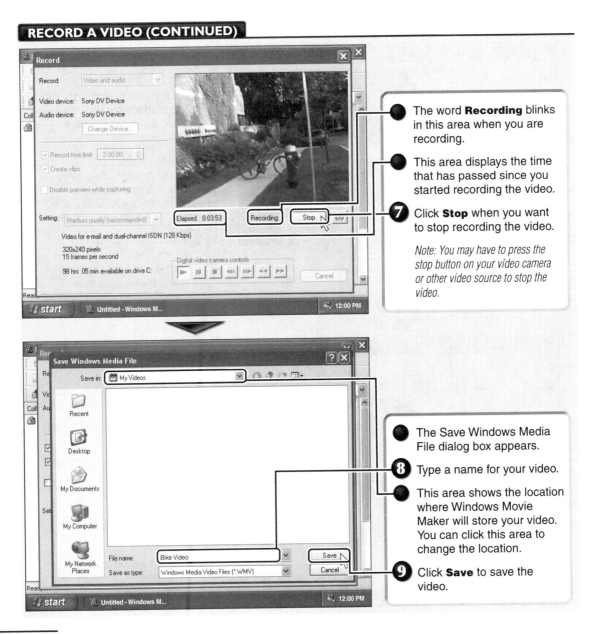

The word **Recording** blinks in this area when you are recording.

This area displays the time that has passed since you started recording the video.

⑦ Click **Stop** when you want to stop recording the video.

*Note: You may have to press the stop button on your video camera or other video source to stop the video.*

The Save Windows Media File dialog box appears.

⑧ Type a name for your video.

This area shows the location where Windows Movie Maker will store your video. You can click this area to change the location.

⑨ Click **Save** to save the video.

in an *Instant*

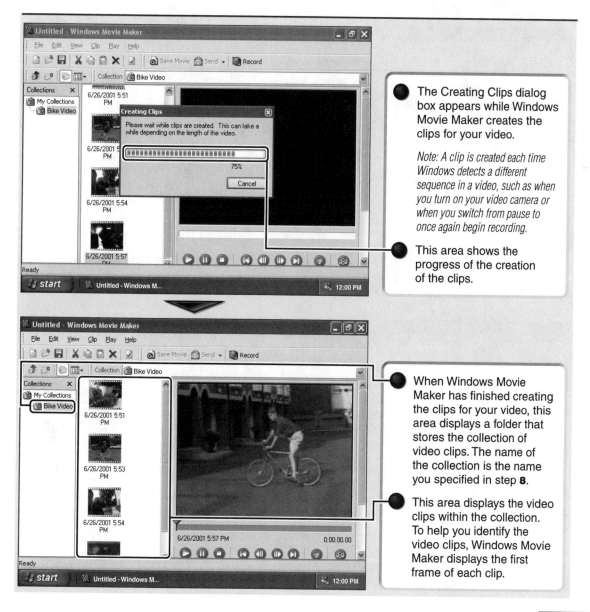

The Creating Clips dialog box appears while Windows Movie Maker creates the clips for your video.

*Note: A clip is created each time Windows detects a different sequence in a video, such as when you turn on your video camera or when you switch from pause to once again begin recording.*

This area shows the progress of the creation of the clips.

When Windows Movie Maker has finished creating the clips for your video, this area displays a folder that stores the collection of video clips. The name of the collection is the name you specified in step **8**.

This area displays the video clips within the collection. To help you identify the video clips, Windows Movie Maker displays the first frame of each clip.

# PLAY A VIDEO CLIP

You can play each video clip that you have recorded on your computer. Playing video clips can help you determine which clips you want to include in your movie. The Windows Movie Maker window displays buttons you can use to control the play of the video clip. For example, you can pause or stop a video clip.

## PLAY A VIDEO CLIP

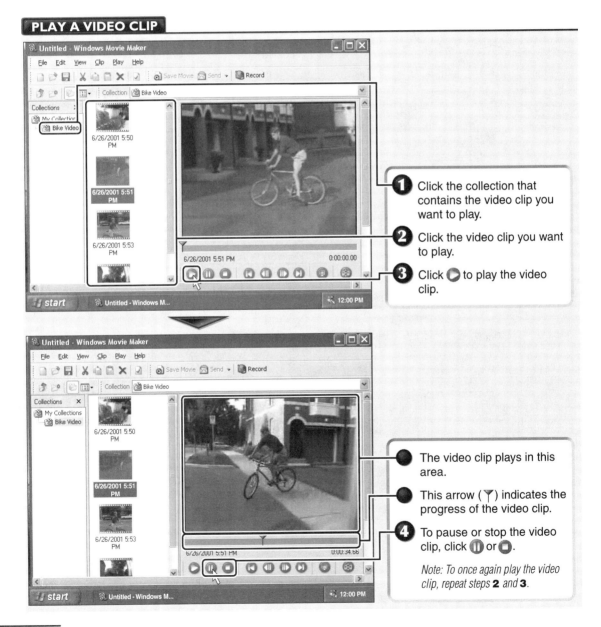

**1** Click the collection that contains the video clip you want to play.

**2** Click the video clip you want to play.

**3** Click ⬤ to play the video clip.

● The video clip plays in this area.

● This arrow (▼) indicates the progress of the video clip.

**4** To pause or stop the video clip, click ⏸ or ⬤.

*Note: To once again play the video clip, repeat steps 2 and 3.*

**136**

# ADD A VIDEO CLIP TO STORYBOARD

You must add each video clip that you want to include in your movie to the storyboard. The storyboard displays the order in which video clips will play in your movie. You can also remove a video clip that you no longer need from the storyboard.

## ADD A VIDEO CLIP TO STORYBOARD

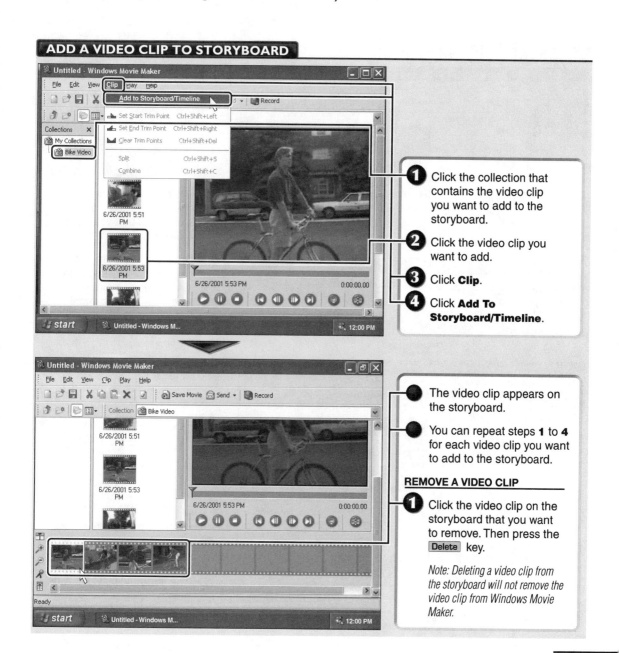

1 Click the collection that contains the video clip you want to add to the storyboard.

2 Click the video clip you want to add.

3 Click **Clip**.

4 Click **Add To Storyboard/Timeline**.

◆ The video clip appears on the storyboard.

◆ You can repeat steps **1** to **4** for each video clip you want to add to the storyboard.

### REMOVE A VIDEO CLIP

1 Click the video clip on the storyboard that you want to remove. Then press the Delete key.

*Note: Deleting a video clip from the storyboard will not remove the video clip from Windows Movie Maker.*

**137**

# REARRANGE VIDEO CLIPS

After adding the video clips you want to use to the storyboard, you can rearrange the video clips to change the order in which the clips will play in your movie. When you move a video clip, the surrounding video clips shift to make room for the clip.

## REARRANGE VIDEO CLIPS

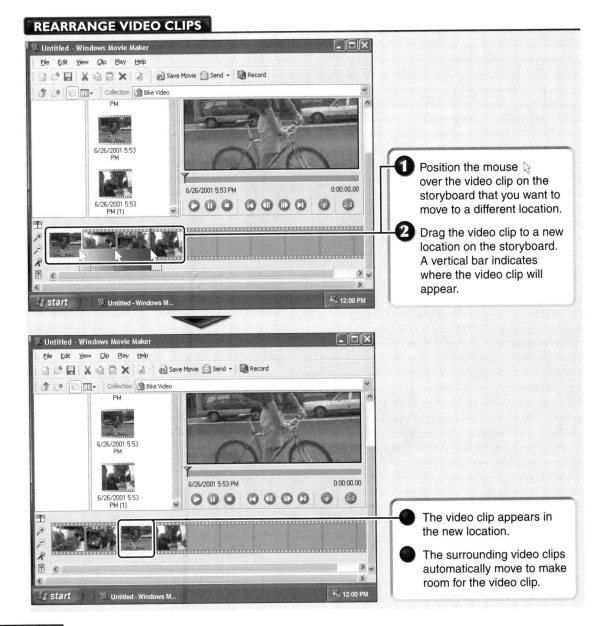

**1** Position the mouse ⤢ over the video clip on the storyboard that you want to move to a different location.

**2** Drag the video clip to a new location on the storyboard. A vertical bar indicates where the video clip will appear.

● The video clip appears in the new location.

● The surrounding video clips automatically move to make room for the video clip.

You can save a project so you can later review and make changes to the project. A project is a rough draft of your movie that contains all the video clips you added to the storyboard. You should regularly save changes you make to a project to avoid losing your work.

## SAVE A PROJECT

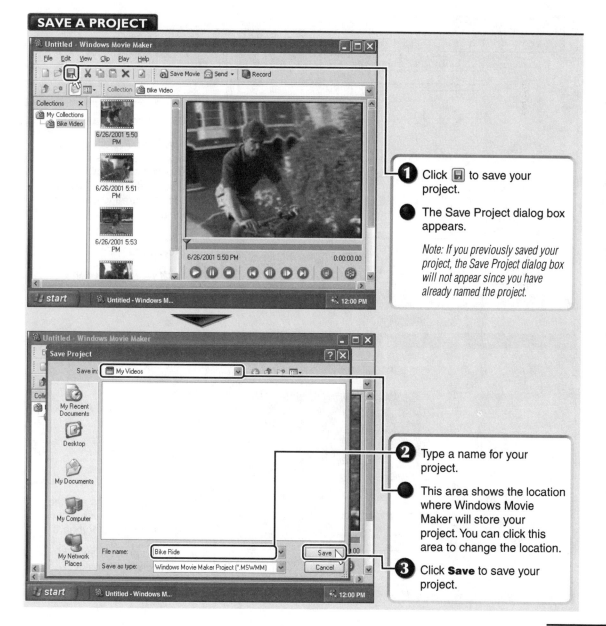

**1** Click 🖫 to save your project.

● The Save Project dialog box appears.

*Note: If you previously saved your project, the Save Project dialog box will not appear since you have already named the project.*

**2** Type a name for your project.

● This area shows the location where Windows Movie Maker will store your project. You can click this area to change the location.

**3** Click **Save** to save your project.

# OPEN A PROJECT

You can open a saved project to display the video clips in the project and review and make changes to the project. A project is a rough draft of your movie that contains all the video clips you added to the storyboard. You can work with only one project at a time, so you should make sure you save the project you are currently working with before opening another project.

## OPEN A PROJECT

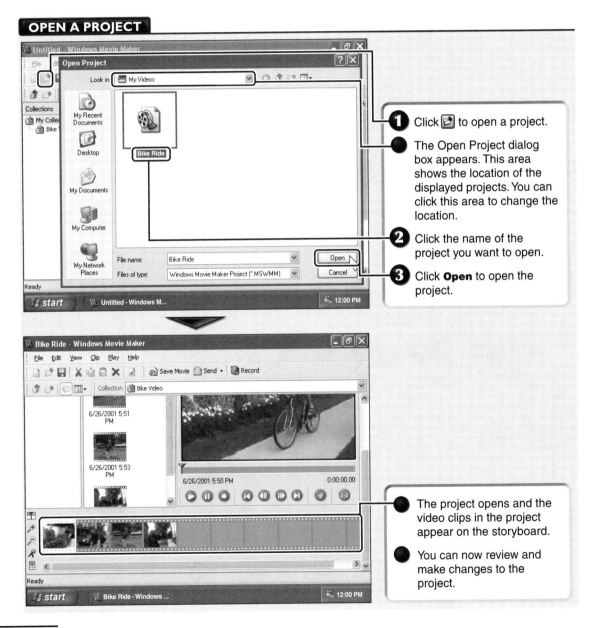

1 Click 🗁 to open a project.

● The Open Project dialog box appears. This area shows the location of the displayed projects. You can click this area to change the location.

2 Click the name of the project you want to open.

3 Click **Open** to open the project.

● The project opens and the video clips in the project appear on the storyboard.

● You can now review and make changes to the project.

You can preview all the video clips you have added to the storyboard as a movie. Previewing a movie is useful if you want to see what the video clips look like together before you save the movie on your computer. When previewing a movie, you can pause or stop the movie at any time.

## PREVIEW A MOVIE

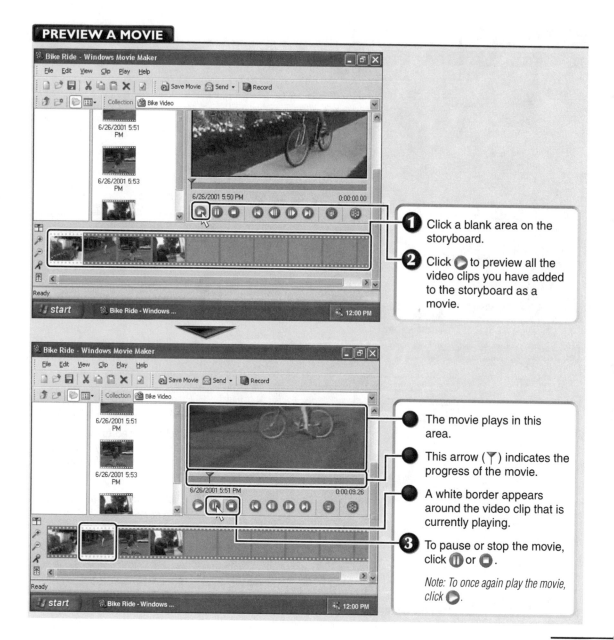

1 Click a blank area on the storyboard.

2 Click ⊙ to preview all the video clips you have added to the storyboard as a movie.

● The movie plays in this area.

● This arrow (Y) indicates the progress of the movie.

● A white border appears around the video clip that is currently playing.

3 To pause or stop the movie, click ⏸ or ⏹.

*Note: To once again play the movie, click ⊙.*

# SAVE A MOVIE

After you add all the video clips that you want to include in your movie to the storyboard, you can save the movie on your computer. Saving a movie allows you to play the movie at any time. You can also share the movie with friends and family by sending it in an e-mail message or publishing the movie to the Web.

## SAVE A MOVIE

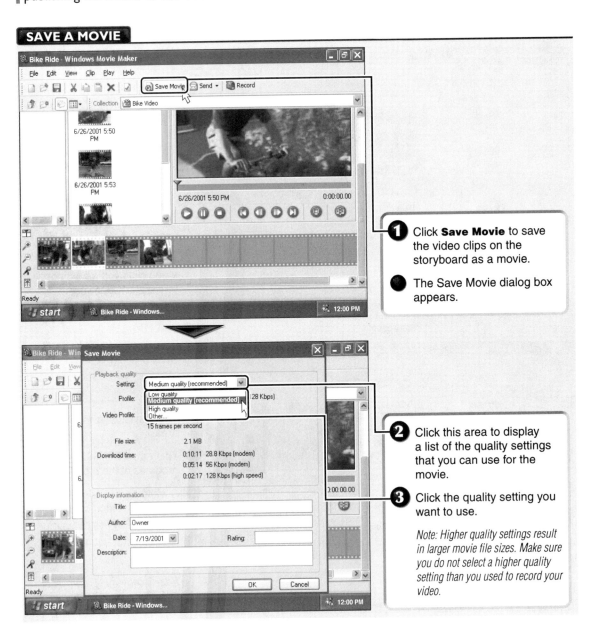

**1** Click **Save Movie** to save the video clips on the storyboard as a movie.

● The Save Movie dialog box appears.

**2** Click this area to display a list of the quality settings that you can use for the movie.

**3** Click the quality setting you want to use.

*Note: Higher quality settings result in larger movie file sizes. Make sure you do not select a higher quality setting than you used to record your video.*

in an *instant*

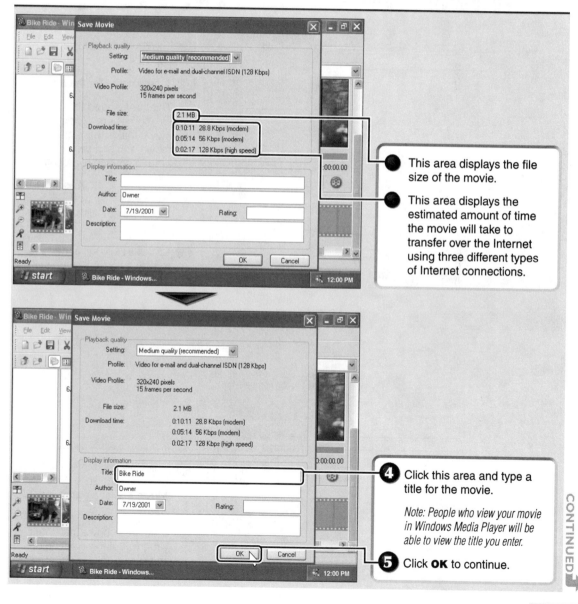

This area displays the file size of the movie.

This area displays the estimated amount of time the movie will take to transfer over the Internet using three different types of Internet connections.

**4** Click this area and type a title for the movie.

*Note: People who view your movie in Windows Media Player will be able to view the title you enter.*

**5** Click **OK** to continue.

CONTINUED

# SAVE A MOVIE

After you save a movie on your computer, you can view the movie in Windows Media Player. You cannot make changes to a movie you have saved. Windows Movie Maker only allows you to make changes to a project, which is a rough draft of a movie.

## SAVE A MOVIE (CONTINUED)

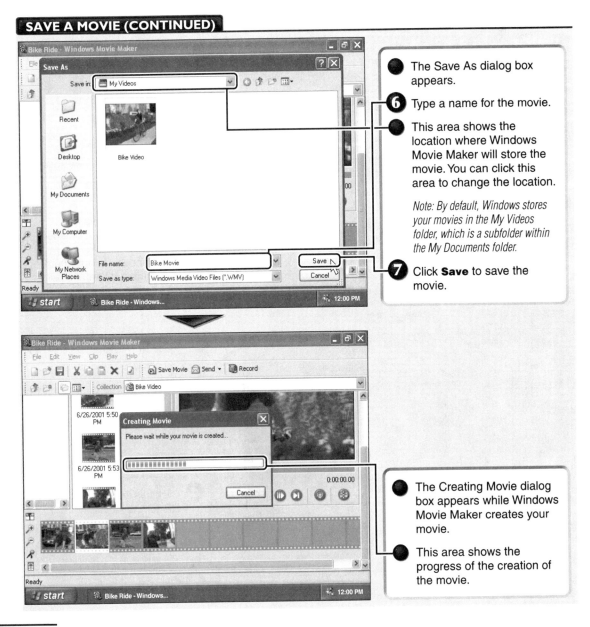

● The Save As dialog box appears.

⑥ Type a name for the movie.

● This area shows the location where Windows Movie Maker will store the movie. You can click this area to change the location.

*Note: By default, Windows stores your movies in the My Videos folder, which is a subfolder within the My Documents folder.*

⑦ Click **Save** to save the movie.

● The Creating Movie dialog box appears while Windows Movie Maker creates your movie.

● This area shows the progress of the creation of the movie.

# in an *instant*

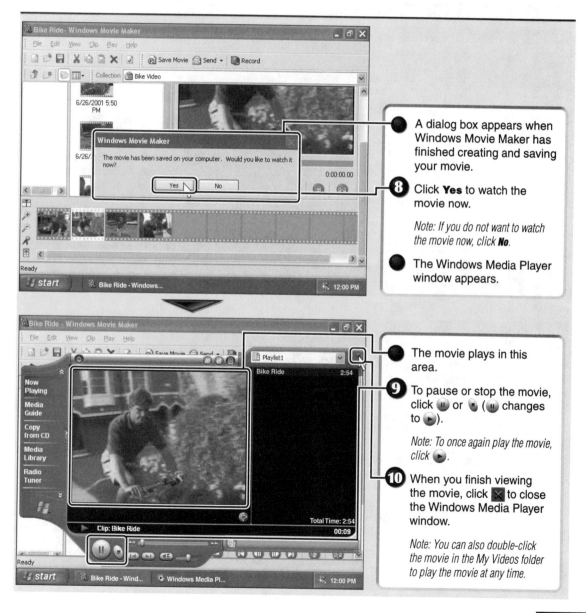

A dialog box appears when Windows Movie Maker has finished creating and saving your movie.

**8** Click **Yes** to watch the movie now.

*Note: If you do not want to watch the movie now, click No.*

The Windows Media Player window appears.

The movie plays in this area.

**9** To pause or stop the movie, click ⏸ or ⏹ (⏸ changes to ▶).

*Note: To once again play the movie, click ▶.*

**10** When you finish viewing the movie, click ✕ to close the Windows Media Player window.

*Note: You can also double-click the movie in the My Videos folder to play the movie at any time.*

# CREATE A USER ACCOUNT

If you share your computer with other people, you can create a personalized user account for each person. Windows will keep your personal files separate from the personal files created by each of the other users. For example, your My Documents folder will display only the files you have created. You must have a computer administrator account to create a user account.

## CREATE A USER ACCOUNT

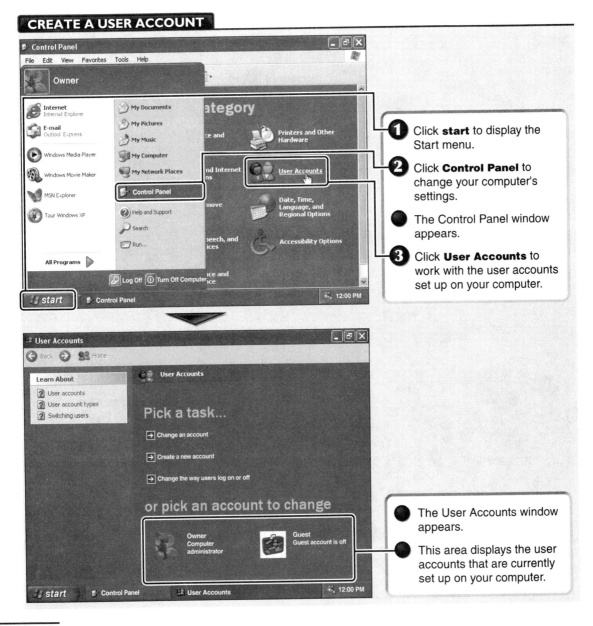

**1** Click **start** to display the Start menu.

**2** Click **Control Panel** to change your computer's settings.

● The Control Panel window appears.

**3** Click **User Accounts** to work with the user accounts set up on your computer.

● The User Accounts window appears.

● This area displays the user accounts that are currently set up on your computer.

# in an *instant*

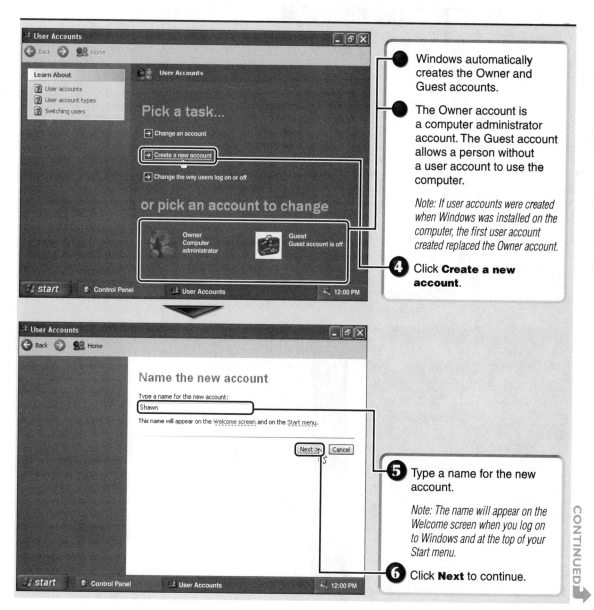

● Windows automatically creates the Owner and Guest accounts.

● The Owner account is a computer administrator account. The Guest account allows a person without a user account to use the computer.

*Note: If user accounts were created when Windows was installed on the computer, the first user account created replaced the Owner account.*

**4** Click **Create a new account**.

**5** Type a name for the new account.

*Note: The name will appear on the Welcome screen when you log on to Windows and at the top of your Start menu.*

**6** Click **Next** to continue.

CONTINUED

# CREATE A USER ACCOUNT

When you create a user account, you must select the type of account you want to create. A computer administrator account allows the user to perform any task on the computer, such as creating and changing all user accounts and installing programs or hardware. A limited account allows the user to perform only certain tasks, such as changing some computer settings.

## CREATE A USER ACCOUNT (CONTINUED)

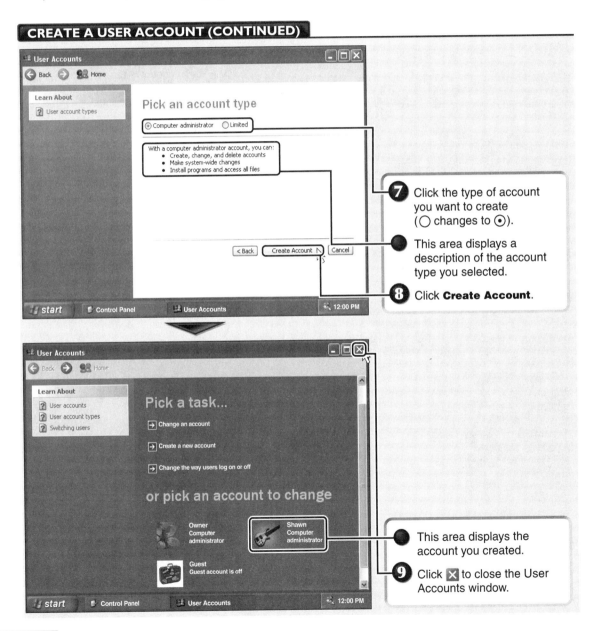

**7** Click the type of account you want to create (○ changes to ⊙).

■ This area displays a description of the account type you selected.

**8** Click **Create Account**.

■ This area displays the account you created.

**9** Click ⊠ to close the User Accounts window.

# DELETE A USER ACCOUNT

If a person no longer uses your computer, you can delete the person's user account from your computer. To ensure that one computer administrator account always exists on the computer, Windows will not allow you to delete the last computer administrator account on your computer. You must have a computer administrator account to delete a user account.

## DELETE A USER ACCOUNT

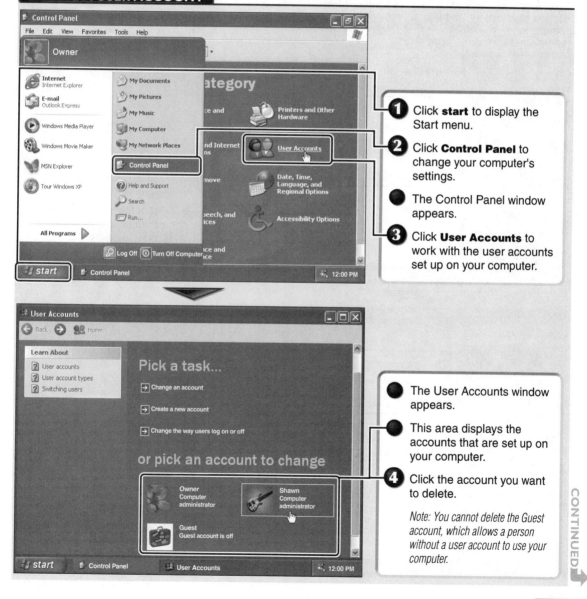

1 Click **start** to display the Start menu.

2 Click **Control Panel** to change your computer's settings.

- The Control Panel window appears.

3 Click **User Accounts** to work with the user accounts set up on your computer.

- The User Accounts window appears.

- This area displays the accounts that are set up on your computer.

4 Click the account you want to delete.

*Note: You cannot delete the Guest account, which allows a person without a user account to use your computer.*

CONTINUED

**149**

When you delete a user account, you can choose to keep or delete the user's personal files. If you choose to keep the personal files, Windows will save the personal files that are stored on the desktop and in the My Documents folder in a new folder that has the same name as the deleted user account.

## DELETE A USER ACCOUNT (CONTINUED)

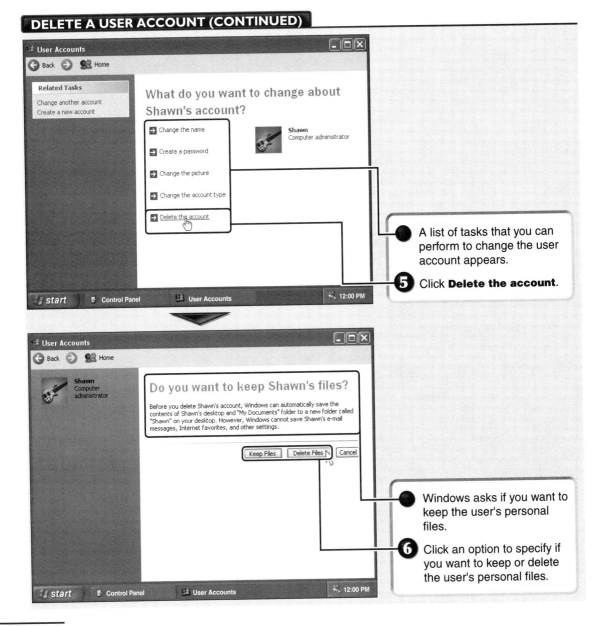

A list of tasks that you can perform to change the user account appears.

**5** Click **Delete the account**.

Windows asks if you want to keep the user's personal files.

**6** Click an option to specify if you want to keep or delete the user's personal files.

# in an instant

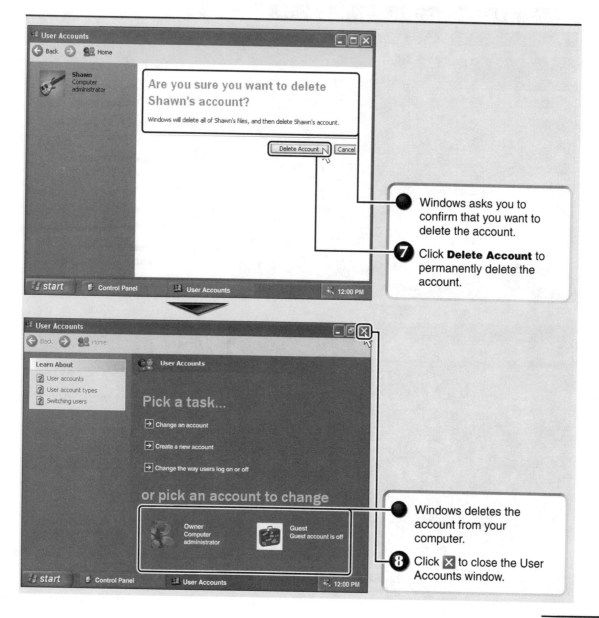

Windows asks you to confirm that you want to delete the account.

**7** Click **Delete Account** to permanently delete the account.

Windows deletes the account from your computer.

**8** Click ☒ to close the User Accounts window.

# ASSIGN A PASSWORD TO A USER ACCOUNT

You can assign a password to your user account to prevent other people from accessing the account. You will need to enter the password each time you want to use Windows. If you have a computer administrator account, you can assign passwords to all accounts. If you have a limited account, you can assign a password only to your own account.

ASSIGN A PASSWORD TO A USER ACCOUNT

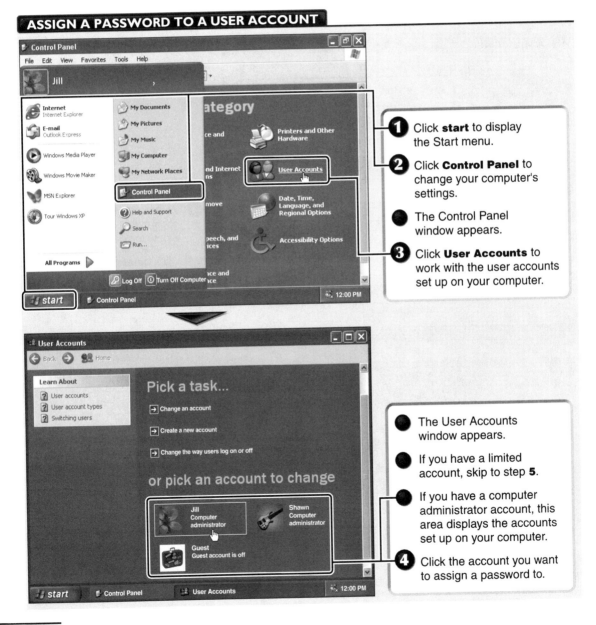

**1** Click **start** to display the Start menu.

**2** Click **Control Panel** to change your computer's settings.

● The Control Panel window appears.

**3** Click **User Accounts** to work with the user accounts set up on your computer.

● The User Accounts window appears.

● If you have a limited account, skip to step **5**.

● If you have a computer administrator account, this area displays the accounts set up on your computer.

**4** Click the account you want to assign a password to.

# in an instant

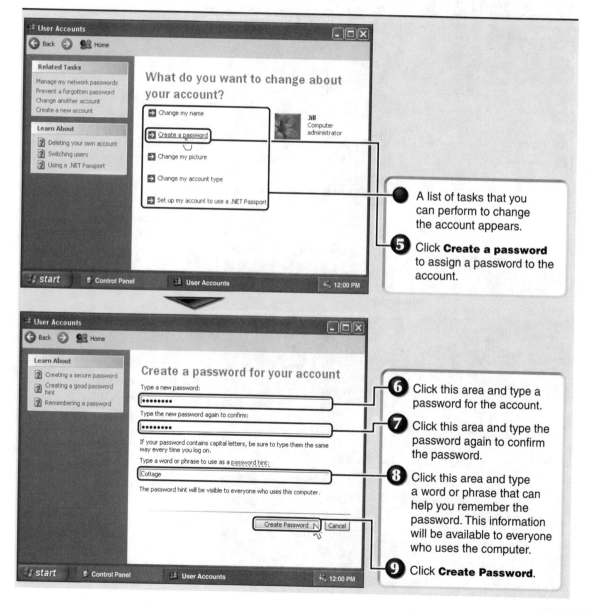

A list of tasks that you can perform to change the account appears.

**5** Click **Create a password** to assign a password to the account.

**6** Click this area and type a password for the account.

**7** Click this area and type the password again to confirm the password.

**8** Click this area and type a word or phrase that can help you remember the password. This information will be available to everyone who uses the computer.

**9** Click **Create Password**.

**153**

# LOG OFF WINDOWS

You can log off Windows so another person can log on to Windows to use the computer. When you log off Windows, you can choose to keep your programs and files open while another person uses the computer. This allows you to quickly return to your programs and files after the other person finishes using the computer.

## LOG OFF WINDOWS

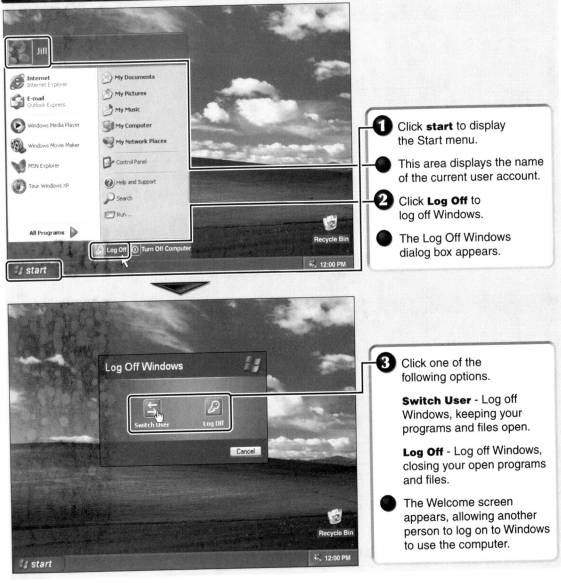

**1** Click **start** to display the Start menu.

● This area displays the name of the current user account.

**2** Click **Log Off** to log off Windows.

● The Log Off Windows dialog box appears.

**3** Click one of the following options.

**Switch User** - Log off Windows, keeping your programs and files open.

**Log Off** - Log off Windows, closing your open programs and files.

● The Welcome screen appears, allowing another person to log on to Windows to use the computer.

If you have set up user accounts on your computer, you will need to log on to Windows to use the computer. You must log on to Windows each time you turn on your computer or log off Windows to switch between user accounts.

## LOG ON TO WINDOWS

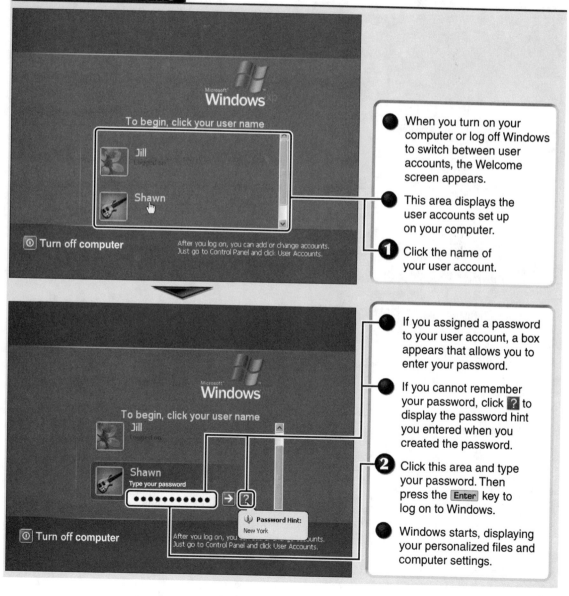

When you turn on your computer or log off Windows to switch between user accounts, the Welcome screen appears.

This area displays the user accounts set up on your computer.

**1** Click the name of your user account.

If you assigned a password to your user account, a box appears that allows you to enter your password.

If you cannot remember your password, click **?** to display the password hint you entered when you created the password.

**2** Click this area and type your password. Then press the **Enter** key to log on to Windows.

Windows starts, displaying your personalized files and computer settings.

# VIEW SHARED FILES

You can view the personal files of every user set up on your computer. In most cases, the contents of every user's My Documents folder and its subfolders are available to all other users. If your computer uses the NTFS file system, you cannot view the personal files of other users if you have a limited user account or users have made their personal folders private.

VIEW SHARED FILES

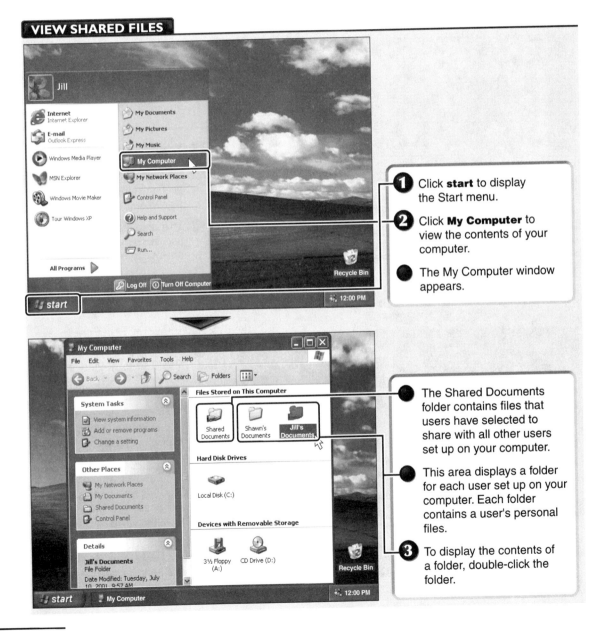

1 Click **start** to display the Start menu.

2 Click **My Computer** to view the contents of your computer.

● The My Computer window appears.

● The Shared Documents folder contains files that users have selected to share with all other users set up on your computer.

● This area displays a folder for each user set up on your computer. Each folder contains a user's personal files.

3 To display the contents of a folder, double-click the folder.

# SHARE FILES

If you want to share files with every user set up on your computer, you can copy the files to the Shared Documents folder. Copying files to the Shared Documents folder is useful when you want to share files that are not stored in the My Documents folder or if your computer uses the NTFS file system and other users are restricted from viewing the contents of your My Documents folder.

## SHARE FILES

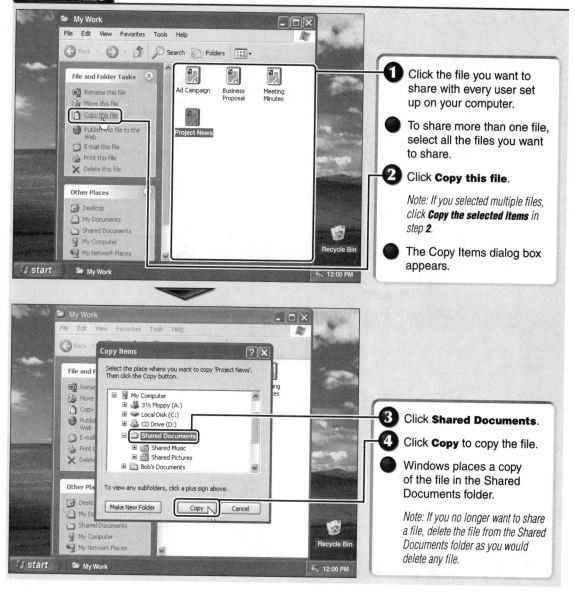

1 Click the file you want to share with every user set up on your computer.

● To share more than one file, select all the files you want to share.

2 Click **Copy this file**.

*Note: If you selected multiple files, click **Copy the selected items** in step 2.*

● The Copy Items dialog box appears.

3 Click **Shared Documents**.

4 Click **Copy** to copy the file.

● Windows places a copy of the file in the Shared Documents folder.

*Note: If you no longer want to share a file, delete the file from the Shared Documents folder as you would delete any file.*

# MAKE YOUR PERSONAL FOLDERS PRIVATE

If your computer uses the NTFS file system, you can make the contents of your personal folders private so that only you can access the files within the folders. By default, the contents of your My Documents folder and its subfolders are available to every user with an administrator account set up on your computer.

## MAKE YOUR PERSONAL FOLDERS PRIVATE

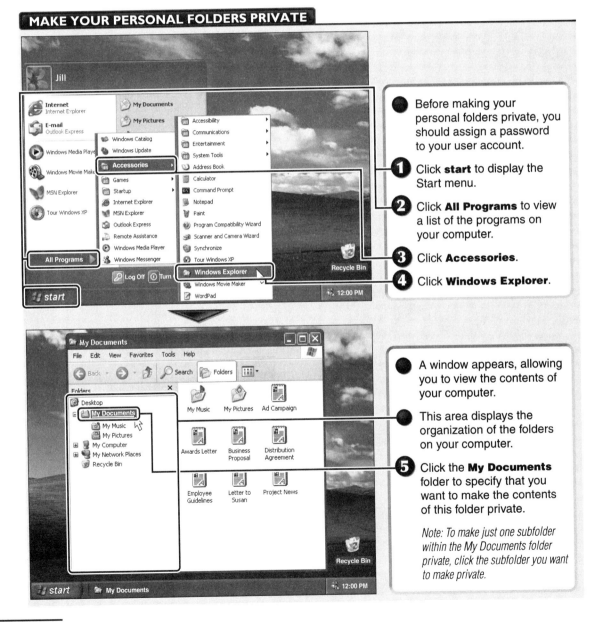

● Before making your personal folders private, you should assign a password to your user account.

**1** Click **start** to display the Start menu.

**2** Click **All Programs** to view a list of the programs on your computer.

**3** Click **Accessories**.

**4** Click **Windows Explorer**.

● A window appears, allowing you to view the contents of your computer.

● This area displays the organization of the folders on your computer.

**5** Click the **My Documents** folder to specify that you want to make the contents of this folder private.

*Note: To make just one subfolder within the My Documents folder private, click the subfolder you want to make private.*

**158**

# in an instant

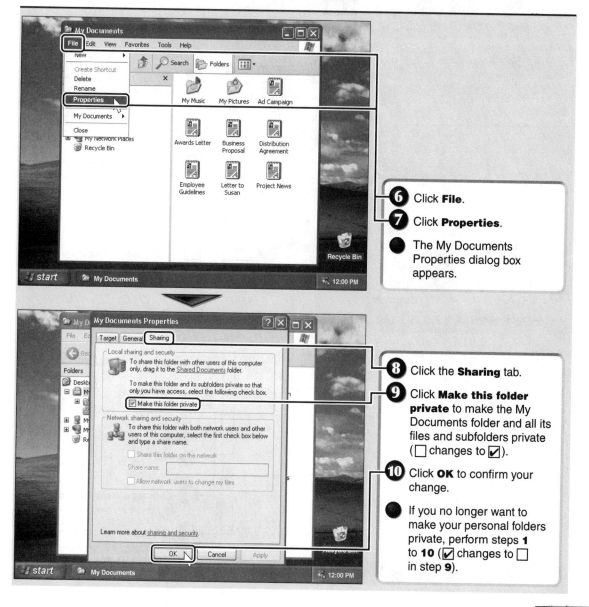

**6** Click **File**.

**7** Click **Properties**.

● The My Documents Properties dialog box appears.

**8** Click the **Sharing** tab.

**9** Click **Make this folder private** to make the My Documents folder and all its files and subfolders private (☐ changes to ☑).

**10** Click **OK** to confirm your change.

● If you no longer want to make your personal folders private, perform steps **1** to **10** (☑ changes to ☐ in step **9**).

# INSTALL A PROGRAM

You can install a program designed for Windows on your computer from floppy disks or CD-ROM discs. Windows will help you locate and run the installation file for the program. To install a program you transferred to your computer from the Internet, you must locate and run the program's installation file. The file is usually named install, setup or the name of the program.

## INSTALL A PROGRAM

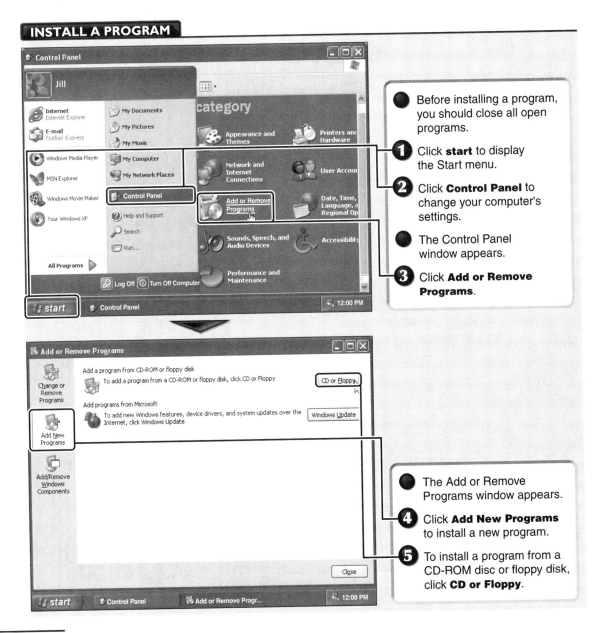

Before installing a program, you should close all open programs.

1 Click **start** to display the Start menu.

2 Click **Control Panel** to change your computer's settings.

The Control Panel window appears.

3 Click **Add or Remove Programs**.

The Add or Remove Programs window appears.

4 Click **Add New Programs** to install a new program.

5 To install a program from a CD-ROM disc or floppy disk, click **CD or Floppy**.

in an *instant*

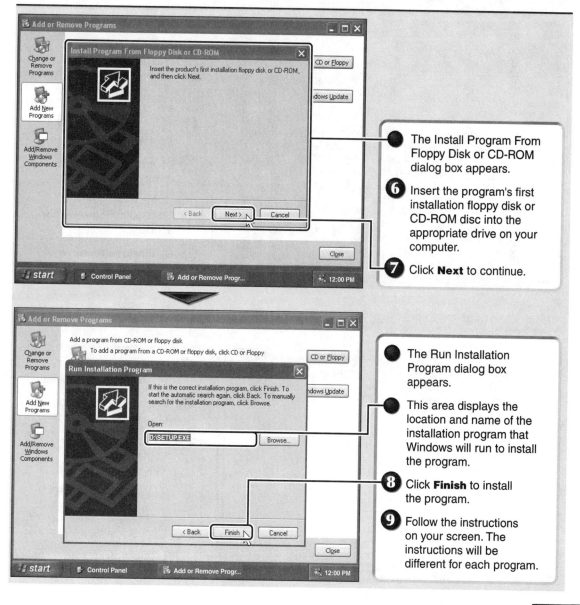

The Install Program From Floppy Disk or CD-ROM dialog box appears.

**6** Insert the program's first installation floppy disk or CD-ROM disc into the appropriate drive on your computer.

**7** Click **Next** to continue.

The Run Installation Program dialog box appears.

This area displays the location and name of the installation program that Windows will run to install the program.

**8** Click **Finish** to install the program.

**9** Follow the instructions on your screen. The instructions will be different for each program.

# REMOVE A PROGRAM

You can remove a program you no longer use to free up space on your computer. You can select the program you want to remove from a list of programs you have installed on the computer to have Windows automatically remove the program.

REMOVE A PROGRAM

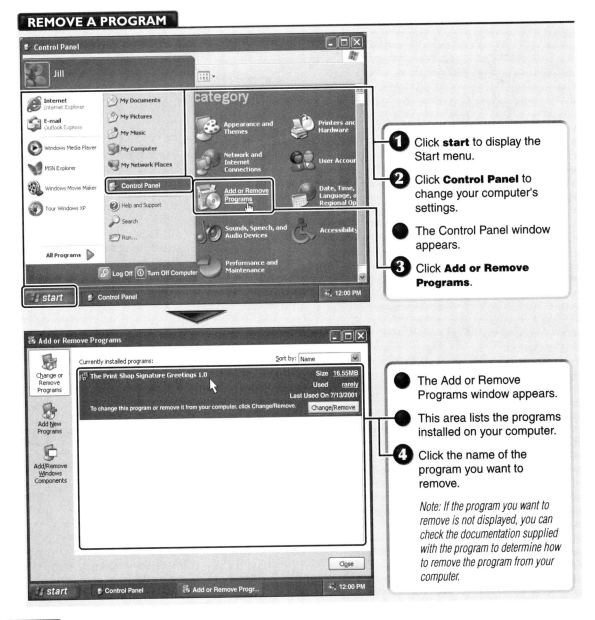

1 Click **start** to display the Start menu.

2 Click **Control Panel** to change your computer's settings.

■ The Control Panel window appears.

3 Click **Add or Remove Programs**.

■ The Add or Remove Programs window appears.

■ This area lists the programs installed on your computer.

4 Click the name of the program you want to remove.

*Note: If the program you want to remove is not displayed, you can check the documentation supplied with the program to determine how to remove the program from your computer.*

in an *instant*

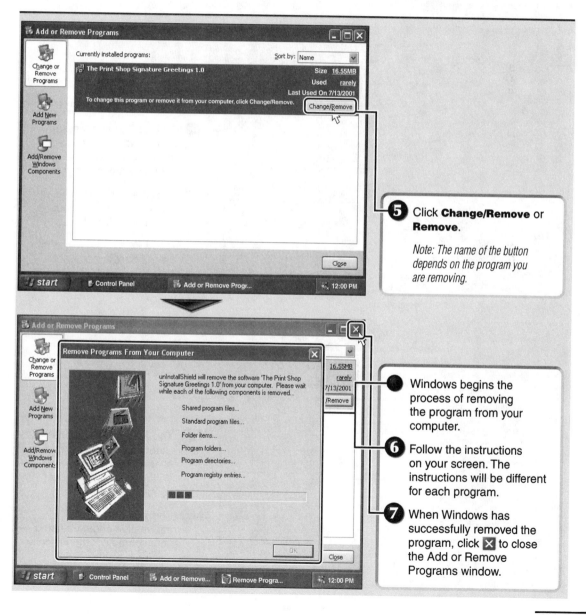

**5** Click **Change/Remove** or **Remove**.

*Note: The name of the button depends on the program you are removing.*

Windows begins the process of removing the program from your computer.

**6** Follow the instructions on your screen. The instructions will be different for each program.

**7** When Windows has successfully removed the program, click ☒ to close the Add or Remove Programs window.

# UPDATE WINDOWS

You can set up Windows to automatically keep your computer up to date with the latest Windows updates available on the Internet. To improve the performance of your computer, Windows can update existing software, fix software problems and add new software. You need an Internet connection for Windows to be able to update your computer automatically.

UPDATE WINDOWS

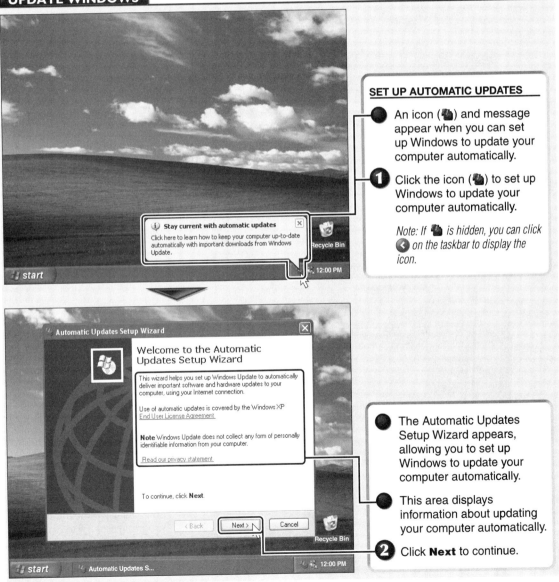

## SET UP AUTOMATIC UPDATES

● An icon (🛡) and message appear when you can set up Windows to update your computer automatically.

**1** Click the icon (🛡) to set up Windows to update your computer automatically.

*Note: If 🛡 is hidden, you can click 🔾 on the taskbar to display the icon.*

● The Automatic Updates Setup Wizard appears, allowing you to set up Windows to update your computer automatically.

● This area displays information about updating your computer automatically.

**2** Click **Next** to continue.

in an *instant*

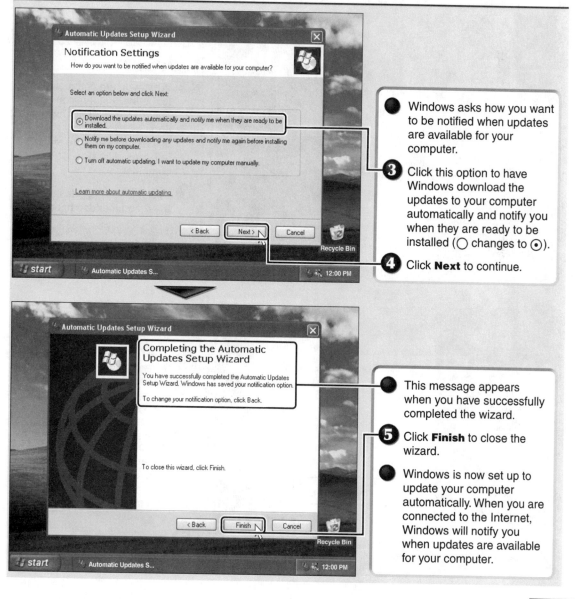

Windows asks how you want to be notified when updates are available for your computer.

**3** Click this option to have Windows download the updates to your computer automatically and notify you when they are ready to be installed ($\bigcirc$ changes to $\odot$).

**4** Click **Next** to continue.

This message appears when you have successfully completed the wizard.

**5** Click **Finish** to close the wizard.

Windows is now set up to update your computer automatically. When you are connected to the Internet, Windows will notify you when updates are available for your computer.

When you are connected to the Internet, Windows will automatically check for updates that apply to your computer and will notify you when the updates are ready to be installed. For example, Windows can obtain updated help information and drivers for your computer. A driver is software that enables your computer to communicate with a hardware device, such as a printer.

## UPDATE WINDOWS (CONTINUED)

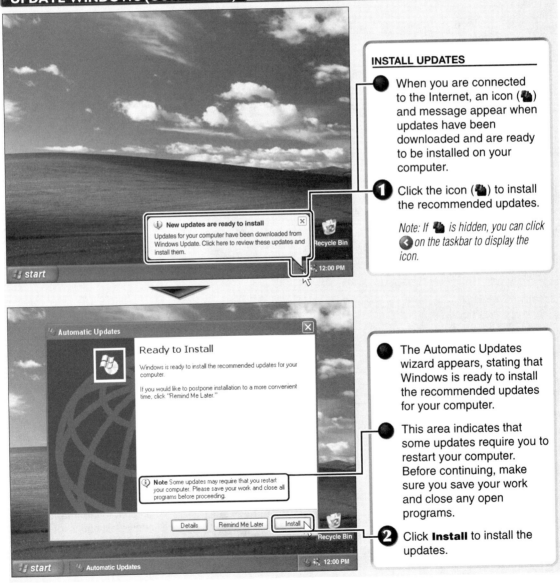

### INSTALL UPDATES

● When you are connected to the Internet, an icon (🔔) and message appear when updates have been downloaded and are ready to be installed on your computer.

**1** Click the icon (🔔) to install the recommended updates.

*Note: If 🔔 is hidden, you can click ◀ on the taskbar to display the icon.*

● The Automatic Updates wizard appears, stating that Windows is ready to install the recommended updates for your computer.

● This area indicates that some updates require you to restart your computer. Before continuing, make sure you save your work and close any open programs.

**2** Click **Install** to install the updates.

# in an Instant

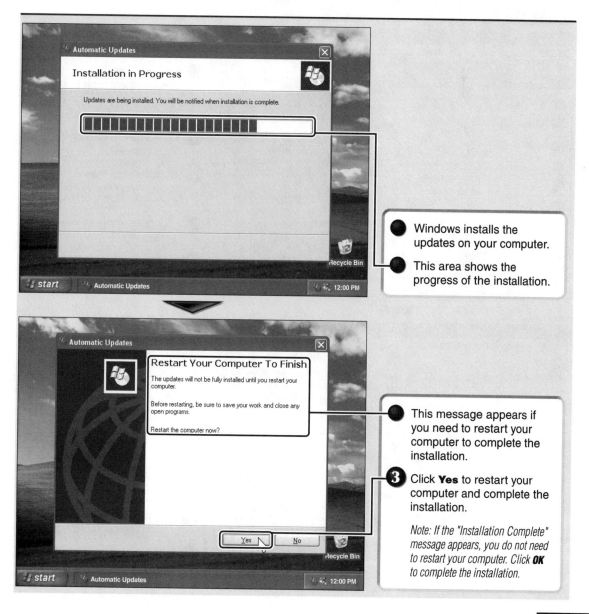

Windows installs the updates on your computer.

This area shows the progress of the installation.

This message appears if you need to restart your computer to complete the installation.

③ Click **Yes** to restart your computer and complete the installation.

*Note: If the "Installation Complete" message appears, you do not need to restart your computer. Click OK to complete the installation.*

# INSTALL A PRINTER

Before you can use a printer attached to your computer, you need to install the printer on your computer. Installing a printer allows you to install the printer driver, which is software that enables Windows to communicate with the printer. Windows provides a wizard that guides you step by step through the process of installing a new printer.

INSTALL A PRINTER

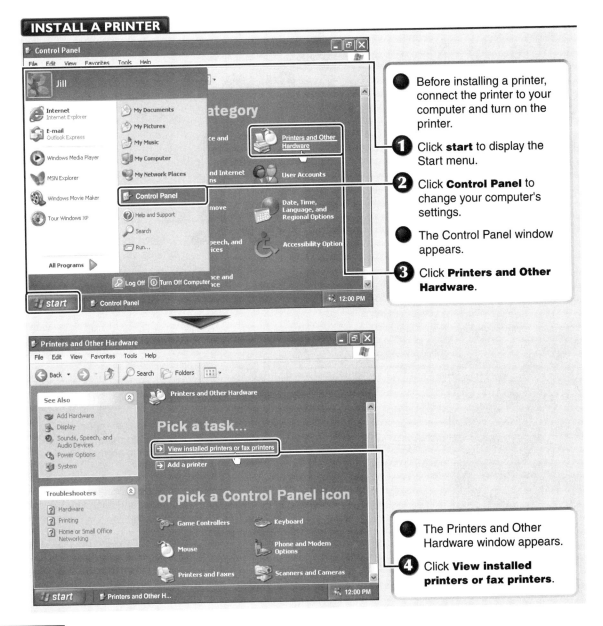

● Before installing a printer, connect the printer to your computer and turn on the printer.

❶ Click **start** to display the Start menu.

❷ Click **Control Panel** to change your computer's settings.

● The Control Panel window appears.

❸ Click **Printers and Other Hardware**.

● The Printers and Other Hardware window appears.

❹ Click **View installed printers or fax printers**.

in an Instant

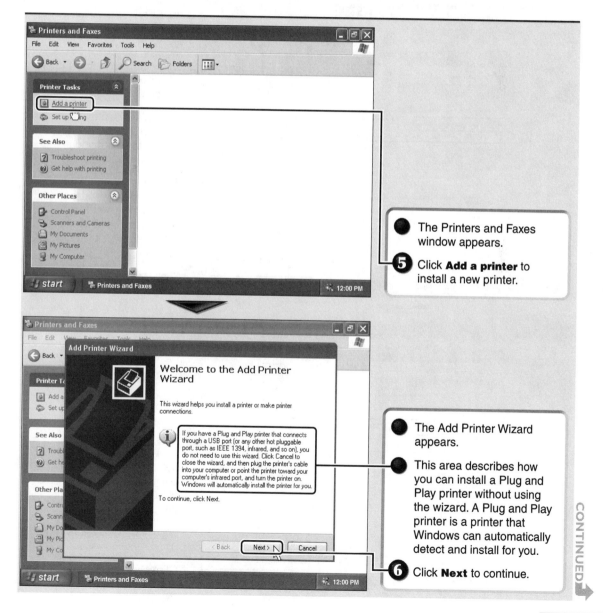

The Printers and Faxes window appears.

**5** Click **Add a printer** to install a new printer.

The Add Printer Wizard appears.

This area describes how you can install a Plug and Play printer without using the wizard. A Plug and Play printer is a printer that Windows can automatically detect and install for you.

**6** Click **Next** to continue.

CONTINUED

# INSTALL A PRINTER

When installing a printer, you need to specify which port you want your printer to use. A port is a socket, usually located at the back of a computer, where you plug in a device. If you already have another printer installed, you can choose to make the new printer the default printer. Files will automatically print to the default printer.

## INSTALL A PRINTER (CONTINUED)

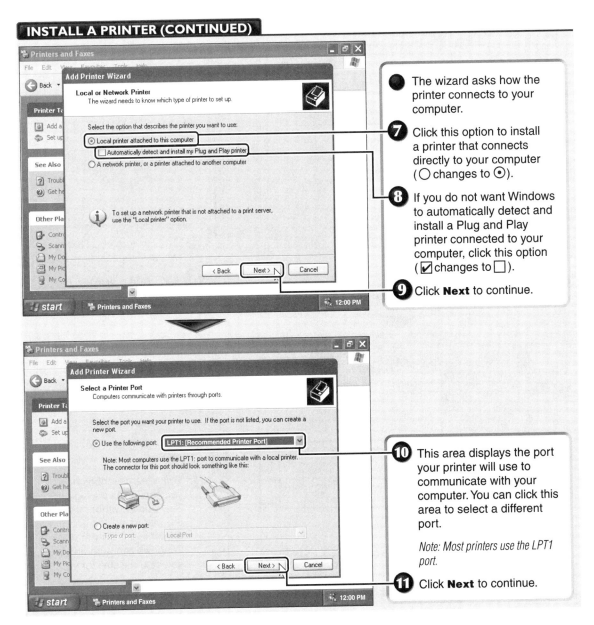

● The wizard asks how the printer connects to your computer.

**7** Click this option to install a printer that connects directly to your computer (○ changes to ⊙).

**8** If you do not want Windows to automatically detect and install a Plug and Play printer connected to your computer, click this option (☑ changes to ☐).

**9** Click **Next** to continue.

**10** This area displays the port your printer will use to communicate with your computer. You can click this area to select a different port.

*Note: Most printers use the LPT1 port.*

**11** Click **Next** to continue.

# in an *instant*

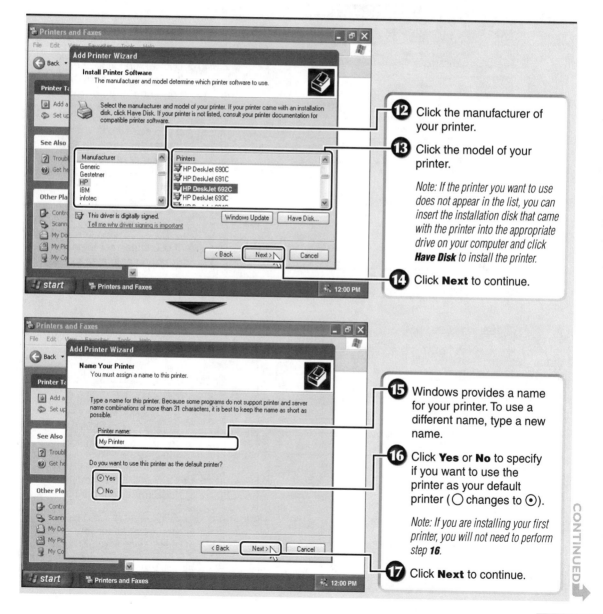

**12** Click the manufacturer of your printer.

**13** Click the model of your printer.

*Note: If the printer you want to use does not appear in the list, you can insert the installation disk that came with the printer into the appropriate drive on your computer and click **Have Disk** to install the printer.*

**14** Click **Next** to continue.

**15** Windows provides a name for your printer. To use a different name, type a new name.

**16** Click **Yes** or **No** to specify if you want to use the printer as your default printer (○ changes to ⊙).

*Note: If you are installing your first printer, you will not need to perform step **16**.*

**17** Click **Next** to continue.

CONTINUED

**171**

# INSTALL A PRINTER

If your computer is set up on a network, you may want to share the printer you are installing with other people on the network. Sharing a printer can save money, since it allows several people on a network to use the same printer. When you view the list of printers installed on your computer, the icon for a printer you shared displays a hand (🖐).

## INSTALL A PRINTER (CONTINUED)

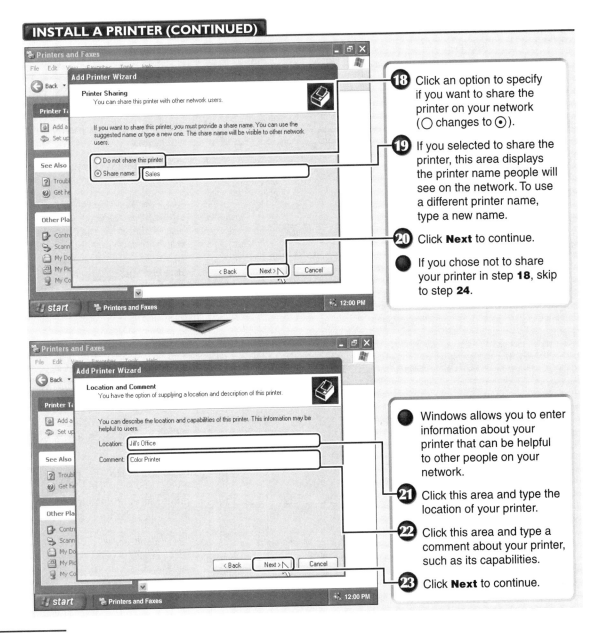

**18** Click an option to specify if you want to share the printer on your network (○ changes to ⊙).

**19** If you selected to share the printer, this area displays the printer name people will see on the network. To use a different printer name, type a new name.

**20** Click **Next** to continue.

● If you chose not to share your printer in step **18**, skip to step **24**.

● Windows allows you to enter information about your printer that can be helpful to other people on your network.

**21** Click this area and type the location of your printer.

**22** Click this area and type a comment about your printer, such as its capabilities.

**23** Click **Next** to continue.

in an *instant*

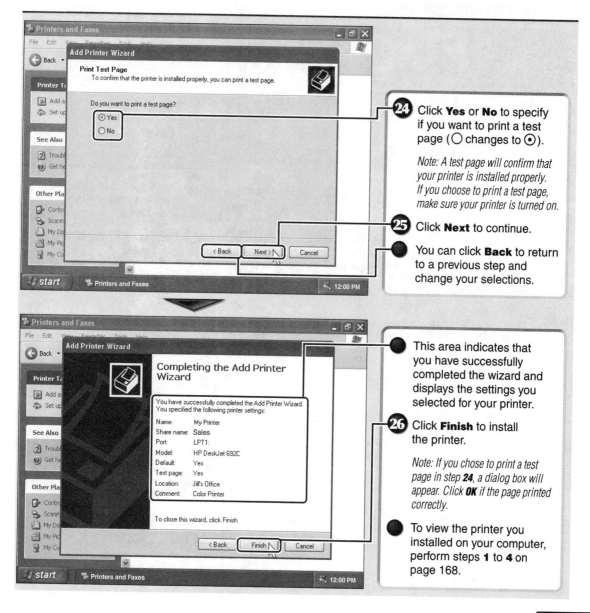

**24** Click **Yes** or **No** to specify if you want to print a test page (○ changes to ⊙).

*Note: A test page will confirm that your printer is installed properly. If you choose to print a test page, make sure your printer is turned on.*

**25** Click **Next** to continue.

You can click **Back** to return to a previous step and change your selections.

This area indicates that you have successfully completed the wizard and displays the settings you selected for your printer.

**26** Click **Finish** to install the printer.

*Note: If you chose to print a test page in step 24, a dialog box will appear. Click OK if the page printed correctly.*

To view the printer you installed on your computer, perform steps **1** to **4** on page 168.

# FORMAT A FLOPPY DISK

You must format a floppy disk before you can use the disk to store information. Floppy disks you buy at computer stores are usually formatted. You may want to later format a floppy disk to erase the information it contains and prepare the disk for storing new information.

## FORMAT A FLOPPY DISK

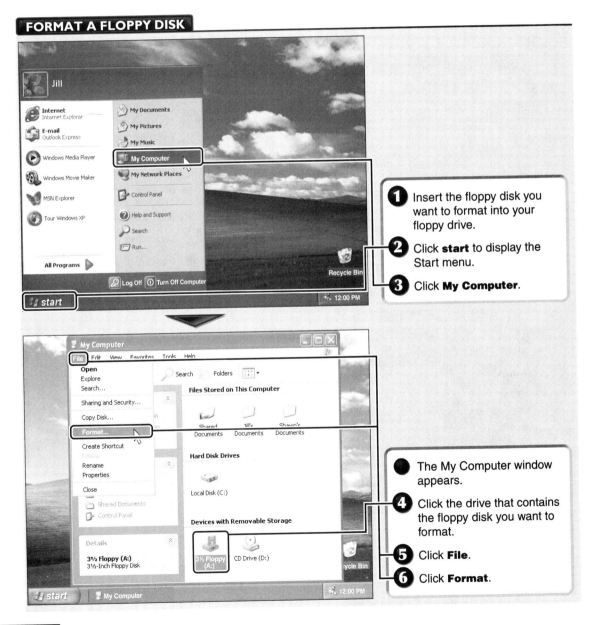

**1** Insert the floppy disk you want to format into your floppy drive.

**2** Click **start** to display the Start menu.

**3** Click **My Computer**.

■ The My Computer window appears.

**4** Click the drive that contains the floppy disk you want to format.

**5** Click **File**.

**6** Click **Format**.

in an **instant**

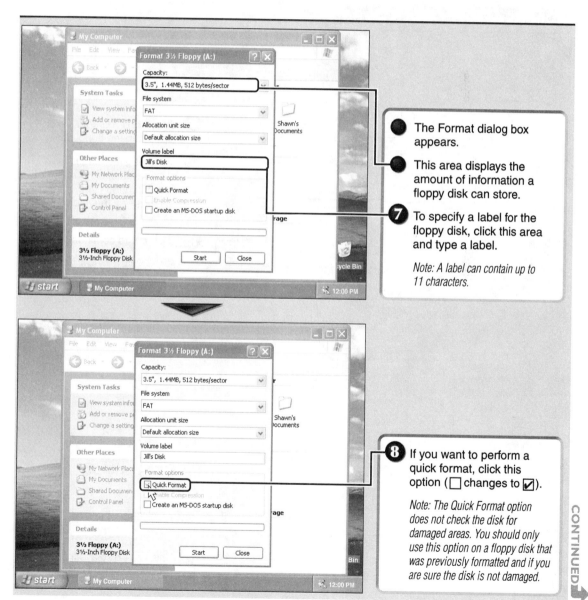

The Format dialog box appears.

This area displays the amount of information a floppy disk can store.

**7** To specify a label for the floppy disk, click this area and type a label.

*Note: A label can contain up to 11 characters.*

**8** If you want to perform a quick format, click this option (☐ changes to ☑).

*Note: The Quick Format option does not check the disk for damaged areas. You should only use this option on a floppy disk that was previously formatted and if you are sure the disk is not damaged.*

CONTINUED

**175**

# FORMAT A FLOPPY DISK

Before formatting a floppy disk, make sure the disk does not contain information you want to keep. Formatting a floppy disk will permanently remove all the information on the disk. After formatting one floppy disk, you can easily format other disks. Formatting several floppy disks at one time helps ensure you always have formatted disks available when you need them.

## FORMAT A FLOPPY DISK (CONTINUED)

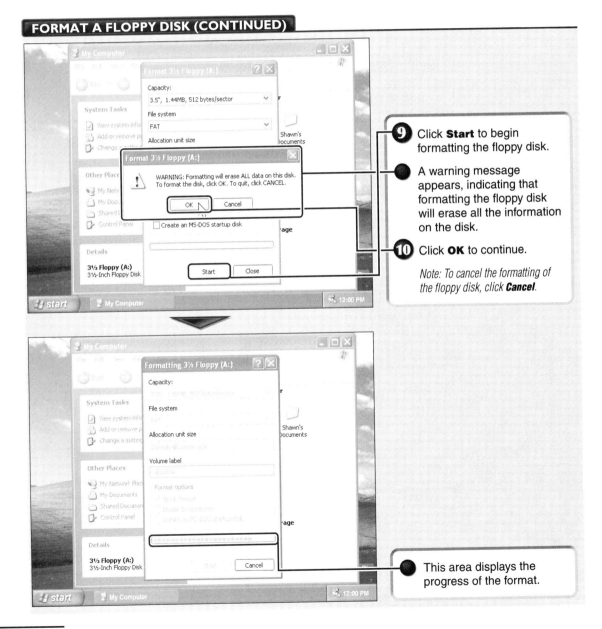

**9** Click **Start** to begin formatting the floppy disk.

● A warning message appears, indicating that formatting the floppy disk will erase all the information on the disk.

**10** Click **OK** to continue.

*Note: To cancel the formatting of the floppy disk, click **Cancel**.*

● This area displays the progress of the format.

in an *instant*

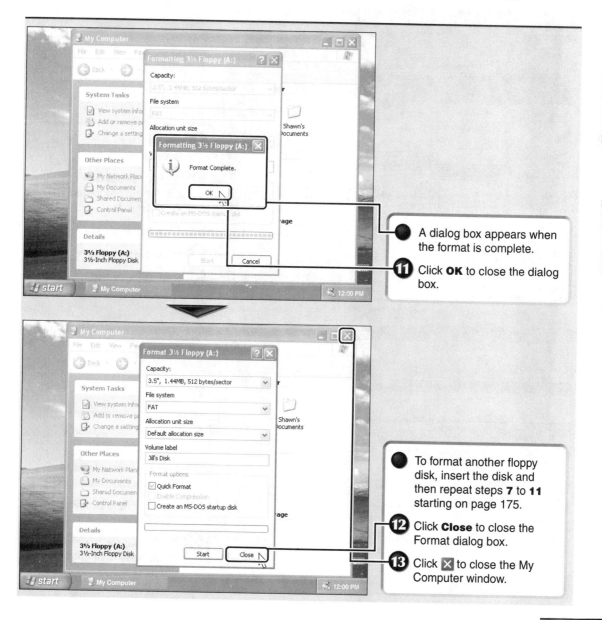

A dialog box appears when the format is complete.

**11** Click **OK** to close the dialog box.

To format another floppy disk, insert the disk and then repeat steps **7** to **11** starting on page 175.

**12** Click **Close** to close the Format dialog box.

**13** Click ✕ to close the My Computer window.

# DEFRAGMENT YOUR HARD DISK

You can improve the performance of your computer by defragmenting your hard disk. Defragmenting your hard disk will allow your programs to run faster and your files to open more quickly. Before defragmenting your hard disk, you should check the amount of free space on the disk. A hard disk must have at least 15% of free space to be properly defragmented.

DEFRAGMENT YOUR HARD DISK

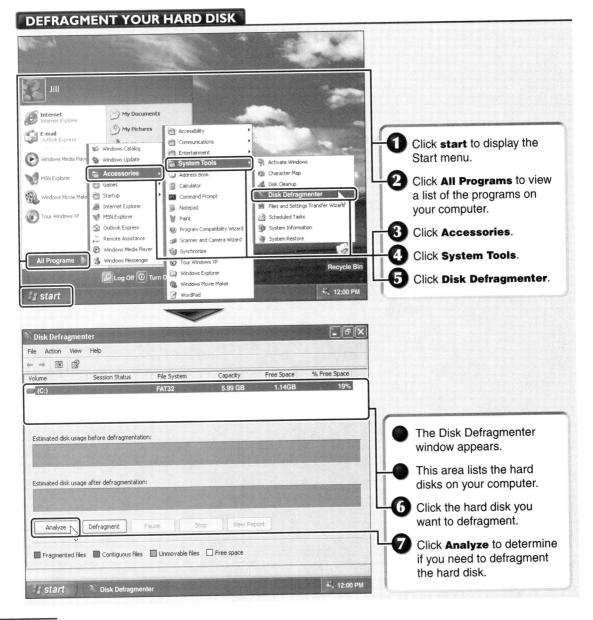

1 Click **start** to display the Start menu.

2 Click **All Programs** to view a list of the programs on your computer.

3 Click **Accessories**.

4 Click **System Tools**.

5 Click **Disk Defragmenter**.

■ The Disk Defragmenter window appears.

■ This area lists the hard disks on your computer.

6 Click the hard disk you want to defragment.

7 Click **Analyze** to determine if you need to defragment the hard disk.

**178**

# in an instant

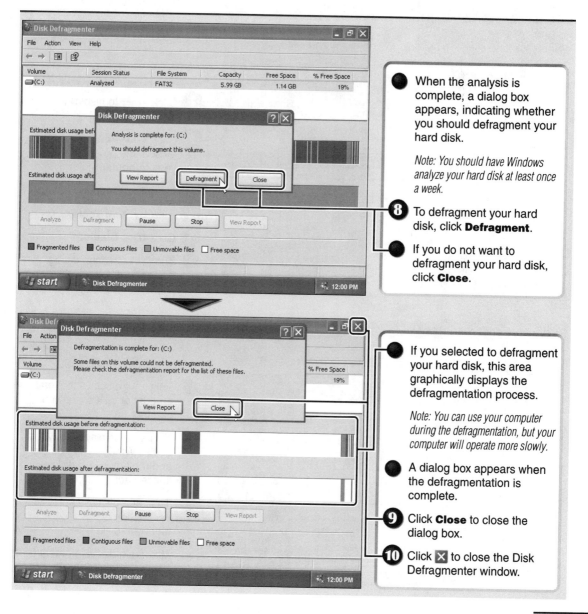

When the analysis is complete, a dialog box appears, indicating whether you should defragment your hard disk.

*Note: You should have Windows analyze your hard disk at least once a week.*

**8** To defragment your hard disk, click **Defragment**.

If you do not want to defragment your hard disk, click **Close**.

If you selected to defragment your hard disk, this area graphically displays the defragmentation process.

*Note: You can use your computer during the defragmentation, but your computer will operate more slowly.*

A dialog box appears when the defragmentation is complete.

**9** Click **Close** to close the dialog box.

**10** Click ☒ to close the Disk Defragmenter window.

# USING DISK CLEANUP

You can use Disk Cleanup to remove unnecessary files from your computer to free up disk space. Disk Cleanup can remove several types of files from your computer, such as temporary Internet files and deleted files stored in your Recycle Bin. Disk Cleanup allows you to display a description of each type of file to help you decide which file types to remove.

## USING DISK CLEANUP

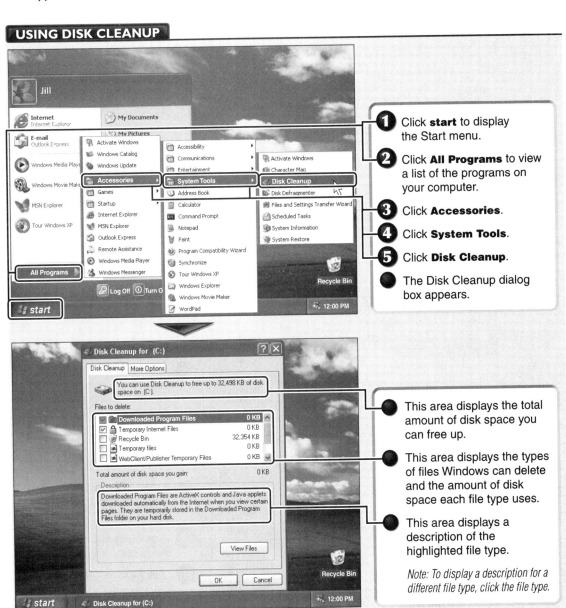

**1** Click **start** to display the Start menu.

**2** Click **All Programs** to view a list of the programs on your computer.

**3** Click **Accessories**.

**4** Click **System Tools**.

**5** Click **Disk Cleanup**.

■ The Disk Cleanup dialog box appears.

● This area displays the total amount of disk space you can free up.

● This area displays the types of files Windows can delete and the amount of disk space each file type uses.

● This area displays a description of the highlighted file type.

*Note: To display a description for a different file type, click the file type.*

in an *instant*

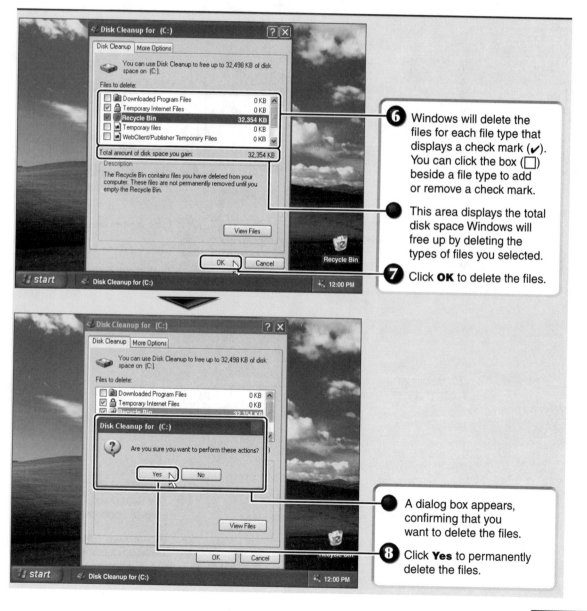

**6** Windows will delete the files for each file type that displays a check mark (✔). You can click the box (☐) beside a file type to add or remove a check mark.

● This area displays the total disk space Windows will free up by deleting the types of files you selected.

**7** Click **OK** to delete the files.

● A dialog box appears, confirming that you want to delete the files.

**8** Click **Yes** to permanently delete the files.

# SCHEDULE TASKS

You can schedule tasks to have Windows automatically run specific programs, such as Disk Cleanup, on a regular basis. Before scheduling a task, you must assign a password to your user account. To have Windows run a program automatically, you will need to enter the password when scheduling the task. To assign a password to your user account, see page 152.

## SCHEDULE TASKS

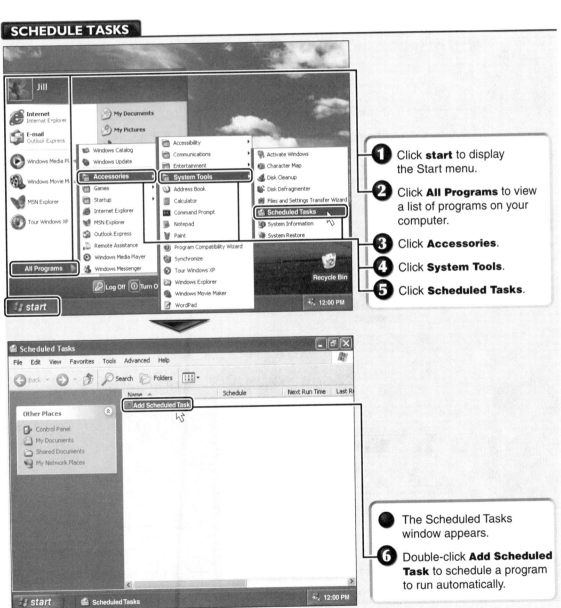

**1** Click **start** to display the Start menu.

**2** Click **All Programs** to view a list of programs on your computer.

**3** Click **Accessories**.

**4** Click **System Tools**.

**5** Click **Scheduled Tasks**.

■ The Scheduled Tasks window appears.

**6** Double-click **Add Scheduled Task** to schedule a program to run automatically.

in an *instant*

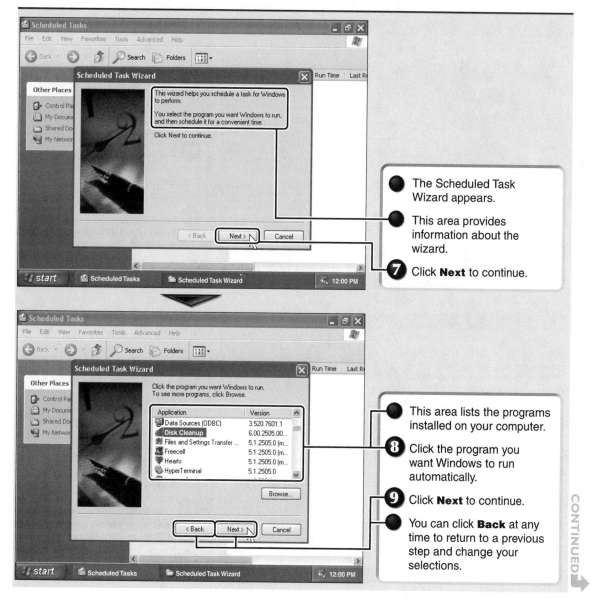

The Scheduled Task Wizard appears.

This area provides information about the wizard.

**7** Click **Next** to continue.

This area lists the programs installed on your computer.

**8** Click the program you want Windows to run automatically.

**9** Click **Next** to continue.

You can click **Back** at any time to return to a previous step and change your selections.

CONTINUED

# SCHEDULE TASKS

When scheduling a program, you can specify the date and time you want Windows to run the program. You should make sure the current date and time are set correctly in your computer. Your computer must also be turned on at the scheduled time in order for the program to run.

## SCHEDULE TASKS (CONTINUED)

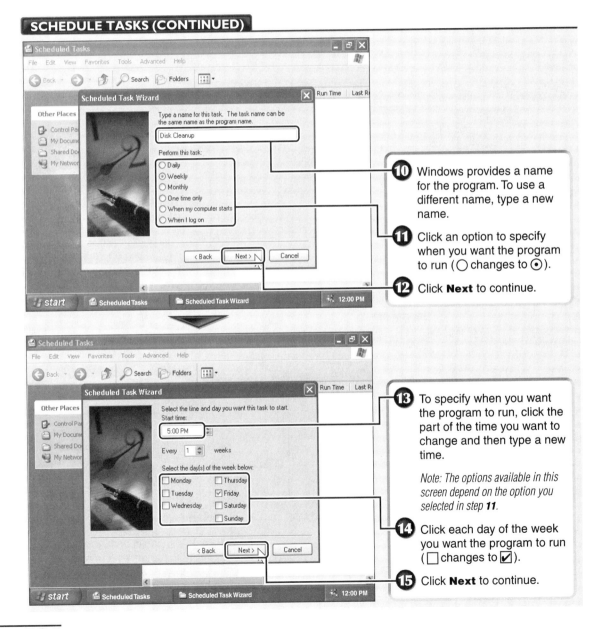

🔟 Windows provides a name for the program. To use a different name, type a new name.

1️⃣1️⃣ Click an option to specify when you want the program to run (○ changes to ⊙).

1️⃣2️⃣ Click **Next** to continue.

1️⃣3️⃣ To specify when you want the program to run, click the part of the time you want to change and then type a new time.

*Note: The options available in this screen depend on the option you selected in step 11.*

1️⃣4️⃣ Click each day of the week you want the program to run (☐ changes to ☑).

1️⃣5️⃣ Click **Next** to continue.

# in an *Instant*

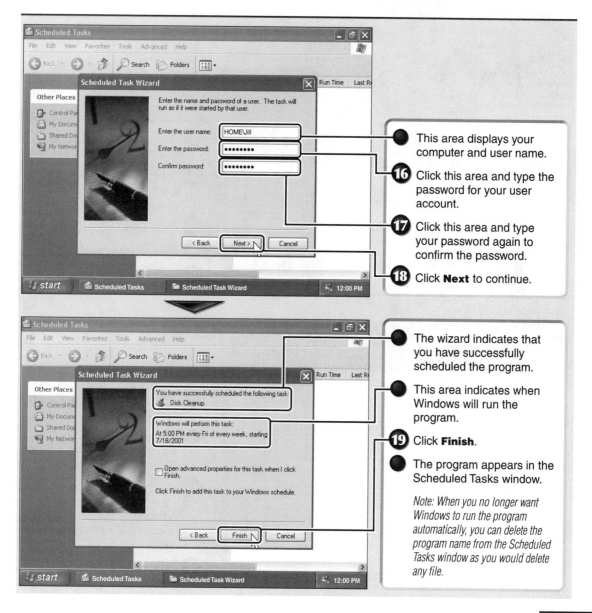

This area displays your computer and user name.

**16** Click this area and type the password for your user account.

**17** Click this area and type your password again to confirm the password.

**18** Click **Next** to continue.

The wizard indicates that you have successfully scheduled the program.

This area indicates when Windows will run the program.

**19** Click **Finish**.

The program appears in the Scheduled Tasks window.

*Note: When you no longer want Windows to run the program automatically, you can delete the program name from the Scheduled Tasks window as you would delete any file.*

# RESTORE YOUR COMPUTER

If you are experiencing problems with your computer, you can use the System Restore feature to return your computer to a time before the problems occurred. For example, if your computer does not work properly after you install a program, you can restore your computer to a time before you installed the program.

## RESTORE YOUR COMPUTER

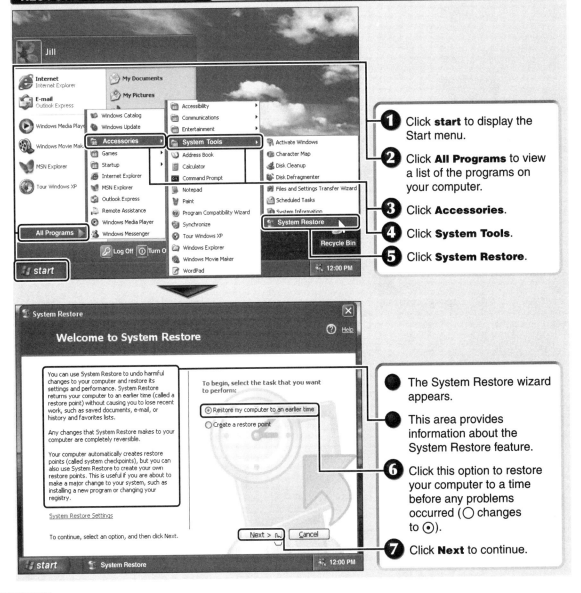

**1** Click **start** to display the Start menu.

**2** Click **All Programs** to view a list of the programs on your computer.

**3** Click **Accessories**.

**4** Click **System Tools**.

**5** Click **System Restore**.

● The System Restore wizard appears.

● This area provides information about the System Restore feature.

**6** Click this option to restore your computer to a time before any problems occurred (○ changes to ⊙).

**7** Click **Next** to continue.

in an *instant*

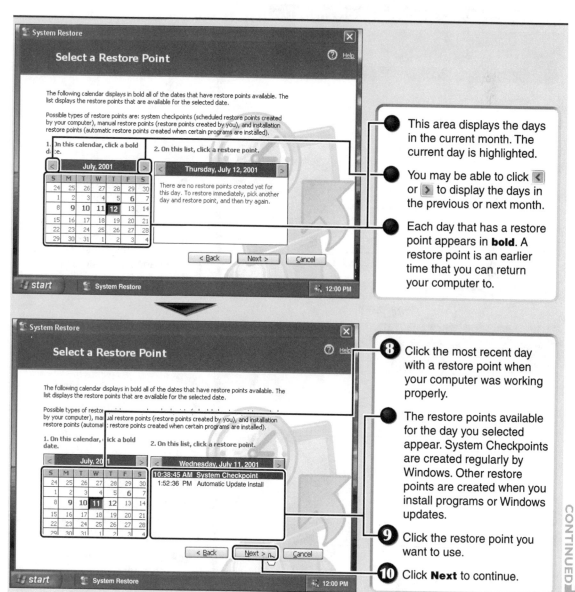

This area displays the days in the current month. The current day is highlighted.

You may be able to click ◀ or ▶ to display the days in the previous or next month.

Each day that has a restore point appears in **bold**. A restore point is an earlier time that you can return your computer to.

**8** Click the most recent day with a restore point when your computer was working properly.

The restore points available for the day you selected appear. System Checkpoints are created regularly by Windows. Other restore points are created when you install programs or Windows updates.

**9** Click the restore point you want to use.

**10** Click **Next** to continue.

CONTINUED

# RESTORE YOUR COMPUTER

When you restore your computer to an earlier time, you will not lose any of your recent work, such as documents or e-mail messages. Before restoring your computer to an earlier time, you should close all open files and programs. Also keep in mind that you may have to re-install any programs you installed after the date to which the computer is being restored.

## RESTORE YOUR COMPUTER (CONTINUED)

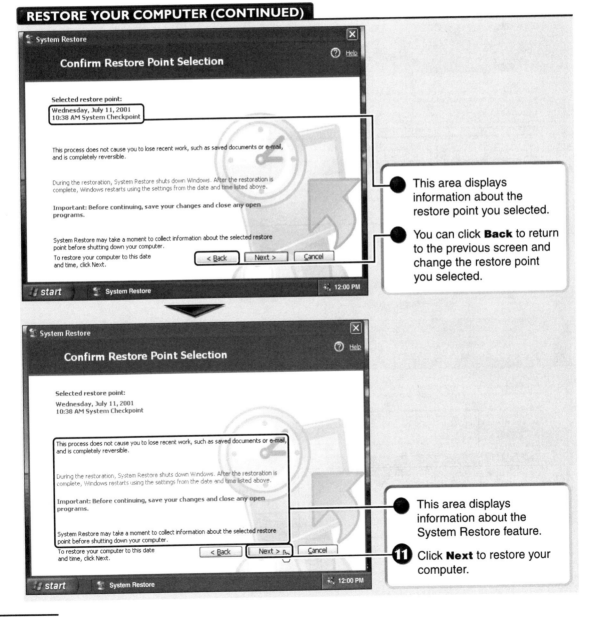

This area displays information about the restore point you selected.

You can click **Back** to return to the previous screen and change the restore point you selected.

This area displays information about the System Restore feature.

⑪ Click **Next** to restore your computer.

# in an *instant*

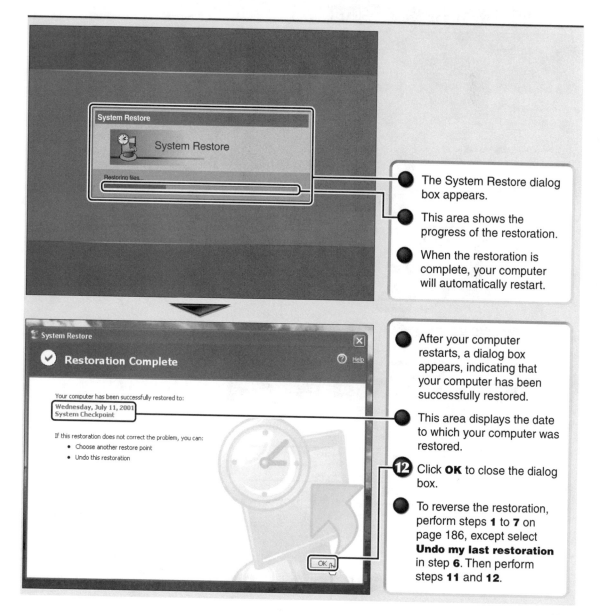

The System Restore dialog box appears.

This area shows the progress of the restoration.

When the restoration is complete, your computer will automatically restart.

After your computer restarts, a dialog box appears, indicating that your computer has been successfully restored.

This area displays the date to which your computer was restored.

**12** Click **OK** to close the dialog box.

To reverse the restoration, perform steps **1** to **7** on page 186, except select **Undo my last restoration** in step **6**. Then perform steps **11** and **12**.

# GET REMOTE ASSISTANCE

You can allow a person at another computer to view your computer screen and chat with you to help you solve a computer problem. With your permission, the other person can control your computer to fix the problem. If either computer is connected to a network, a firewall may prevent you from using Remote Assistance. A firewall protects a network from unauthorized access.

GET REMOTE ASSISTANCE

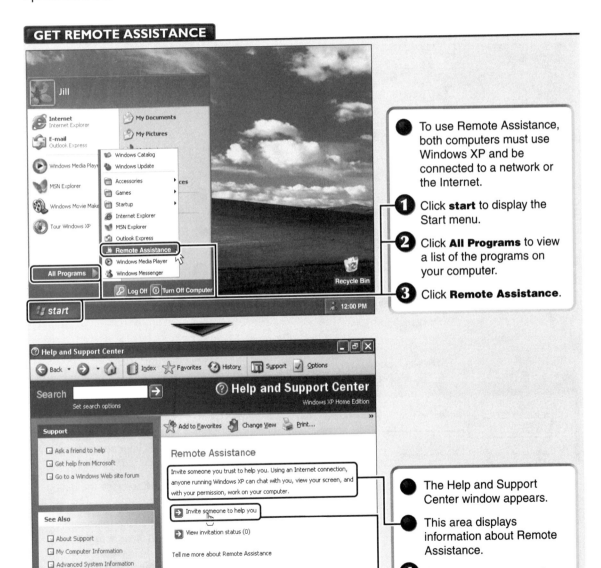

To use Remote Assistance, both computers must use Windows XP and be connected to a network or the Internet.

**1** Click **start** to display the Start menu.

**2** Click **All Programs** to view a list of the programs on your computer.

**3** Click **Remote Assistance**.

The Help and Support Center window appears.

This area displays information about Remote Assistance.

**4** Click **Invite someone to help you**.

# in an *instant*

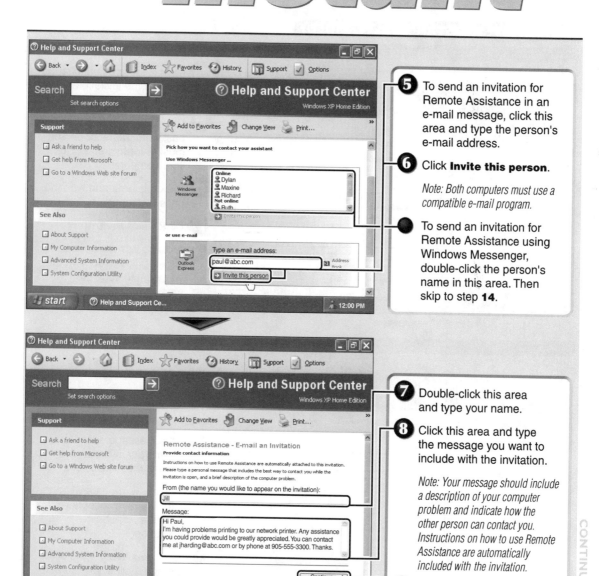

**5** To send an invitation for Remote Assistance in an e-mail message, click this area and type the person's e-mail address.

**6** Click **Invite this person**.

*Note: Both computers must use a compatible e-mail program.*

● To send an invitation for Remote Assistance using Windows Messenger, double-click the person's name in this area. Then skip to step **14**.

**7** Double-click this area and type your name.

**8** Click this area and type the message you want to include with the invitation.

*Note: Your message should include a description of your computer problem and indicate how the other person can contact you. Instructions on how to use Remote Assistance are automatically included with the invitation.*

**9** Click **Continue**.

CONTINUED

# GET REMOTE ASSISTANCE

When sending a Remote Assistance invitation in an e-mail message, you can specify when you want the invitation to expire and a password the other person must enter to connect to your computer. You must tell the other person the password you specified.

## GET REMOTE ASSISTANCE (CONTINUED)

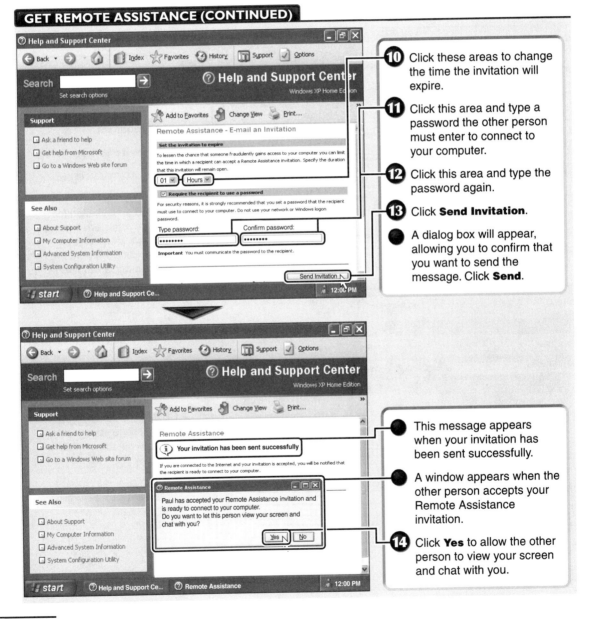

**10** Click these areas to change the time the invitation will expire.

**11** Click this area and type a password the other person must enter to connect to your computer.

**12** Click this area and type the password again.

**13** Click **Send Invitation**.

● A dialog box will appear, allowing you to confirm that you want to send the message. Click **Send**.

● This message appears when your invitation has been sent successfully.

● A window appears when the other person accepts your Remote Assistance invitation.

**14** Click **Yes** to allow the other person to view your screen and chat with you.

in an *instant*

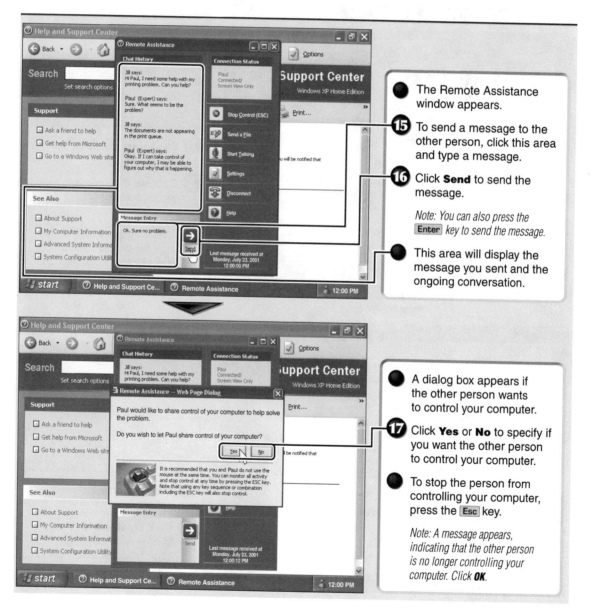

The Remote Assistance window appears.

15 To send a message to the other person, click this area and type a message.

16 Click **Send** to send the message.

*Note: You can also press the* **Enter** *key to send the message.*

This area will display the message you sent and the ongoing conversation.

A dialog box appears if the other person wants to control your computer.

17 Click **Yes** or **No** to specify if you want the other person to control your computer.

To stop the person from controlling your computer, press the **Esc** key.

*Note: A message appears, indicating that the other person is no longer controlling your computer. Click **OK**.*

# BROWSE THROUGH A NETWORK

You can use My Network Places to browse through the information available on your network. You can work with the files available on your network as you would work with files stored on your own computer. To access a folder on your network, the computer that stores the folder must be turned on and the owner of the computer must have shared the folder.

## BROWSE THROUGH A NETWORK

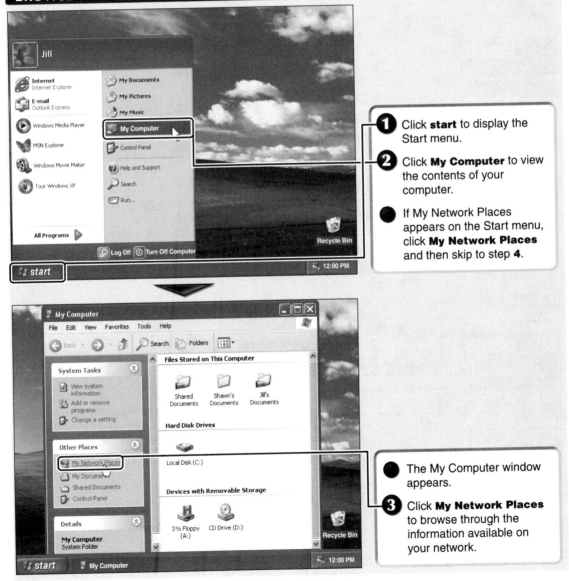

1 Click **start** to display the Start menu.

2 Click **My Computer** to view the contents of your computer.

● If My Network Places appears on the Start menu, click **My Network Places** and then skip to step **4**.

● The My Computer window appears.

3 Click **My Network Places** to browse through the information available on your network.

# in an Instant

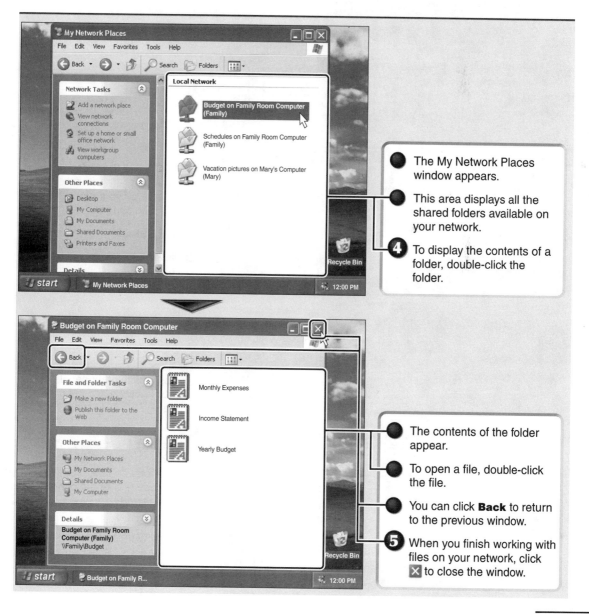

The My Network Places window appears.

This area displays all the shared folders available on your network.

4 To display the contents of a folder, double-click the folder.

The contents of the folder appear.

To open a file, double-click the file.

You can click **Back** to return to the previous window.

5 When you finish working with files on your network, click X to close the window.

# SHARE INFORMATION

You can specify the information on your computer that you want to share with other people on your network. Sharing information is useful when people on a network need to access the same files. Before you can share information on your computer with other people on your network, your computer must be set up on the network.

## SHARE INFORMATION

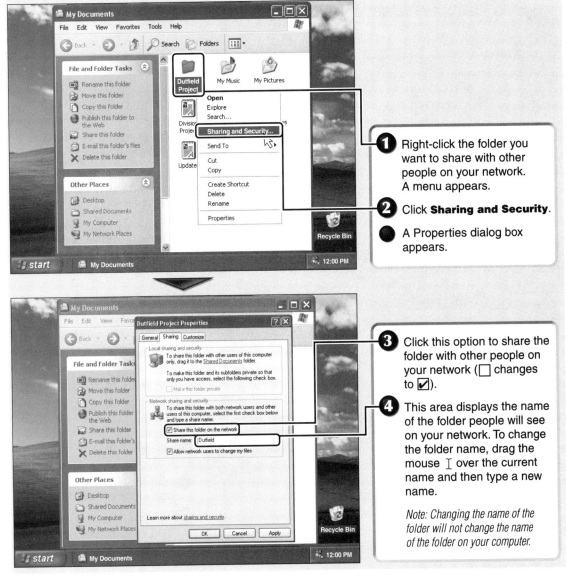

**1** Right-click the folder you want to share with other people on your network. A menu appears.

**2** Click **Sharing and Security**.

● A Properties dialog box appears.

**3** Click this option to share the folder with other people on your network (☐ changes to ☑).

**4** This area displays the name of the folder people will see on your network. To change the folder name, drag the mouse I over the current name and then type a new name.

*Note: Changing the name of the folder will not change the name of the folder on your computer.*

# in an instant

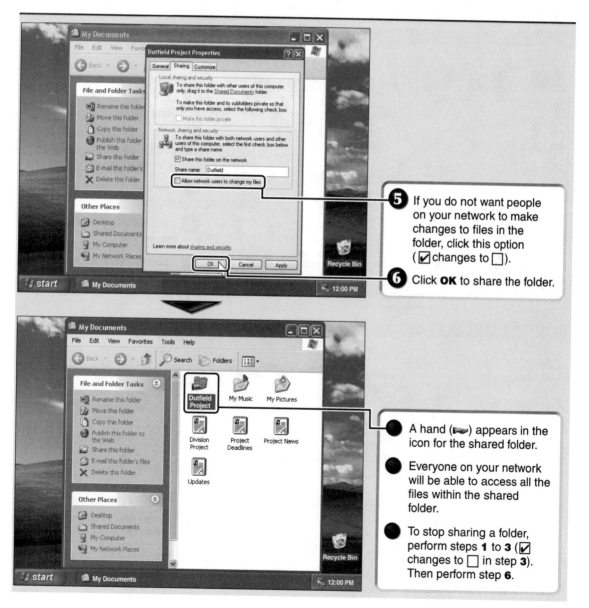

**5** If you do not want people on your network to make changes to files in the folder, click this option (☑ changes to ☐).

**6** Click **OK** to share the folder.

● A hand (☞) appears in the icon for the shared folder.

● Everyone on your network will be able to access all the files within the shared folder.

● To stop sharing a folder, perform steps **1** to **3** (☑ changes to ☐ in step **3**). Then perform step **6**.

# SHARE A PRINTER

You can share your printer with other people on a network.
Sharing a printer allows others to use your printer to print
documents. You should make sure your computer and the
shared printer are turned on when other people want to use
the printer. Your computer must be set up on a network
before you can share your printer.

## SHARE A PRINTER

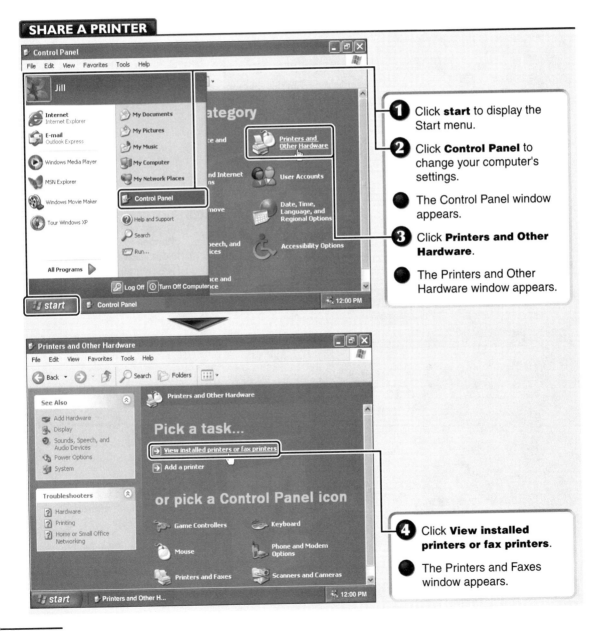

1 Click **start** to display the Start menu.

2 Click **Control Panel** to change your computer's settings.

● The Control Panel window appears.

3 Click **Printers and Other Hardware**.

● The Printers and Other Hardware window appears.

4 Click **View installed printers or fax printers**.

● The Printers and Faxes window appears.

# in an *instant*

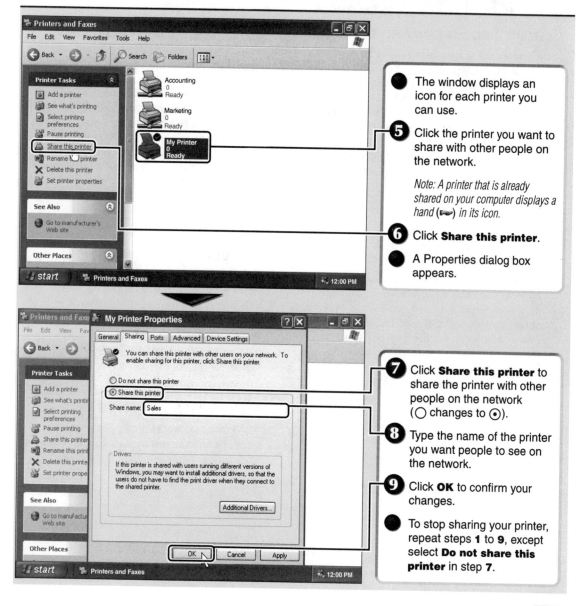

The window displays an icon for each printer you can use.

**5** Click the printer you want to share with other people on the network.

*Note: A printer that is already shared on your computer displays a hand (☜) in its icon.*

**6** Click **Share this printer**.

A Properties dialog box appears.

**7** Click **Share this printer** to share the printer with other people on the network (○ changes to ⊙).

**8** Type the name of the printer you want people to see on the network.

**9** Click **OK** to confirm your changes.

To stop sharing your printer, repeat steps **1** to **9**, except select **Do not share this printer** in step **7**.

# SET UP A HOME NETWORK

If you have more than one computer at home, you can set up a network so the computers can exchange information and share equipment. There are many advantages to setting up your own network at home.

## ADVANTAGES OF HOME NETWORKS

### SHARE INFORMATION AND RESOURCES

A home network enables several family members to share information such as schedules and resources such as printers and storage devices. Sharing equipment allows you to save money since several people on the network can use the same equipment. Home networks are also useful for re-using old computers and equipment. While an older computer may not have the power to play the latest games, it may still be adequate for tasks such as printer sharing.

### SHARE AN INTERNET CONNECTION

You can set up a computer to share its Internet connection with other computers on the network. All the computers on the network can use the shared Internet connection to access the Internet at the same time. The computer that shares the Internet connection must be turned on when other computers on the network want to access the Internet.
Your Internet Service Provider (ISP), which is the company that gives you access to the Internet, may charge extra or not allow multiple computers to share a single Internet connection. You can contact your ISP for more information.

### RESTRICT CHILDREN'S INTERNET ACCESS

Parents can set up the computer that shares its Internet connection to restrict access to the Internet for some users on the network. This can allow parents to restrict children from downloading files or accessing inappropriate Web sites on the Internet. Windows XP allows you to restrict some Internet activities, but you can also purchase restriction programs, such as Net Nanny (www.netnanny.com) and Cyber Patrol (www.cyberpatrol.com).

### PROTECT YOUR NETWORK

When you set up a network, Windows will install firewall software on the computer that shares its Internet connection. The firewall software is designed to protect your network from unauthorized access when computers on the network are connected to the Internet.

### PLAY MULTI-PLAYER GAMES

Many games allow several people on a network and the Internet to compete against each other. You can obtain multi-player games at computer stores and on the Internet.

# in an *instant*

## NETWORK HARDWARE

You need to install and set up your network hardware to enable the computers on the network to communicate.

### NETWORK INTERFACE CARDS

Most networks use Network Interface Cards (NICs) to connect each computer to the network and control the flow of information between the computers on the network. An NIC is typically installed inside a computer. The edge of the NIC can be seen at the back of the computer and has a port where the network cable plugs in.

### COMPUTERS

You will need two or more computers to set up a network. One computer on your network must use Windows XP. All the other computers on your network must use Windows 98, Windows Me or Windows XP.

### HUB

A network may require a hub, which provides a central location where the cables on the network meet. The speed of the hub determines the speed of the NICs that can be used on the home network.

### CABLES

Cables are the wires that connect computers and resources on a network. Many different kinds of cables can be used, depending on the type and size of a network. The type of cable used often determines how quickly information will transfer through the network.

### INTERNET CONNECTION DEVICE

If you want all the computers on your network to share an Internet connection, one computer on the network will need a device, such as a modem, to connect to the Internet. The computer that shares its Internet connection should be using Windows XP.

### WIRING A HOUSE

In most recently built houses, it is relatively easy to run network cables through the walls to create network connections in different locations in the house. Each connection allows you to connect a computer to the hub. Connectors and cabling are available at most good electronic stores. For difficult installations, a professional cable installer should be consulted.

# SET UP A HOME NETWORK

Windows provides the Network Setup Wizard that will take you step by step through the process of setting up a computer on your home network. You must run the Network Setup Wizard on each computer you want to set up on your home network. If the computers will share an Internet connection, you should run the wizard on the computer that has the Internet connection first.

## SET UP A HOME NETWORK

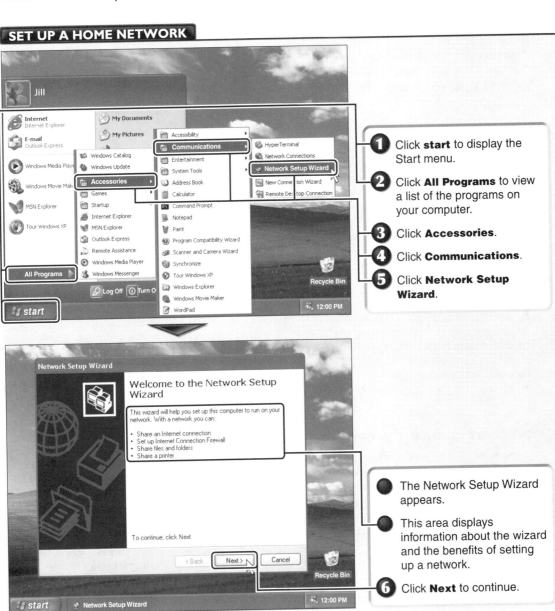

1 Click **start** to display the Start menu.

2 Click **All Programs** to view a list of the programs on your computer.

3 Click **Accessories**.

4 Click **Communications**.

5 Click **Network Setup Wizard**.

● The Network Setup Wizard appears.

● This area displays information about the wizard and the benefits of setting up a network.

6 Click **Next** to continue.

# in an instant

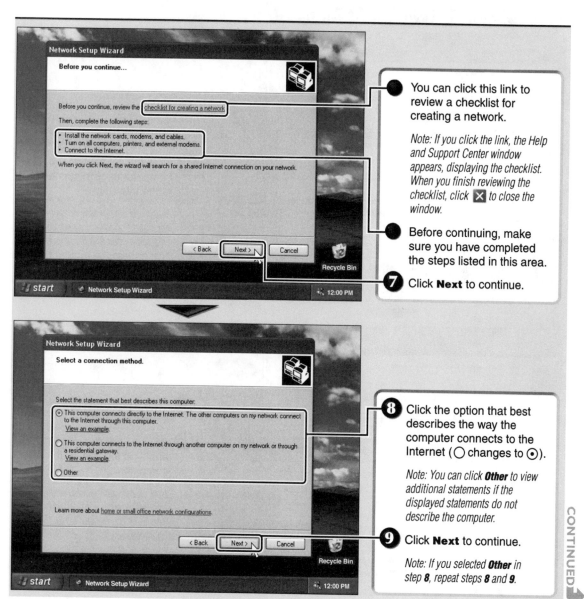

You can click this link to review a checklist for creating a network.

*Note: If you click the link, the Help and Support Center window appears, displaying the checklist. When you finish reviewing the checklist, click ☒ to close the window.*

Before continuing, make sure you have completed the steps listed in this area.

**7** Click **Next** to continue.

**8** Click the option that best describes the way the computer connects to the Internet (○ changes to ⊙).

*Note: You can click **Other** to view additional statements if the displayed statements do not describe the computer.*

**9** Click **Next** to continue.

*Note: If you selected **Other** in step 8, repeat steps 8 and 9.*

CONTINUED

When setting up a computer on your network, you need to provide a description, computer name and workgroup name for the computer. Each computer on the network must have a different name, but should have the same workgroup name. The company that gives you access to the Internet may require you to use a specific name for the computer that shares its Internet connection.

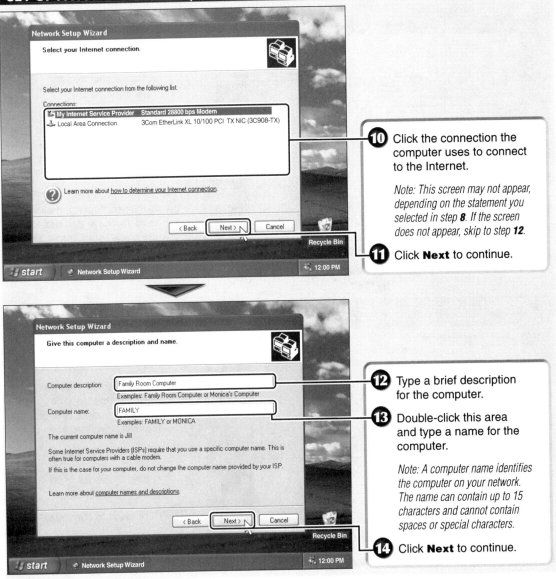

**10** Click the connection the computer uses to connect to the Internet.

*Note: This screen may not appear, depending on the statement you selected in step 8. If the screen does not appear, skip to step 12.*

**11** Click **Next** to continue.

**12** Type a brief description for the computer.

**13** Double-click this area and type a name for the computer.

*Note: A computer name identifies the computer on your network. The name can contain up to 15 characters and cannot contain spaces or special characters.*

**14** Click **Next** to continue.

# in an instant

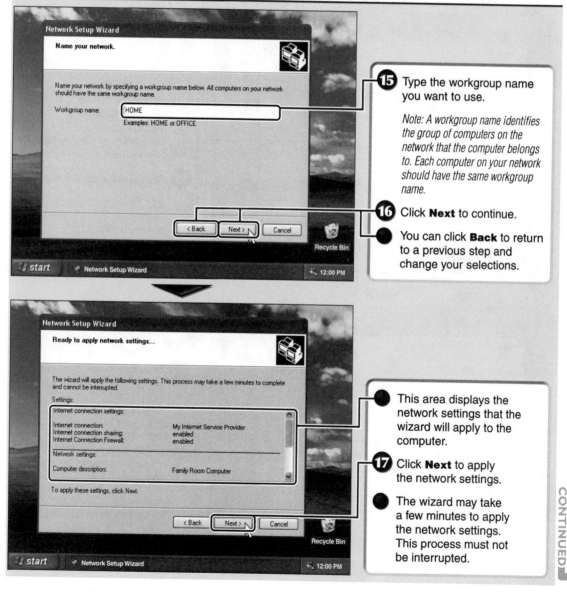

**15** Type the workgroup name you want to use.

*Note: A workgroup name identifies the group of computers on the network that the computer belongs to. Each computer on your network should have the same workgroup name.*

**16** Click **Next** to continue.

● You can click **Back** to return to a previous step and change your selections.

● This area displays the network settings that the wizard will apply to the computer.

**17** Click **Next** to apply the network settings.

● The wizard may take a few minutes to apply the network settings. This process must not be interrupted.

CONTINUED

# SET UP A HOME NETWORK

You need to specify how you want to set up other computers on your home network. To set up computers that use Windows 98 or Windows Me, you can create a Network Setup disk or use the CD you used to install Windows XP. To set up other computers that use Windows XP, run the Network Setup Wizard on each computer.

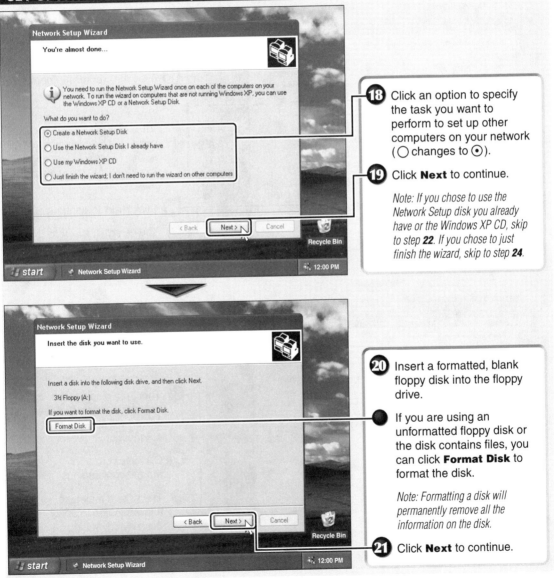

**18** Click an option to specify the task you want to perform to set up other computers on your network (○ changes to ⊙).

**19** Click **Next** to continue.

Note: If you chose to use the Network Setup disk you already have or the Windows XP CD, skip to step **22**. If you chose to just finish the wizard, skip to step **24**.

**20** Insert a formatted, blank floppy disk into the floppy drive.

● If you are using an unformatted floppy disk or the disk contains files, you can click **Format Disk** to format the disk.

Note: Formatting a disk will permanently remove all the information on the disk.

**21** Click **Next** to continue.

in an *instant*

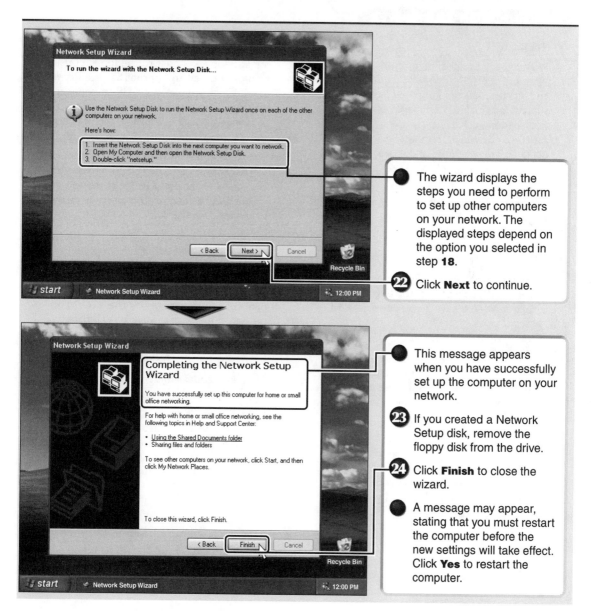

The wizard displays the
steps you need to perform
to set up other computers
on your network. The
displayed steps depend on
the option you selected in
step **18**.

**22** Click **Next** to continue.

This message appears
when you have successfully
set up the computer on your
network.

**23** If you created a Network
Setup disk, remove the
floppy disk from the drive.

**24** Click **Finish** to close the
wizard.

A message may appear,
stating that you must restart
the computer before the
new settings will take effect.
Click **Yes** to restart the
computer.

# INTRODUCTION TO THE WEB

The World Wide Web is part of the Internet and consists of a huge collection of documents stored on computers around the world. The World Wide Web is commonly called the Web.

## INTRODUCTION TO THE WEB

### WEB PAGE

A Web page is a document on the Web. Web pages can include text, pictures, sounds and videos. You can find Web pages on every subject imaginable. Web pages can offer information such as newspaper and magazine articles, movie clips, recipes, Shakespearean plays, airline schedules and more.

A Web site is a collection of Web pages created and maintained by a college, university, government agency, company, organization or individual.

### URL

Each Web page has a unique address, called a Uniform Resource Locator (URL). You can display any Web page if you know its URL.

### WEB SERVER

A Web server is a computer that stores Web pages and makes the pages available on the Web for other people to view.

### WEB BROWSER

A Web browser is a program that allows you to view and explore information on the Web. Windows XP comes with the Microsoft Internet Explorer Web browser.

### CONNECTING TO THE INTERNET

Most people connect to the Internet using a company called an Internet Service Provider (ISP). Once you pay your ISP to connect to the Internet, you can view and exchange information on the Internet free of charge.

Most individuals use a modem to connect to the Internet, although cable modems and Digital Subscriber Line (DSL) modems are becoming more popular. Most schools and businesses connect to the Internet through a network connection.

### LINK

Web pages contain links, or hyperlinks, which are highlighted text or images that connect to other pages on the Web. You can select a link to display a Web page located on the same computer or on a computer across the city, country or world. You can easily identify links on a Web page. Text links appear underlined and in color.

Links save you time since you do not have to enter the URL of each Web page you want to view. Links also allow you to easily navigate through a vast amount of information by jumping from one Web page to another. This is known as "browsing the Web."

# START INTERNET EXPLORER

You can start Internet Explorer to browse through the information on the Web. The first time you start Internet Explorer, the New Connection Wizard will appear if you have not yet set up your connection to the Internet. Follow the instructions in the wizard to set up your Internet connection.

## START INTERNET EXPLORER

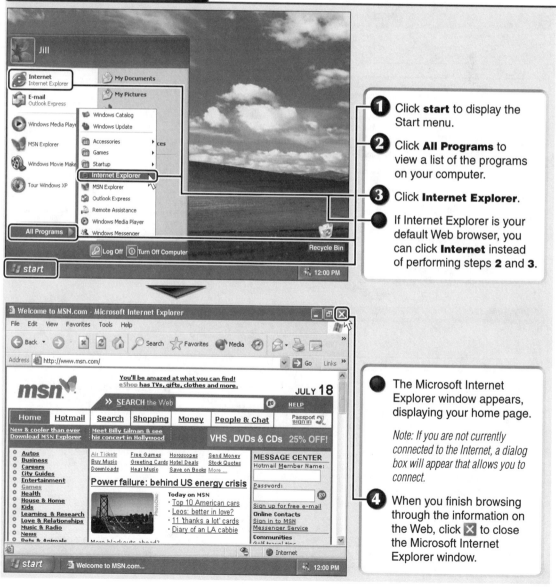

**1** Click **start** to display the Start menu.

**2** Click **All Programs** to view a list of the programs on your computer.

**3** Click **Internet Explorer**.

■ If Internet Explorer is your default Web browser, you can click **Internet** instead of performing steps **2** and **3**.

■ The Microsoft Internet Explorer window appears, displaying your home page.

*Note: If you are not currently connected to the Internet, a dialog box will appear that allows you to connect.*

**4** When you finish browsing through the information on the Web, click 🗙 to close the Microsoft Internet Explorer window.

# DISPLAY A SPECIFIC WEB PAGE

You can display a page on the Web that you have heard or read about. Each page on the Web has a unique address, called a Uniform Resource Locator (URL). You must specify the URL of a Web page in order to display the page. Internet Explorer remembers the addresses of Web pages you recently visited so you can quickly redisplay a Web page.

## DISPLAY A SPECIFIC WEB PAGE

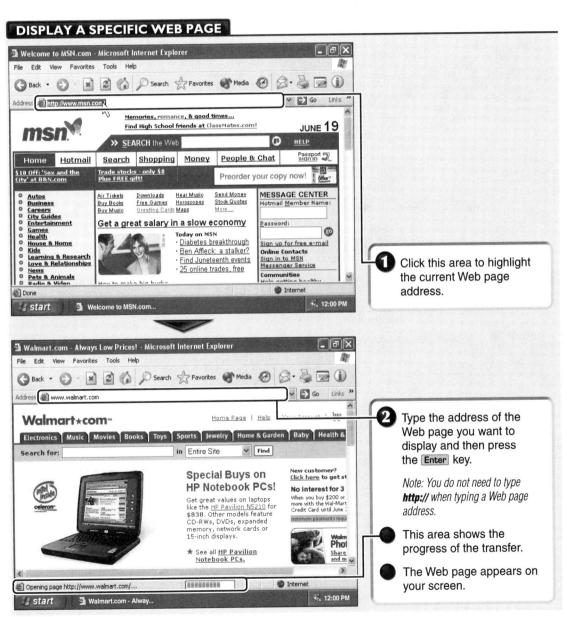

**1** Click this area to highlight the current Web page address.

**2** Type the address of the Web page you want to display and then press the Enter key.

*Note: You do not need to type **http://** when typing a Web page address.*

● This area shows the progress of the transfer.

● The Web page appears on your screen.

# in an Instant

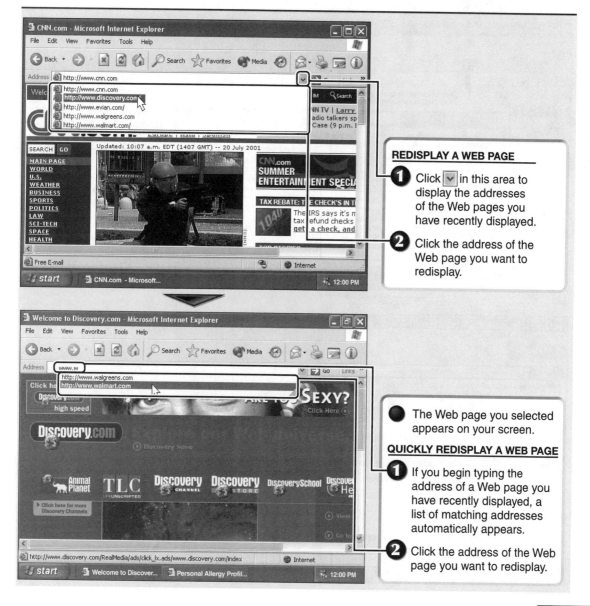

### REDISPLAY A WEB PAGE

**1** Click ⌄ in this area to display the addresses of the Web pages you have recently displayed.

**2** Click the address of the Web page you want to redisplay.

● The Web page you selected appears on your screen.

### QUICKLY REDISPLAY A WEB PAGE

**1** If you begin typing the address of a Web page you have recently displayed, a list of matching addresses automatically appears.

**2** Click the address of the Web page you want to redisplay.

# SELECT A LINK

A link connects text or an image on one Web page to another Web page. When you select the text or image, the linked Web page appears. Links allow you to easily navigate through a vast amount of information by jumping from one Web page to another. Links are also known as hyperlinks.

## SELECT A LINK

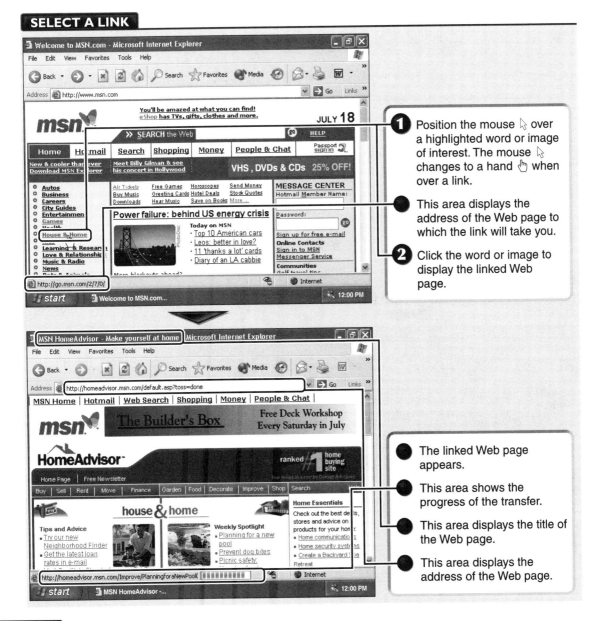

**1** Position the mouse ⊵ over a highlighted word or image of interest. The mouse ⊵ changes to a hand ⟨ᵐ⟩ when over a link.

This area displays the address of the Web page to which the link will take you.

**2** Click the word or image to display the linked Web page.

The linked Web page appears.

This area shows the progress of the transfer.

This area displays the title of the Web page.

This area displays the address of the Web page.

You can easily move back and forth through the Web pages you have viewed since you last started Internet Explorer. Using the buttons in Internet Explorer to move through Web pages you have viewed saves you time, since you do not have to retype a Web page address to redisplay the page.

## MOVE THROUGH WEB PAGES

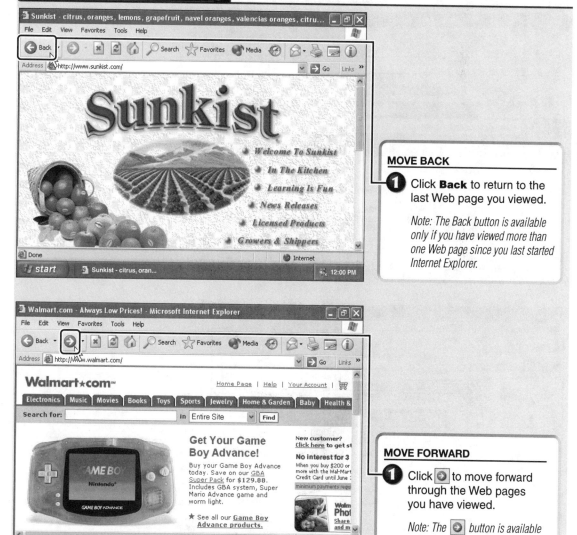

### MOVE BACK

**1** Click **Back** to return to the last Web page you viewed.

*Note: The Back button is available only if you have viewed more than one Web page since you last started Internet Explorer.*

### MOVE FORWARD

**1** Click ⬢ to move forward through the Web pages you have viewed.

*Note: The ⬢ button is available only after you use the Back button to return to a Web page.*

# DISPLAY AND CHANGE YOUR HOME PAGE

You can display and change the Web page that appears each time you start Internet Explorer. This page is called your home page. When setting a new home page, you may want to choose a page that provides a good starting point for exploring the Web, such as www.yahoo.com, or a page that provides information about your personal interests or work.

## DISPLAY AND CHANGE YOUR HOME PAGE

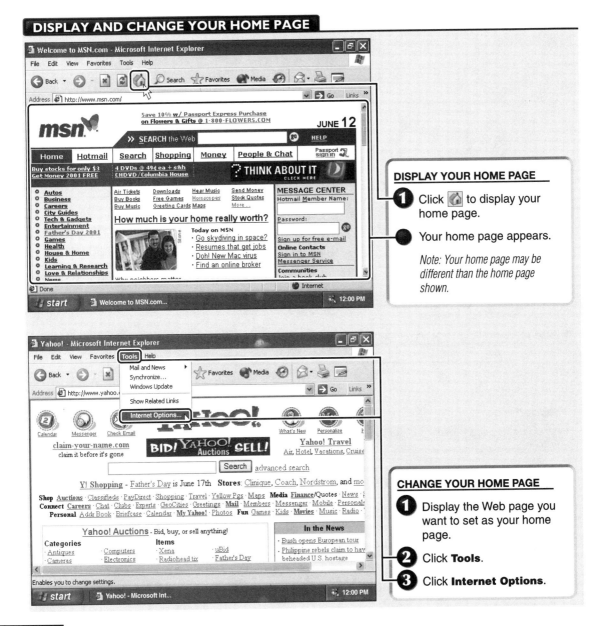

### DISPLAY YOUR HOME PAGE

1 Click the home icon to display your home page.

■ Your home page appears.

*Note: Your home page may be different than the home page shown.*

### CHANGE YOUR HOME PAGE

1 Display the Web page you want to set as your home page.

2 Click **Tools**.

3 Click **Internet Options**.

# in an Instant

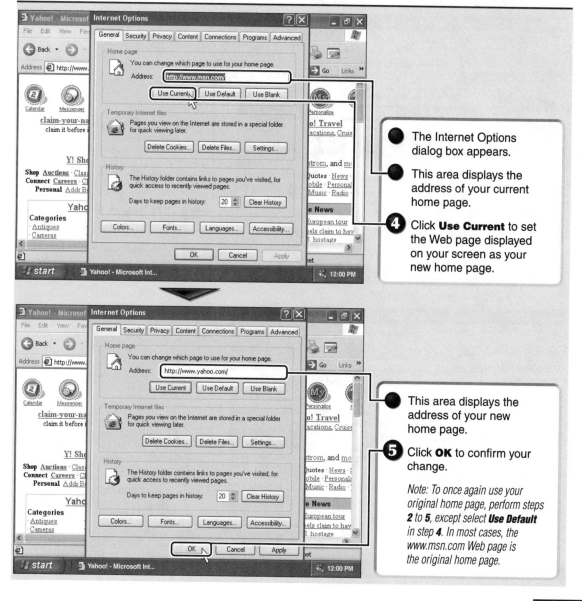

The Internet Options dialog box appears.

This area displays the address of your current home page.

**4** Click **Use Current** to set the Web page displayed on your screen as your new home page.

This area displays the address of your new home page.

**5** Click **OK** to confirm your change.

*Note: To once again use your original home page, perform steps 2 to 5, except select **Use Default** in step 4. In most cases, the www.msn.com Web page is the original home page.*

# SEARCH THE WEB

You can search for Web pages that discuss topics of interest to you. Internet Explorer uses the MSN search tool to help you find Web pages, but you can also use other search tools, such as Google (www.google.com) and Yahoo! (www.yahoo.com), to search for pages on the Web. A search tool is a service on the Web that catalogs Web pages.

## SEARCH THE WEB

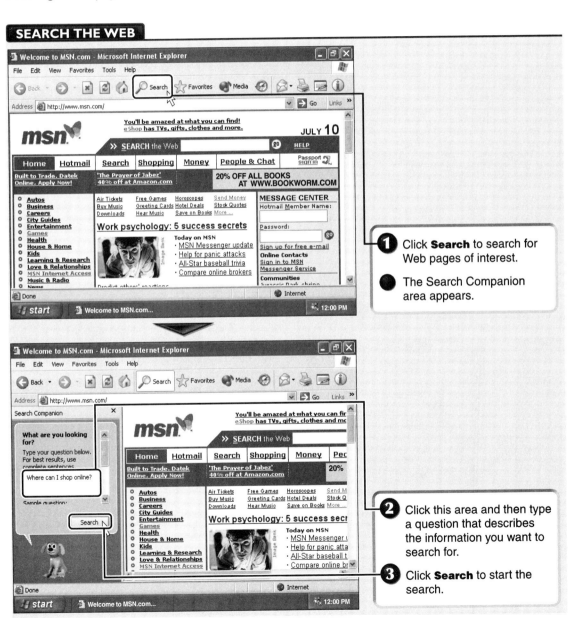

**1** Click **Search** to search for Web pages of interest.

● The Search Companion area appears.

**2** Click this area and then type a question that describes the information you want to search for.

**3** Click **Search** to start the search.

# in an *Instant*

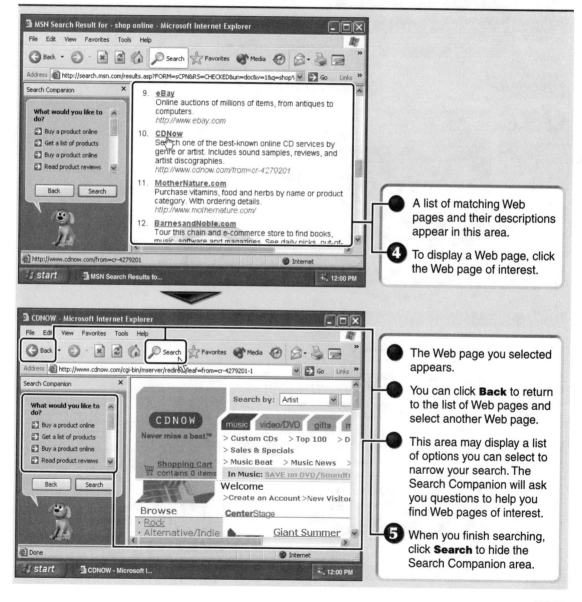

A list of matching Web pages and their descriptions appear in this area.

**4** To display a Web page, click the Web page of interest.

The Web page you selected appears.

You can click **Back** to return to the list of Web pages and select another Web page.

This area may display a list of options you can select to narrow your search. The Search Companion will ask you questions to help you find Web pages of interest.

**5** When you finish searching, click **Search** to hide the Search Companion area.

# ADD A WEB PAGE TO FAVORITES

You can use the Favorites feature to create a list of Web pages that you frequently visit. Internet Explorer also automatically adds items, such as the MSN.com Web site and the Radio Station Guide, to your list of favorites. You can select a Web page from the list of favorites to quickly display the Web page at any time.

## ADD A WEB PAGE TO FAVORITES

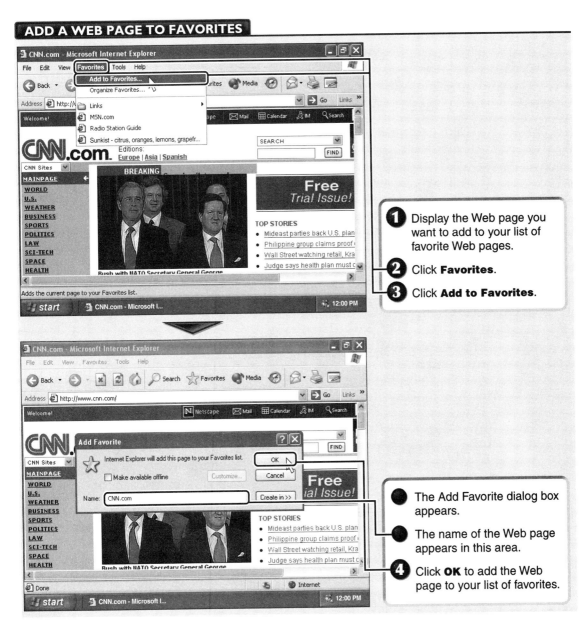

1 Display the Web page you want to add to your list of favorite Web pages.

2 Click **Favorites**.

3 Click **Add to Favorites**.

■ The Add Favorite dialog box appears.

■ The name of the Web page appears in this area.

4 Click **OK** to add the Web page to your list of favorites.

# in an *instant*

## VIEW A FAVORITE WEB PAGE

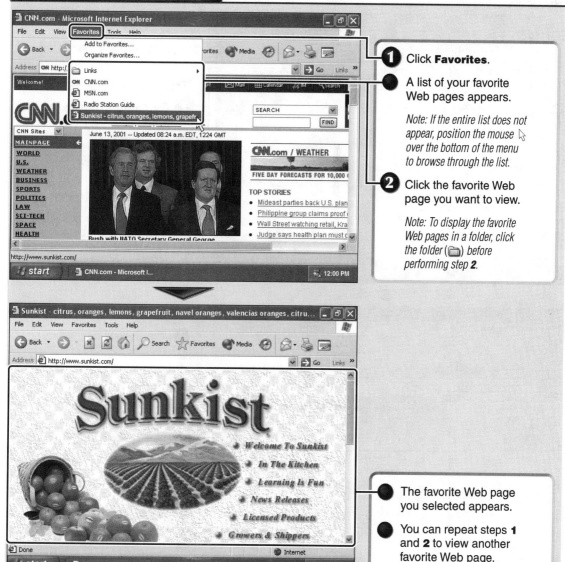

1 Click **Favorites**.

● A list of your favorite Web pages appears.

*Note: If the entire list does not appear, position the mouse over the bottom of the menu to browse through the list.*

2 Click the favorite Web page you want to view.

*Note: To display the favorite Web pages in a folder, click the folder (📁) before performing step 2.*

● The favorite Web page you selected appears.

● You can repeat steps 1 and 2 to view another favorite Web page.

**219**

# READ MESSAGES

You can start Outlook Express to open and read the contents of your e-mail messages. The first time you start Outlook Express, a wizard will appear if you have not yet set up your Internet connection or e-mail account. Follow the instructions in the wizard to set up your Internet connection and/or e-mail account.

## READ MESSAGES

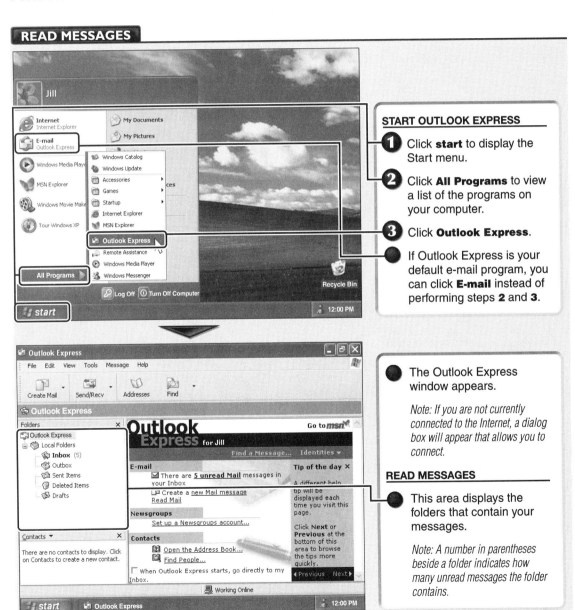

### START OUTLOOK EXPRESS

**1** Click **start** to display the Start menu.

**2** Click **All Programs** to view a list of the programs on your computer.

**3** Click **Outlook Express**.

● If Outlook Express is your default e-mail program, you can click **E-mail** instead of performing steps **2** and **3**.

● The Outlook Express window appears.

*Note: If you are not currently connected to the Internet, a dialog box will appear that allows you to connect.*

### READ MESSAGES

● This area displays the folders that contain your messages.

*Note: A number in parentheses beside a folder indicates how many unread messages the folder contains.*

in an *instant*

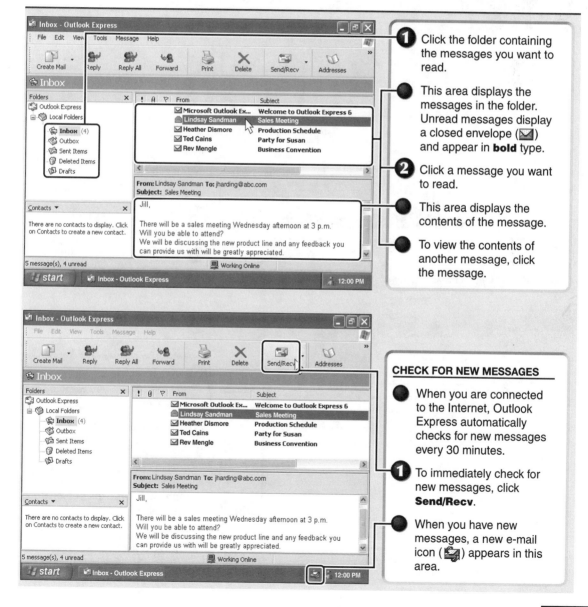

**1** Click the folder containing the messages you want to read.

This area displays the messages in the folder. Unread messages display a closed envelope (📩) and appear in **bold** type.

**2** Click a message you want to read.

This area displays the contents of the message.

To view the contents of another message, click the message.

**CHECK FOR NEW MESSAGES**

When you are connected to the Internet, Outlook Express automatically checks for new messages every 30 minutes.

**1** To immediately check for new messages, click **Send/Recv**.

When you have new messages, a new e-mail icon (📩) appears in this area.

# SEND A MESSAGE

You can send a message to express an idea or request information. When sending a message, you should always use uppercase and lowercase letters. A message written in all capital letters is annoying and difficult to read. To practice sending a message, you can send a message to yourself.

## SEND A MESSAGE

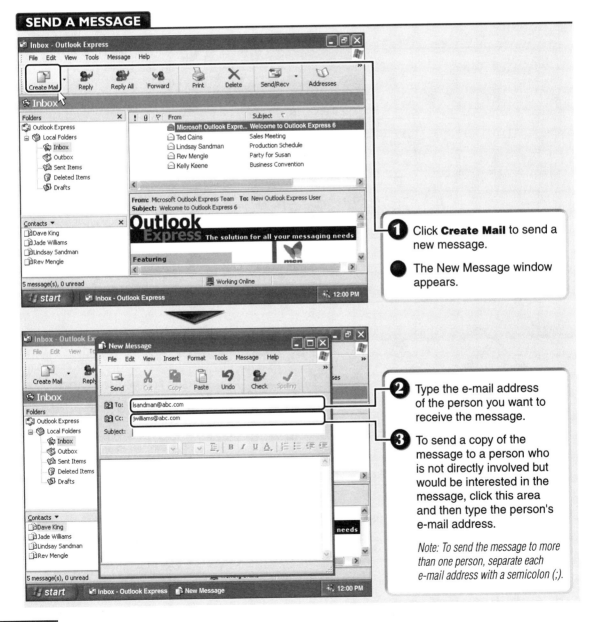

1 Click **Create Mail** to send a new message.

● The New Message window appears.

2 Type the e-mail address of the person you want to receive the message.

3 To send a copy of the message to a person who is not directly involved but would be interested in the message, click this area and then type the person's e-mail address.

*Note: To send the message to more than one person, separate each e-mail address with a semicolon (;).*

# in an *instant*

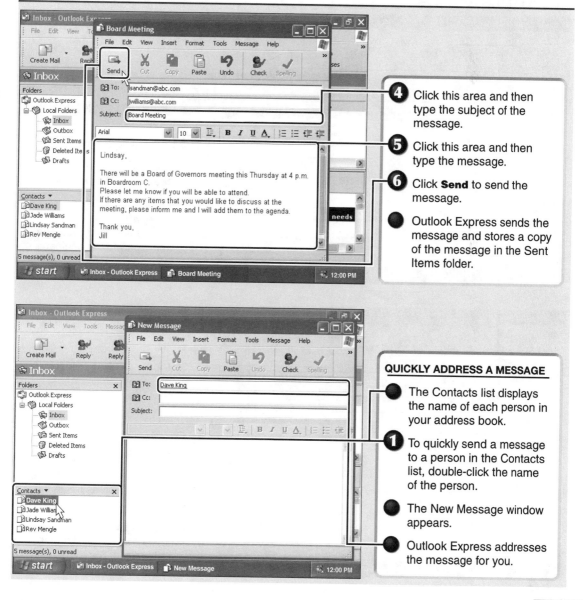

**4** Click this area and then type the subject of the message.

**5** Click this area and then type the message.

**6** Click **Send** to send the message.

● Outlook Express sends the message and stores a copy of the message in the Sent Items folder.

## QUICKLY ADDRESS A MESSAGE

● The Contacts list displays the name of each person in your address book.

**1** To quickly send a message to a person in the Contacts list, double-click the name of the person.

● The New Message window appears.

● Outlook Express addresses the message for you.

# REPLY TO A MESSAGE

You can reply to a message you received. You can reply to only the sender of the original message or to the sender and everyone who received the original message. When you reply to a message, the contents of the original message automatically appear in your reply. This helps the reader identify which message you are replying to.

## REPLY TO A MESSAGE

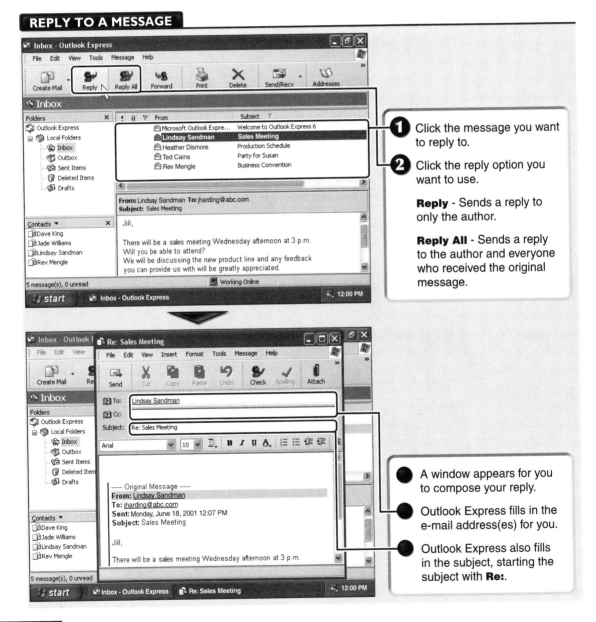

**1** Click the message you want to reply to.

**2** Click the reply option you want to use.

**Reply** - Sends a reply to only the author.

**Reply All** - Sends a reply to the author and everyone who received the original message.

■ A window appears for you to compose your reply.

■ Outlook Express fills in the e-mail address(es) for you.

■ Outlook Express also fills in the subject, starting the subject with **Re:**.

in an *instant*

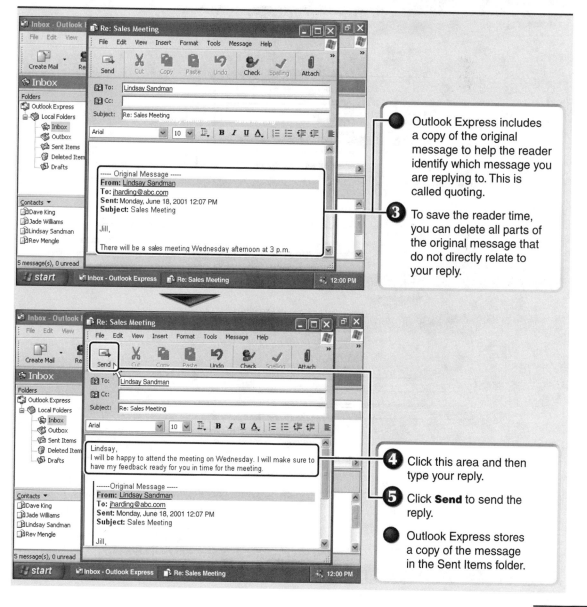

Outlook Express includes a copy of the original message to help the reader identify which message you are replying to. This is called quoting.

**3** To save the reader time, you can delete all parts of the original message that do not directly relate to your reply.

**4** Click this area and then type your reply.

**5** Click **Send** to send the reply.

Outlook Express stores a copy of the message in the Sent Items folder.

# FORWARD A MESSAGE

After reading a message, you can forward the message to another person. When you forward a message, you can add your own comments to the original message. Forwarding a message is useful when you know another person would be interested in the contents of a message you received.

## FORWARD A MESSAGE

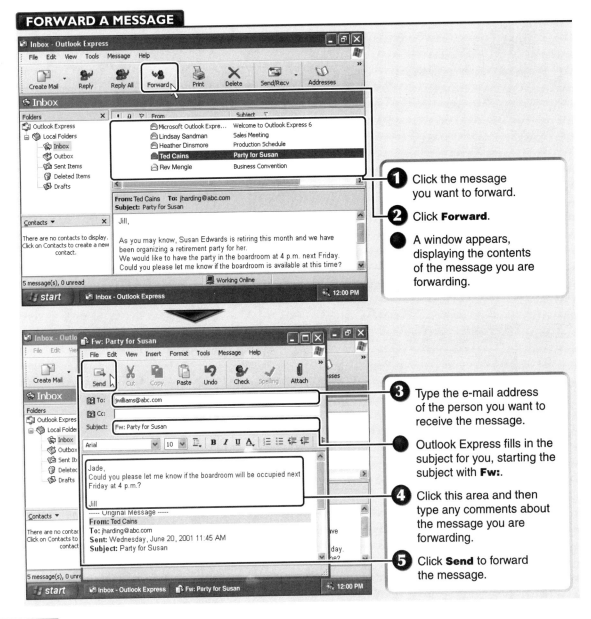

1 Click the message you want to forward.

2 Click **Forward**.

● A window appears, displaying the contents of the message you are forwarding.

3 Type the e-mail address of the person you want to receive the message.

● Outlook Express fills in the subject for you, starting the subject with **Fw:**.

4 Click this area and then type any comments about the message you are forwarding.

5 Click **Send** to forward the message.

# PRINT A MESSAGE

You can produce a paper copy of a message. A printed message is useful when you need a copy of the message for reference. Outlook Express prints the page number and total number of pages at the top of each page. The current date prints at the bottom of each page.

## PRINT A MESSAGE

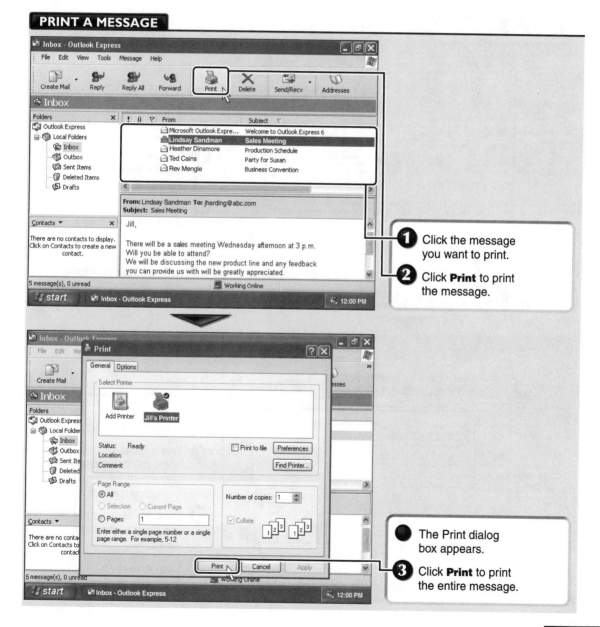

1 Click the message you want to print.

2 Click **Print** to print the message.

● The Print dialog box appears.

3 Click **Print** to print the entire message.

# ATTACH A FILE TO A MESSAGE

You can attach a file to a message you are sending to include additional information with the message. You can attach many types of files to a message, including documents, pictures, videos, sounds and programs. The computer receiving the message must have the necessary hardware and software installed to display or play the file you attach.

## ATTACH A FILE TO A MESSAGE

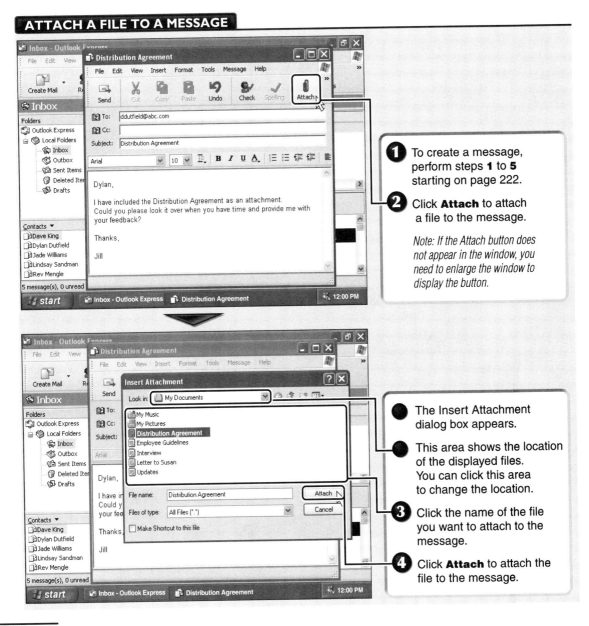

**1** To create a message, perform steps **1** to **5** starting on page 222.

**2** Click **Attach** to attach a file to the message.

*Note: If the Attach button does not appear in the window, you need to enlarge the window to display the button.*

■ The Insert Attachment dialog box appears.

■ This area shows the location of the displayed files. You can click this area to change the location.

**3** Click the name of the file you want to attach to the message.

**4** Click **Attach** to attach the file to the message.

# in an *instant*

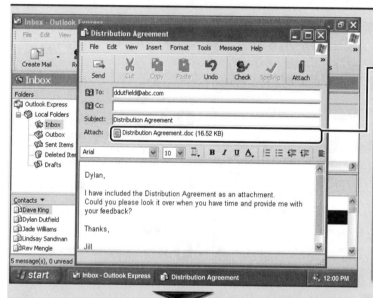

This area displays the name and size of the file you selected.

To attach additional files to the message, perform steps **2** to **4** for each file you want to attach.

*Note: You should determine whether the company that provides your e-mail account limits the size of messages you can send over the Internet. Most companies do not allow you to send or receive messages larger than 2 MB.*

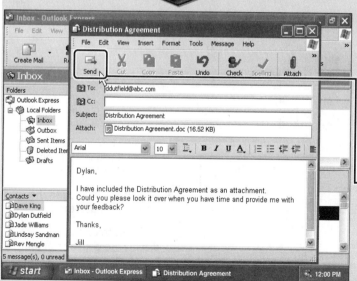

**5** Click **Send** to send the message.

Outlook Express will send the message and the attached file(s) to the e-mail address(es) you specified.

# OPEN AN ATTACHED FILE

You can easily open a file attached to a message you receive. Since some files can contain viruses which can damage the information on your computer, you should make sure an attached file is from a reliable source before opening the file. You can use an anti-virus program, such as McAfee VirusScan, to check files for viruses.

## OPEN AN ATTACHED FILE

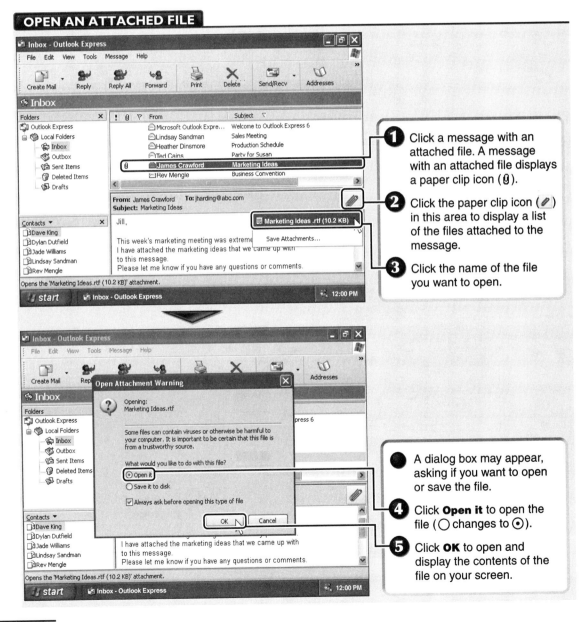

■ Click a message with an attached file. A message with an attached file displays a paper clip icon (📎).

② Click the paper clip icon (📎) in this area to display a list of the files attached to the message.

③ Click the name of the file you want to open.

● A dialog box may appear, asking if you want to open or save the file.

④ Click **Open it** to open the file (○ changes to ⊙).

⑤ Click **OK** to open and display the contents of the file on your screen.

You can delete a message you no longer need. Deleting messages prevents your folders from becoming cluttered with messages. When you delete a message, Outlook Express places the deleted message in the Deleted Items folder. When you are ready to permanently remove the message from your computer, you can delete the message from the Deleted Items folder.

## DELETE A MESSAGE

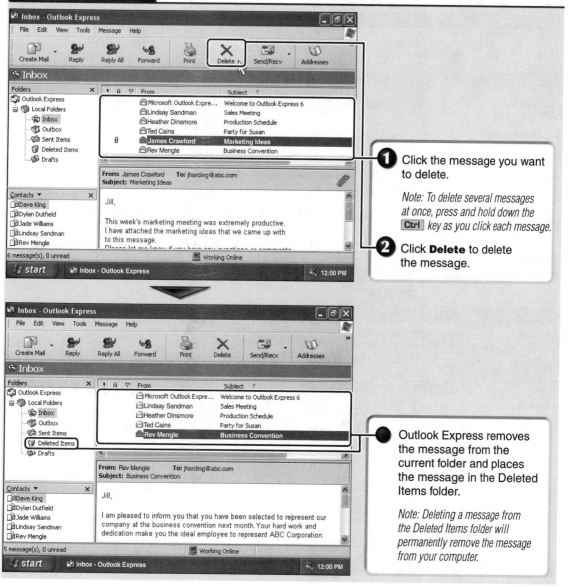

**1** Click the message you want to delete.

*Note: To delete several messages at once, press and hold down the* **Ctrl** *key as you click each message.*

**2** Click **Delete** to delete the message.

Outlook Express removes the message from the current folder and places the message in the Deleted Items folder.

*Note: Deleting a message from the Deleted Items folder will permanently remove the message from your computer.*

**231**

# ADD A NAME TO THE ADDRESS BOOK

You can store the names and e-mail addresses of people to whom you frequently send messages in Outlook Express's address book. Each time you reply to a message, the name and e-mail address of the person who sent the message is also automatically added to your address book.

## ADD A NAME TO THE ADDRESS BOOK

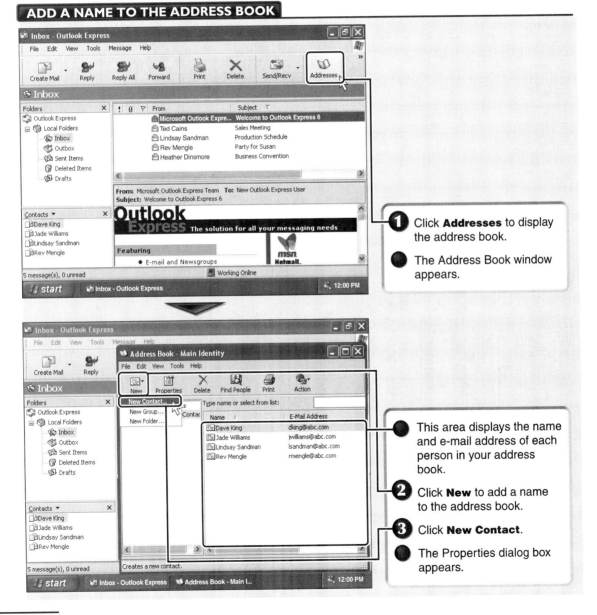

**1** Click **Addresses** to display the address book.

● The Address Book window appears.

● This area displays the name and e-mail address of each person in your address book.

**2** Click **New** to add a name to the address book.

**3** Click **New Contact**.

● The Properties dialog box appears.

# in an instant

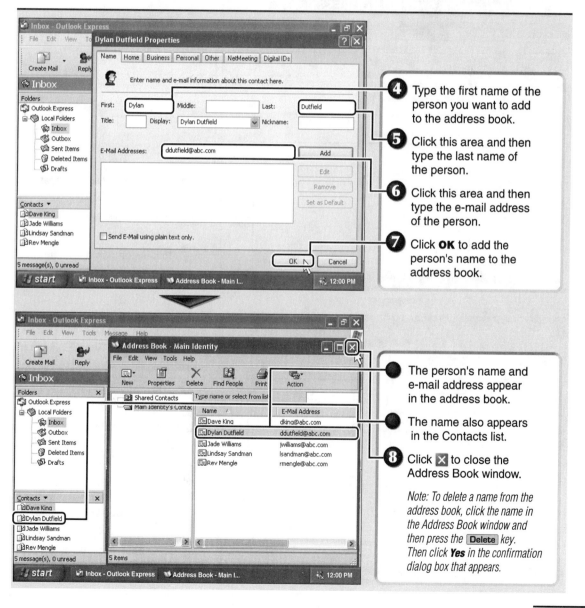

**4** Type the first name of the person you want to add to the address book.

**5** Click this area and then type the last name of the person.

**6** Click this area and then type the e-mail address of the person.

**7** Click **OK** to add the person's name to the address book.

● The person's name and e-mail address appear in the address book.

● The name also appears in the Contacts list.

**8** Click ☒ to close the Address Book window.

*Note: To delete a name from the address book, click the name in the Address Book window and then press the* Delete *key. Then click* **Yes** *in the confirmation dialog box that appears.*

When sending a message, you can select the name of the person you want to receive the message from the address book. You can also use the address book to send carbon copies or blind carbon copies of the message to other people. A blind carbon copy sends a copy of the message to a person without anyone else knowing that the copy was sent.

## SELECT A NAME FROM THE ADDRESS BOOK

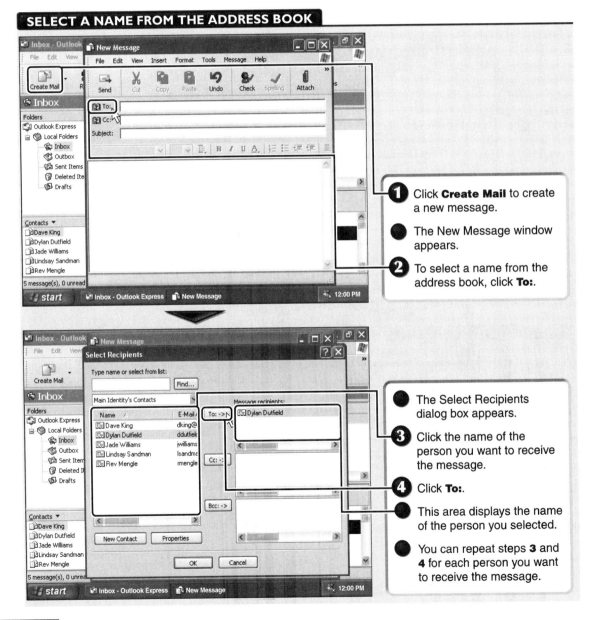

1 Click **Create Mail** to create a new message.

● The New Message window appears.

2 To select a name from the address book, click **To:**.

● The Select Recipients dialog box appears.

3 Click the name of the person you want to receive the message.

4 Click **To:**.

● This area displays the name of the person you selected.

● You can repeat steps **3** and **4** for each person you want to receive the message.

in an *instant*

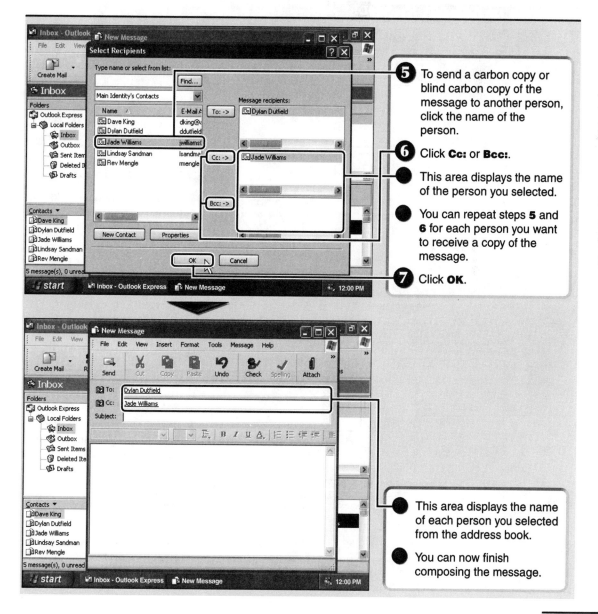

**5** To send a carbon copy or blind carbon copy of the message to another person, click the name of the person.

**6** Click **Cc:** or **Bcc:**.

● This area displays the name of the person you selected.

● You can repeat steps **5** and **6** for each person you want to receive a copy of the message.

**7** Click **OK**.

● This area displays the name of each person you selected from the address book.

● You can now finish composing the message.

# START WINDOWS MESSENGER

You can use Windows Messenger to see when your friends are
online and exchange instant messages and files with them. The
first time you start Windows Messenger, a wizard appears to
help you add a Passport to your user account. You must add
a Passport to your user account to use Windows Messenger.

## START WINDOWS MESSENGER

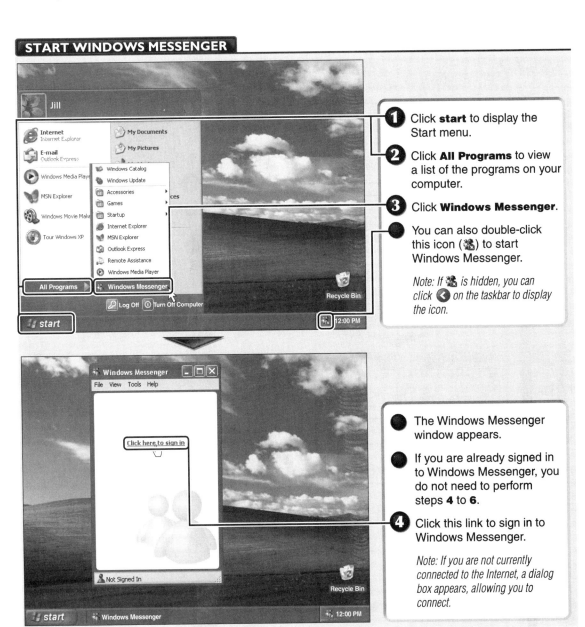

① Click **start** to display the
Start menu.

② Click **All Programs** to view
a list of the programs on your
computer.

③ Click **Windows Messenger**.

● You can also double-click
this icon (🐧) to start
Windows Messenger.

*Note: If 🐧 is hidden, you can
click ◀ on the taskbar to display
the icon.*

● The Windows Messenger
window appears.

● If you are already signed in
to Windows Messenger, you
do not need to perform
steps **4** to **6**.

④ Click this link to sign in to
Windows Messenger.

*Note: If you are not currently
connected to the Internet, a dialog
box appears, allowing you to
connect.*

# in an *instant*

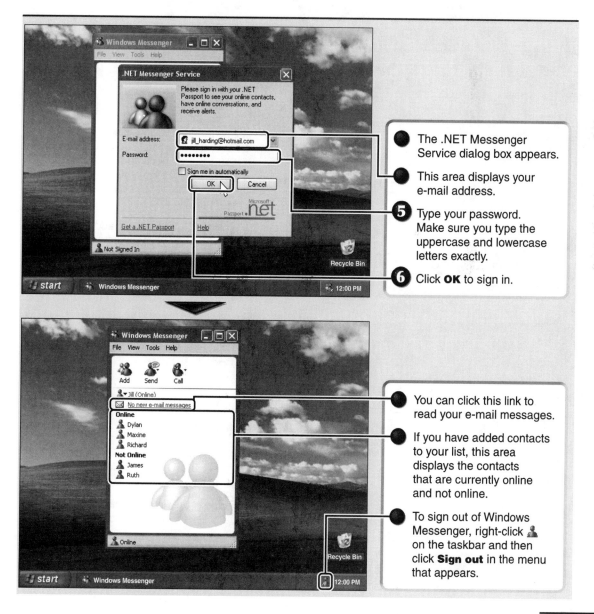

The .NET Messenger Service dialog box appears.

This area displays your e-mail address.

**5** Type your password. Make sure you type the uppercase and lowercase letters exactly.

**6** Click **OK** to sign in.

You can click this link to read your e-mail messages.

If you have added contacts to your list, this area displays the contacts that are currently online and not online.

To sign out of Windows Messenger, right-click 🔒 on the taskbar and then click **Sign out** in the menu that appears.

# ADD A CONTACT

You can add a person to your contact list to see when they are online and available to exchange instant messages. Each person you want to add to your contact list requires a Passport. A Passport is obtained when Windows Messenger is set up on a computer. People using a program that is compatible with Windows Messenger can obtain a Passport at the passport.com Web site.

## ADD A CONTACT

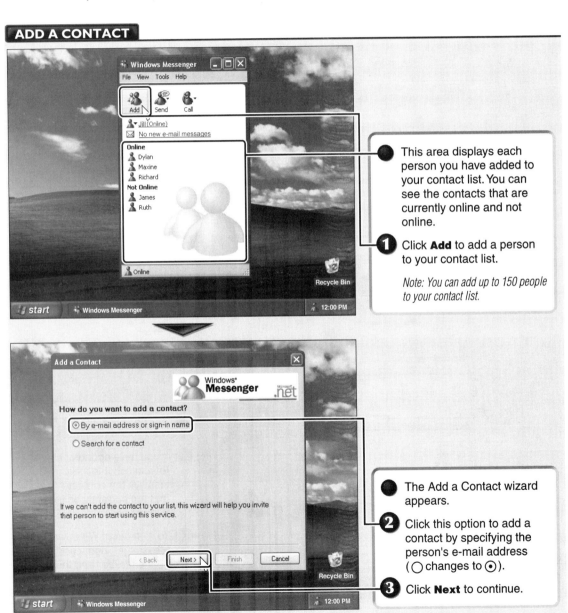

This area displays each person you have added to your contact list. You can see the contacts that are currently online and not online.

**1** Click **Add** to add a person to your contact list.

*Note: You can add up to 150 people to your contact list.*

The Add a Contact wizard appears.

**2** Click this option to add a contact by specifying the person's e-mail address ( ○ changes to ⊙ ).

**3** Click **Next** to continue.

# in an *instant*

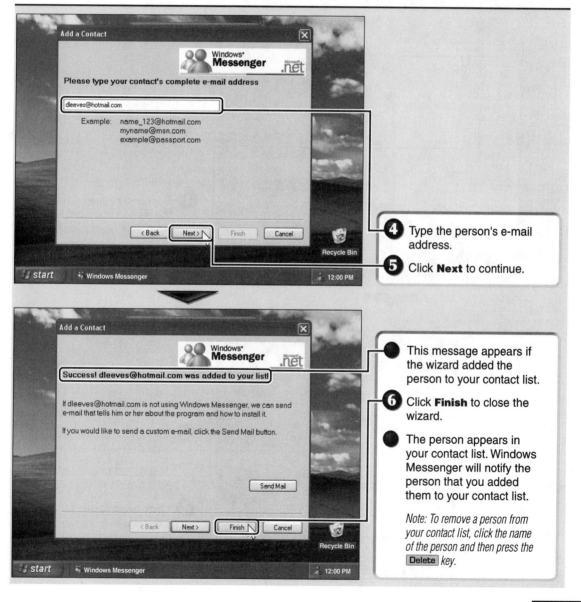

**4** Type the person's e-mail address.

**5** Click **Next** to continue.

This message appears if the wizard added the person to your contact list.

**6** Click **Finish** to close the wizard.

The person appears in your contact list. Windows Messenger will notify the person that you added them to your contact list.

*Note: To remove a person from your contact list, click the name of the person and then press the* Delete *key.*

**239**

# SEND AN INSTANT MESSAGE

You can send an instant message to a person in your contact list who is currently signed in to Windows Messenger. When typing an instant message, you should use upper and lower case letters to make the message easy to read. You should never give out your password or credit card information in an instant message.

## SEND AN INSTANT MESSAGE

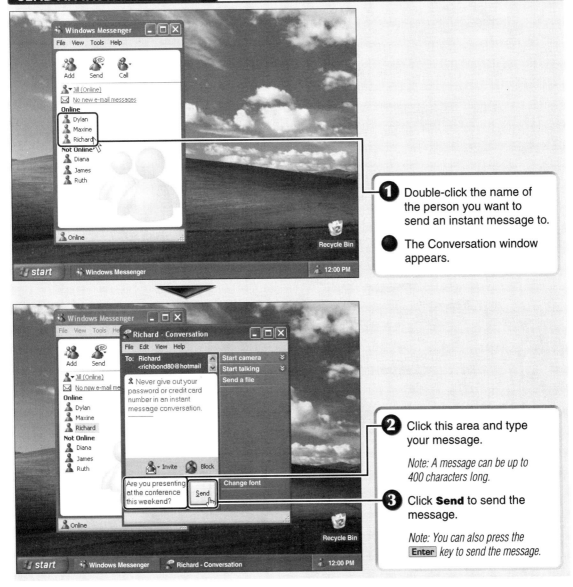

**1** Double-click the name of the person you want to send an instant message to.

● The Conversation window appears.

**2** Click this area and type your message.

*Note: A message can be up to 400 characters long.*

**3** Click **Send** to send the message.

*Note: You can also press the* Enter *key to send the message.*

# in an *instant*

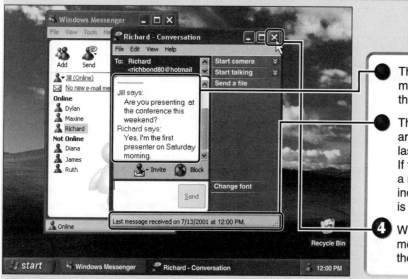

This area displays the message you sent and the ongoing conversation.

This area displays the date and time the other person last sent you a message. If the other person is typing a message, this area indicates that the person is typing.

**4** When you finish exchanging messages, click ✕ to close the Conversation window.

## RECEIVE AN INSTANT MESSAGE

When you receive an instant message that is not part of an ongoing conversation, your computer makes a sound and briefly displays a box containing the first part of the message.

**1** To display the entire message in the Conversation window, click inside the box.

*Note: You can also click the Conversation button on the taskbar to display the entire message.*

While exchanging instant messages with another person, you can send the person a file. You can send many types of files, including documents, pictures and videos. The computer receiving the file must have the necessary hardware and software installed to display or play the file. If your computer is connected to a network with a firewall, you may not be able to send a file.

## SEND A FILE

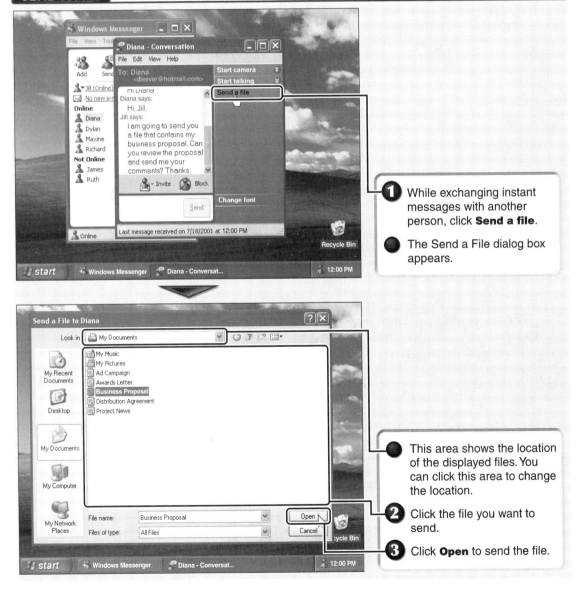

① While exchanging instant messages with another person, click **Send a file**.

● The Send a File dialog box appears.

● This area shows the location of the displayed files. You can click this area to change the location.

② Click the file you want to send.

③ Click **Open** to send the file.

# in an *instant*

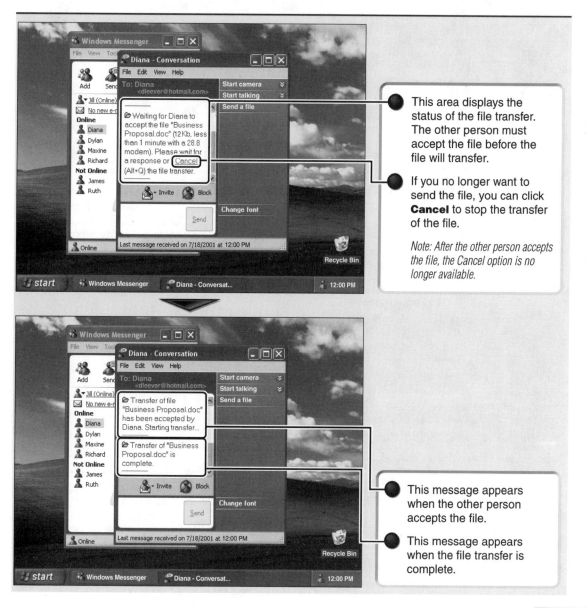

This area displays the status of the file transfer. The other person must accept the file before the file will transfer.

If you no longer want to send the file, you can click **Cancel** to stop the transfer of the file.

*Note: After the other person accepts the file, the Cancel option is no longer available.*

This message appears when the other person accepts the file.

This message appears when the file transfer is complete.

While exchanging instant messages with another person, you can receive a file from the other person. Before opening a file you received, you should use an anti-virus program, such as McAfee VirusScan, to check the file for viruses. Some files may contain viruses, which can damage the information on your computer. You should be very cautious of files you receive from people you do not know.

**RECEIVE A FILE**

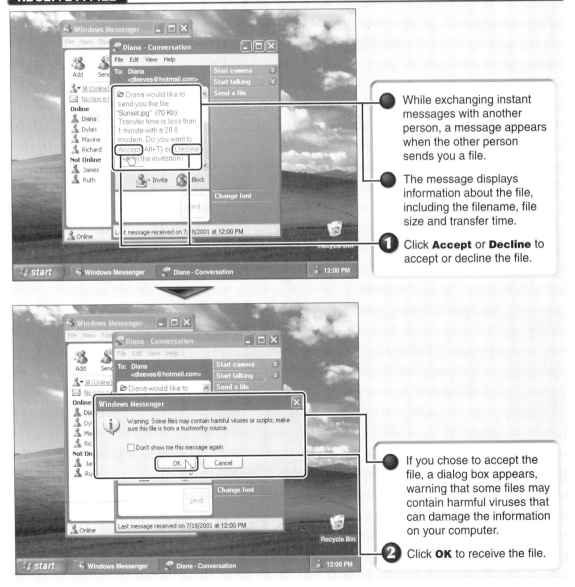

■ While exchanging instant messages with another person, a message appears when the other person sends you a file.

■ The message displays information about the file, including the filename, file size and transfer time.

**1** Click **Accept** or **Decline** to accept or decline the file.

■ If you chose to accept the file, a dialog box appears, warning that some files may contain harmful viruses that can damage the information on your computer.

**2** Click **OK** to receive the file.

# in an *instant*

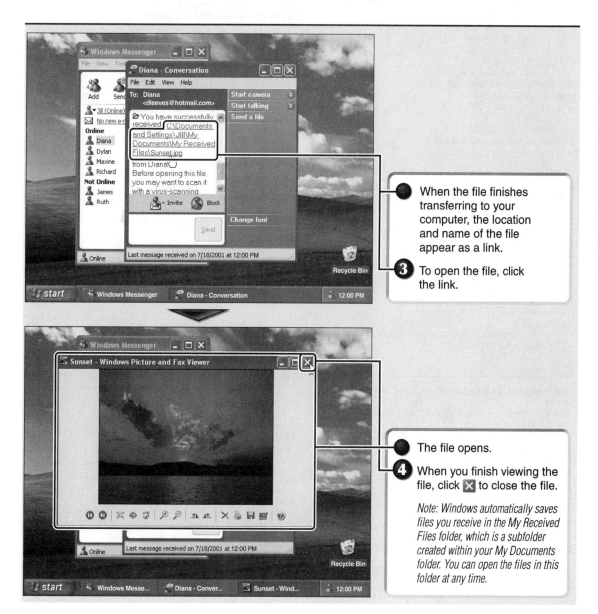

When the file finishes transferring to your computer, the location and name of the file appear as a link.

**3** To open the file, click the link.

The file opens.

**4** When you finish viewing the file, click ⊠ to close the file.

*Note: Windows automatically saves files you receive in the My Received Files folder, which is a subfolder created within your My Documents folder. You can open the files in this folder at any time.*

# INDEX

# INDEX

# INDEX

# INDEX

# INDEX

# New from the Award-Winning Visual™ Series

## Fast
## Focused
## Visual
## —and a great value!

- Zeroes in on the core tools and tasks of each application
- Features hundreds of large, super-crisp screenshots
- Straight-to-the-point explanations get you up and running—instantly

### Titles In Series

Dreamweaver® 4 In an Instant
  (0-7645-3628-1)
Flash™ 5 In an Instant
  (0-7645-3624-9)
FrontPage® 2002 In an Instant
  (0-7645-3626-5)
HTML In an Instant
  (0-7645-3627-3)

Office XP In an Instant
  (0-7645-3637-0)
Photoshop® 6 In an Instant
  (0-7645-3629-X)
Windows® XP In an Instant
  (0-7645-3625-7)

## Other Visual Series That Help You Read Less - Learn More™

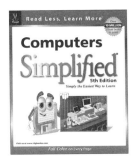

Simplified®

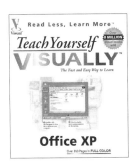

Teach Yourself VISUALLY™

Master VISUALLY™

Visual Blueprint

## Available wherever books are sold

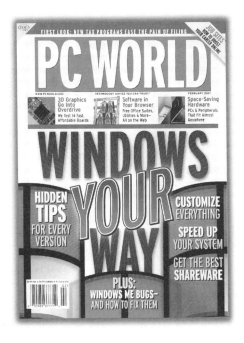